Discarded
Memphis Public Library

# How to Use Your Mac

*Gene Steinberg*

**SAMS**
A Division of Macmillan USA
201 W. 103rd Street
Indianapolis, Indiana 46290

# How to Use Your Mac

Copyright © 2000 by Sams Publishing

All rights reserved. No part of this book shall be reproduced, stored in a retrieval system, or transmitted by any means, electronic, mechanical, photocopying, recording, or otherwise, without written permission from the publisher. No patent liability is assumed with respect to the use of the information contained herein. Although every precaution has been taken in the preparation of this book, the publisher and author assume no responsibility for errors or omissions. Neither is any liability assumed for damages resulting from the use of the information contained herein.

International Standard Book Number: 0-672-31827-X

Library of Congress Catalog Card Number: 99-69270

Printed in the United States of America

First Printing: May 2000

03  02  01  00        4  3  2  1

## Trademarks

All terms mentioned in this book that are known to be trademarks or service marks have been appropriately capitalized. Sams Publishing cannot attest to the accuracy of this information. Use of a term in this book should not be regarded as affecting the validity of any trademark or service mark. America Online is a registered trademark of America Online, Inc.

*Attack of the Rockoids* © 2000 Gene Steinberg & Grayson Steinberg. Excerpts used with permission.

Screen reproductions in this book were created on an Apple iMac using SnapzPro from Ambrosia Software, Inc. and edited in Graphic Converter from Lemke Software and Adobe Photoshop from Adobe Systems, Inc.

All photographs taken by the Nikon CoolPix 950, courtesy Nikon, Inc.

## Warning and Disclaimer

Every effort has been made to make this book as complete and as accurate as possible, but no warranty or fitness is implied. The information provided is on an "as is" basis. The author and the publisher shall have neither liability nor responsibility to any person or entity with respect to any loss or damages arising from the information contained in this book.

**Acquisitions Editor**
Betsy Brown

**Development Editor**
Marta M. Justak

**Managing Editor**
Charlotte Clapp

**Project Editor**
Andy Beaster

**Copy Editors**
Marta M. Justak
Mike Henry

**Indexer**
Greg Pearson

**Proofreader**
Tony Reitz

**Technical Editors**
Jeff Keller
Mike W. Perry

**Team Coordinator**
Amy Patton

**Interior Designers**
Nathan Clement
Ruth Lewis

**Cover Designers**
Aren Howell
Nathan Clement

**Copywriter**
Eric Borgert

# Contents at a Glance

| | | |
|---|---|---|
| 1 | How to Set Up Your Mac | 5 |
| 2 | Discovering the Mac OS | 19 |
| 3 | Opening and Saving Stuff | 39 |
| 4 | Finding and Moving Files | 51 |
| 5 | Working with Documents | 61 |
| 6 | Getting Connected to the Internet | 73 |
| 7 | Exploring the System Folder | 93 |
| 8 | Installing and Removing Programs | 105 |
| 9 | Customizing Your Mac's Look and Feel | 117 |
| 10 | Printing from Your Mac | 137 |
| 11 | Hard Drive Setup and Maintenance | 153 |
| 12 | Adding Accessories to Your Mac | 167 |
| 13 | Networking Your Mac | 181 |
| 14 | Working with the System | 193 |
| 15 | Solving Problems | 205 |
| G | Glossary | 223 |
| I | Index | 231 |

# Contents

## 1 How to Set Up Your Mac  5
How to Hook Your Mac Up and Turn It On  6
How to Use the Mac OS Setup Assistant  8
How to Use Your Desktop  12
How to Use Tutorials  14
How to Restart and Shut Down  16

## 2 Discovering the Mac OS  19
How to Navigate a Window  20
How to Organize Windows and Icons  22
How to Identify Desktop Icons  24
How to Change Folder Views  26
How to Use the Menu Bar  28
How to Use a Dialog Box and Contextual Menus  30
How to Make an Alias and Rename a File  32
How to Launch and Quit an Application  34
How to Trash a File  36

## 3 Opening and Saving Stuff  39
How to Use the Standard Open Dialog Box  40
How to Use the New Open Dialog Box  42
How to Use the Standard Save As Dialog Box  44
How to Use the New Save As Dialog Box  46
How to Find a Place to Save Your File  48

## 4 Finding and Moving Files  51
How to Use Sherlock 2 to Find a File  52
How to Use Sherlock 2 to Find a File's Text  54
How to Use Sherlock 2 to Search the Internet  56
How to Select, Copy, and Move Folders and Files  58

## 5 Working with Documents  61
How to Create a New Document and Enter and Select Text  62
How to Move, Copy, and Paste Text  64
How to Undo and Redo an Action  66
How to Drag Items from One Place to Another  68
How to Export and Import Data Between Documents  70

## 6 Getting Connected to the Internet  73
How to Run the Internet Assistant  74
How to Use a Web Browser  78
How to Search Online  82
How to Use an Email Program  86
How to Prepare and Send Email  90

## 7 Exploring the System Folder  93
How to Identify and Use Extensions Folder Items  94
How to Identify and Use the Contextual Menu Items and Control Strip Modules Folders  96
How to Identify and Use Control Panels Folder Items  98
How to Use the Preferences Folder  100
How to Identify and Use Other System Folder Items  102

## 8 Installing and Removing Applications  105
How to Use the Installer  106
How to Use ReadMe Files  108
How to Set Up Application Preferences  110
How to Give an Application More Memory  112
How to Remove Applications  114

## 9 Customizing Your Mac's Look and Feel  *117*

- How to Change the Appearance Control Panel  118
- How to Adjust Mouse Tracking Speed  120
- How to Use the Date & Time Control Panel  122
- How to Pick System Alert Sounds  126
- How to Record System Alert Sounds  128
- How to Use the Energy Saver  130
- How to Adjust Your Display Settings  132
- How to Customize for Multiple Users  134

## 10 Printing from Your Mac  *137*

- How to Set Up a Printer  138
- How to Use the Page Setup Dialog  140
- How to Use the Print Dialog  142
- How to Stop and Resume a Print Job  144
- How to Use Desktop Printing  146
- How to Use PrintMonitor  148
- How to Cope with Printer Problems  150

## 11 Hard Drive Setup and Maintenance  *153*

- How to Hook Up a New Drive  154
- How to Format a New Drive  156
- How to Start from Another Drive  158
- How to Check for Hard Drive Damage  160
- How to Optimize a Hard Drive  162
- How to Back Up a Drive  164

## 12 Adding Accessories to Your Mac  *167*

- How to Install a Scanner  168
- How to Install a Keyboard or Pointing Device  170
- How to Install a Desktop or Digital Camera  172
- How to Install a New Modem  174
- How to Add Speakers  176
- How to Add a Hub  178

## 13 Networking Your Mac  *181*

- How to Connect to a Network  182
- How to Set Up File Sharing  184
- How to Set Permission Levels  186
- How to Turn Off File Sharing  188
- How to Diagnose Network Problems  190

## 14 Working with the System  *193*

- How to Install the Mac Operating System  194
- How to Do a Clean System Install  196
- How to Merge System Folders  198
- How to Do a System Update  202

## 15 Solving Problems  *205*

- How to Deal with System Crashes  206
- How to Use the Extensions Manager  208
- How to Find Extension Conflicts  210
- How to Deal with Memory Problems  212
- How to Rebuild the Desktop  214
- How to Free Space on a Hard Drive  216
- How to Cope with a Hard Drive Crash  218
- How to Use Virus Software  220

## G Glossary  *223*

## I Index  *231*

## About the Author

**Gene Steinberg** first used a Mac in 1984 and never looked back. He is a fact and science fiction writer as well as a computer software and systems consultant. His more than 20 computer-related books include *Sams Teach Yourself the iMac in 24 Hours* and *Sams Teach Yourself the iBook in 24 Hours*. Gene's commentaries and product reviews appear in *MacHome* magazine and in his "Mac Reality Check Column" for the *Arizona Republic's* Arizona Central Computing page. He's also a regularly featured guest on Craig Crossman's "Computer America" radio show. In his spare time, Gene and his son, Grayson, are developing a new science fiction adventure series, *Attack of the Rockoids*.

## Dedication

*For my family, who made everything possible.*

## Acknowledgements

I cannot begin to list everyone who has helped make this book a success. In addition to my patient family, my son, Grayson, and wonderful wife, Barbara, a host of people helped me to check and test and confirm and reconfirm all the information you are reading in this book.

I am also indebted to the folks at Apple Computer for developing the great products that have revitalized the company and kept the expectations of Mac users alive and well.

Among those people is Apple's PR team, who has provided me with a steady flow of information about their new products.

In addition, I'd like to thank the folks at Macmillan USA for giving me this opportunity and making sure that everything in this book came out just perfect.

# Tell Us What You Think!

As the reader of this book, *you* are our most important critic and commentator. We value your opinion and want to know what we're doing right, what we could do better, what areas you'd like to see us publish in, and any other words of wisdom you're willing to pass our way.

You can email or write me directly to let me know what you did or didn't like about this book—as well as what we can do to make our books stronger.

*Please note that I cannot help you with technical problems related to the topic of this book, and that due to the high volume of mail I receive, I might not be able to reply to every message.*

When you write, please be sure to include this book's title and author as well as your name and phone or fax number. I will carefully review your comments and share them with the author and editors who worked on the book.

Email:         `internet_sams@mcp.com`

Mail:          Mark Taber
               Associate Publisher
               Sams Publishing
               201 West 103rd Street
               Indianapolis, IN 46290 USA

# How To Use This Book

## The Complete Visual Reference

Each chapter of this book is made up of a series of short, instructional tasks, designed to help you understand all the information that you need to get the most out of your computer hardware and software.

**Click:** Click the mouse button once.

**Double-click:** Click the mouse button twice in rapid succession.

**Pointer Arrow:** Highlights an item on the screen you need to point to or focus on in the step or task.

**Selection:** Highlights the area on-screen discussed in the step or task.

**Click and Type:** Click once where indicated and begin typing to enter your text or data.

**How to Drag:** Point to the starting place or object. Hold down the mouse button, move the mouse to the new location, and then release the button.

Each task includes a series of easy-to-understand steps designed to guide you through the procedure.

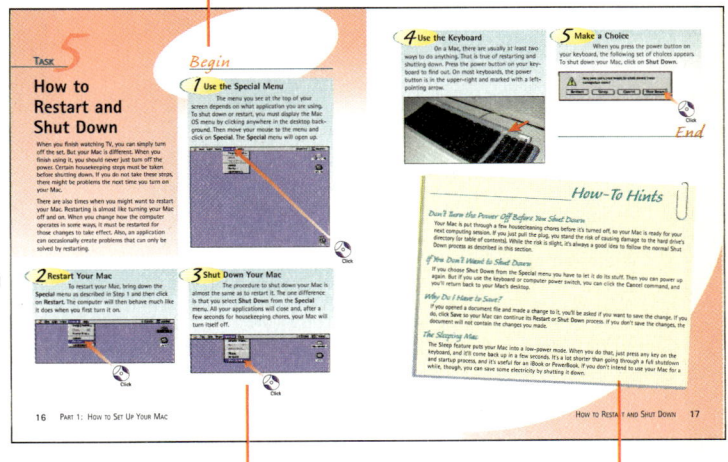

Each step is fully illustrated to show you how it looks onscreen.

Extra hints that tell you how to accomplish a goal are provided in most tasks.

Menus and items you click are shown in **bold**.

If you see this symbol, it means the task you're in continues on the next page.

# Introduction

*D*o you remember when Wall Street considered the Mac a lost cause? It wasn't so very long ago, either. Apple wasn't relevant anymore, they said.

But things have changed.

In 1998, Apple made history again, by introducing the iMac, a consumer desktop computer with a unique look and with an advertising campaign that was equally innovative.

Hundreds of thousands of folks ordered iMacs from the very beginning, and it soared to the upper echelons of the sales charts, right next to those computers from the "Dark Side."

Apple followed with the iBook, faster and faster G3 and G4 Power Macs, and a new variation on the iMac design, the DV series, which lets you easily edit your home videos with near broadcast-quality results.

The results have been phenomenal. Apple Computer is the darling of Wall Street again, and more and more PC-only companies are signing in with new Mac products.

## About This Book

A great many of the folks buying Macs never used a personal computer before. It is a whole new world, but it's a world that shouldn't be intimidating or frustrating.

*How to Use Your Mac* is designed to teach you how to master your Mac quickly and easily.

This book is written in the true spirit of the Mac. Instead of reading pages and pages of text, I'll show you how to learn your Mac by using color pictures and simple descriptions.

You'll start with unpacking your Mac and hooking it up for the first time. Then you'll discover the magic of the Mac operating system, where icons are used to represent the computer's functions. You'll learn what files and folders are all about, and how to use your programs, so you can put your Mac to work as quickly as possible.

Once you've begun to run your programs on your Mac, you'll learn how to save your files and where you should put them.

You'll then discover how to locate files on your Mac's drive, in seconds, even if you can't remember where you put them.

From there, I'll show you how to edit your documents and even how easy it is to move information from one document to another.

A lot of you bought a Mac to get on the Internet, and I've devoted a whole section in the book to getting connected. You'll learn how to set up your Internet access. And once you're hooked up, you'll discover the World Wide Web and email.

Armed with these basics, I'll introduce you to the nuts and bolts of your Mac. You'll be taken on a tour of the System Folder, and you'll see what secrets lie within that folder and what all those files are there for.

You'll learn how to install and remove a program, and how to customize your Mac's look and feel, including changing the desktop background.

This book will also show you how to set up and use a printer, how to check your hard drive for problems, and how to back up your files, so you know they're safe.

A Mac shouldn't stay alone. In addition to adding a printer, there are many other accessories you can buy to extend your Mac's capabilities. I'll tell you about installing extra drives for backups, how to add a different keyboard or mouse, a scanner, a digital camera, and even a better set of loudspeakers.

The Mac is also a computer that's easy to network. I'll show you how to hook it up to a computer network in minutes, and then how to share files between your Mac and other computers.

Of course, no personal computer is perfect, and so problems sometimes arise. So I conclude this book with a hands-on troubleshooting guide. You'll find that you can actually solve most computer problems by yourself, in minutes. And even if you have to make a phone call to get further assistance, you'll be able to give the technical support person the right information to help you resolve the problem as quickly as possible.

## Task

1. How to Hook Your Mac Up and Turn it On  6

2. How to Use the Mac OS Setup Assistant  8

3. How to Use Your Desktop  12

4. How to Use Tutorials  14

5. How to Restart and Shut Down  16

PART

# How to Set Up Your Mac

1

**R**ight out of the box, your Mac is a powerful personal computer that, without a lot of complex setup, is designed to perform a variety of complex tasks with relative ease.

In this book, I'll show you how to hook up your Mac, and then take you on a guided tour of all its features.

Beginning in this section, you'll learn how to get your Mac up and running, and then begin to explore all its features. You'll also be guided to Apple's own tutorials that will help you learn basic mouse and other Mac skills.

Once you have progressed past the basics, you'll discover how to make your Mac do your bidding, and if trouble arises, what you can do to solve any problems.

Now we do what you want to do most-get your hands on that new computer and start using it. You will be going through a series of easy-to-follow tasks. The first series prepares your Macintosh computer to be turned on. The second takes you through steps that fit your Mac to your own particular circumstances. (Macs really do let you "have it you way.") Then, beginning with Task 3, you will learn how to use your Mac to the things you want to do.

Ready? Then let's get started!

## Task 1

# How to Hook Your Mac Up and Turn It On

Here's your new Mac. Whether it's a fully outfitted Power Macintosh G4 or an iMac, the basic techniques of getting it ready to run are pretty much the same.

## Begin

### 1 Find a Place to Set It Up

Place your Mac on a table or desk.

### 2 Plug It In

Plug one end of the power cord into your Mac and the other end into an AC outlet. You might want to purchase a surge protector for the best protection against power surges (due to weather or other conditions) that can possibly damage the delicate electronics of your Mac and the rest of your system. One major manufacturer of such a product is Tripp Lite.

### 3 Attach the Keyboard

Take the keyboard cable and plug it into your Mac. If it's an older Mac without a USB jack, check the installation diagram for the correct location.

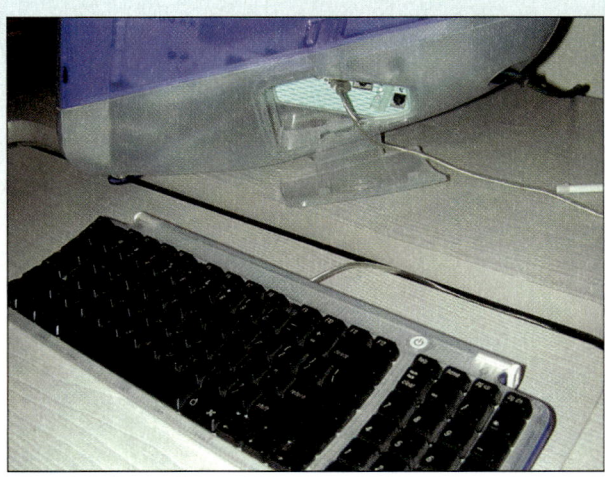

6    Part 1: How to Set Up Your Mac

## 4 Connect the Mouse

Take the mouse that came with your Mac and plug it into the keyboard. On some keyboards, there will be a jack at each end. On others, it'll be in the rear.

## 5 Hook Up the Modem

If your Mac has a built-in modem for Internet access, attach a modular phone plug to the Mac and plug it in at the other end to the wall jack or to the external phone jack of a fax machine or an office phone.

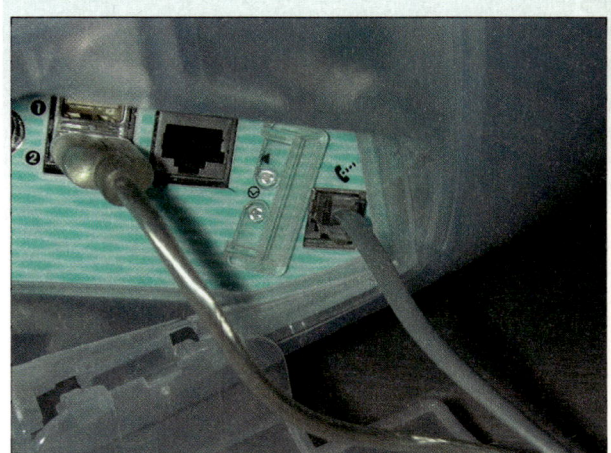

## 6 Turn It On

Press the **power on** switch on the keyboard or Mac to switch it on. You should hear a startup tone, which sounds like a musical chord, that will announce that the Mac is up and running. In a minute or two, you'll see a **Welcome to Mac OS** or **Welcome to Mac OS 9** message on your Mac's display.

## How-To Hints

### Got an Apple Laptop?

If your new Mac is an iBook or PowerBook, the only thing you have to plug in when you first set it up is the AC power adapter. When the unit ships from the factory, the battery power is usually depleted. Once plugged in, press the **power button** to turn the unit on. Even if you will be turning it off soon, leave it connected for a few hours to fully charge the battery.

### What If It Doesn't Start?

If you don't hear a startup tone, recheck your connections. Then switch it on again. If you're using a power strip for AC power, make sure that the switch, if any, is on, and that the other end is plugged into a wall socket. It's not uncommon for these units to get disconnected during housecleaning.

End

TASK 2

# How to Use the Mac OS Setup Assistant

At the beginning of your new Mac's startup process, you'll see a procession of little icons appearing on the bottom of the screen. These are little programs, called **Extensions**, which provide essential features when your Mac is running.

*Begin*

## 1 Launch Mac OS Setup Assistant

When you turn on a new Mac, or after reinstalling the Mac operating system, a program called **Mac OS Setup Assistant** will launch. It's designed to do some initial setups of your Mac. You'll want to answer the little questionnaire first; then point your **mouse** and click on the **right arrow** to continue each step of the way.

Click

## 2 Regional Preferences

Each country has its own way of handling things such as date and time. Your Mac knows about these differences. Using the mouse, point to and click on the country whose format best suits your needs and then click on the **right arrow** in the lower-right corner.

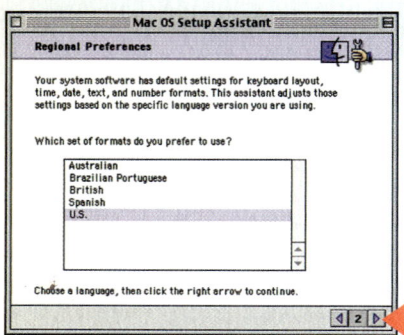

Click

## 3 Identify Yourself

The **Mac OS Setup Assistant** will ask for your name and the name of your company. If you're using the computer at home, you can leave the company part blank.

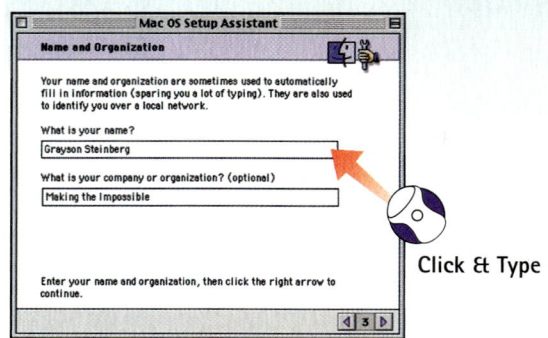
Click & Type

## 4 Set Time and Date

From the factory, the Mac doesn't know which geographic location and time zone you live in. You'll be asked to specify the date and time. You'll also indicate whether Daylight Savings Time is in effect.

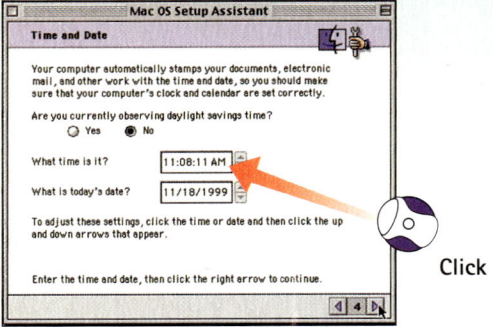
Click

## 5 Geographic Location

To handle time differences, your Mac needs to know the time zone you are in. Find and click on a city close to you and in your time zone. (Hint: Type the first letters of a city's name and the list will go to that city.) Then click on the **right arrow**.

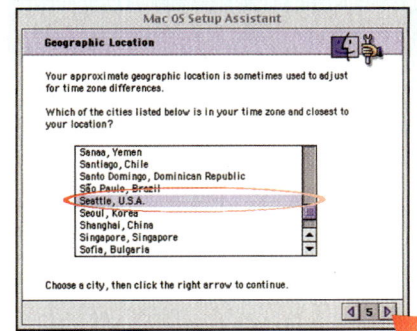

Click

## 6 Set Finder Preferences

Don't worry about this option. Just leave it as it is. Click the **right** arrow to move on.

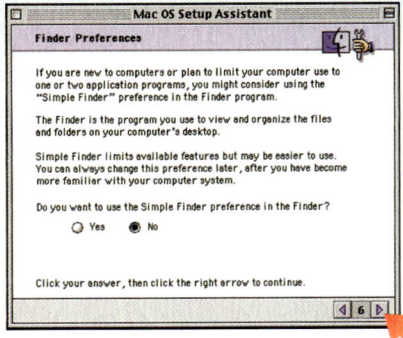

Click

## 7 Name Your Computer

If your Mac is on a network, it needs its own unique name and password. Make up a **password** and type it in, write them down and keep them in a safe place. The next question, about a Shared Folder, can be ignored. Just click the **next** arrow to move on.

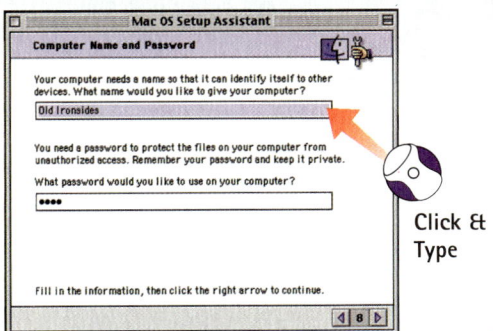
Click & Type

*Continues*

## How to Use the Mac OS Setup Assistnt Continued

### 8 Set Printer Connection

If you have a personal printer, such as a Canon, Epson, or HP, or any printer plugged into a USB jack, choose **Direct Connection**. Otherwise, it'll be a networked printer, in which case you pick **Network Connection**. Just click the **right** arrow to pass this by if you don't have a printer. If you have a printer, you'll be asked to pick its **name** from the list (even if there's only one). If the printer's name isn't displayed, just pick one from the list for now. You can reselect your printer with **Apple's Chooser** (available from the **Apple** menu) later, before you're ready to print.

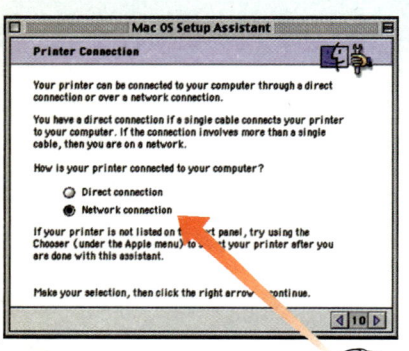
Click

### 9 The Finsih Line

The final screen will show your choices. Click **Go Ahead** to activate the settings. Click the **left** (back) arrow if you need to redo anything. When you're done, click **Quit** to finish. If you want to set up an Internet account, click **Continue** and proceed to Part 6 of this book.

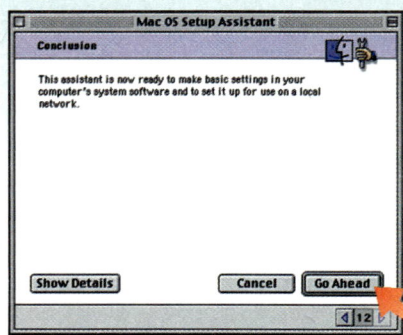

Click

*End*

## How-To Hints

### No Mac OS Setup Assistant
If a service technician sets up your Mac or it has been used previously, the Mac OS Setup Assistant won't appear when you start your Mac. You can find it located in a folder on your Mac's hard drive, called **Assistants**. Just open that folder, point the mouse at the **Mac OS Setup Assistant** icon, and double-click it to begin the setup process.

### Need to Make a Change?
No problem. You can relaunch **Mac OS Setup Assistant** at any time and switch the settings to the ones you want. You may want to do this if the computer is being transferred to another user or another network setup.

TASK 3

# How to Use Your Desktop

Now that your Mac is properly set up, turn your attention to your computer screen and tell yourself, "I'm looking at a desktop." Why? Because in the Mac world, your screen is much like the top of a desk. On an old-fashioned desktop, people kept office tools, such as a typewriter, along with folders in which they kept printed documents. The Mac desktop is the same except the tools are called applications (programs). Folders and documents keep their names and work much like their namesakes.

## Begin

### 1 Exploring Your Desktop

Look at your desktop. On your desktop are small pictures called *icons*. You use the mouse to place a pointer (which looks like an arrow) on top of an icon. Look in the upper-right corner for a rectangular icon labeled **Macintosh HD**. Click that icon once and notice that it turns dark. By clicking the icon once, you "selected" it. We'll say more about selecting later.

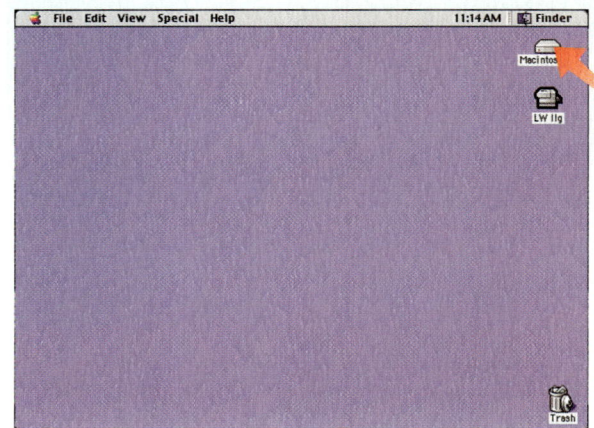

### 2 Open Your Hard Drive

The **Macintosh HD** icon you clicked on represents the hard drive inside your computer. Like a file cabinet, a hard disk stores information that your Mac uses. Point your mouse arrow at the hard disk icon again, but this time click the icon twice. A window should open up on your desktop. You have opened your hard drive.

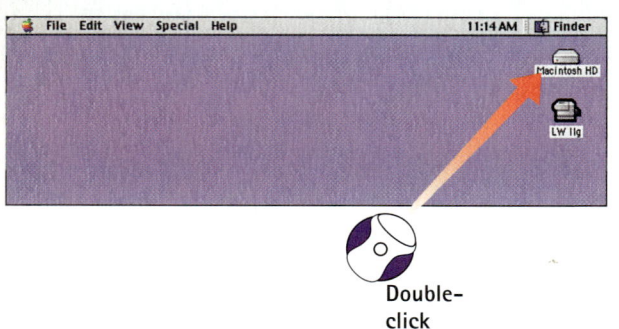

### 3 Explore a Window

Look more closely at the window you have opened. Its icons reveal what is on your hard drive. Notice that many of the icons look like file folders turned sideways. Mac users call these icons—you guessed it—*folders*. Now find the folder labeled **Assistants** and double-click on it.

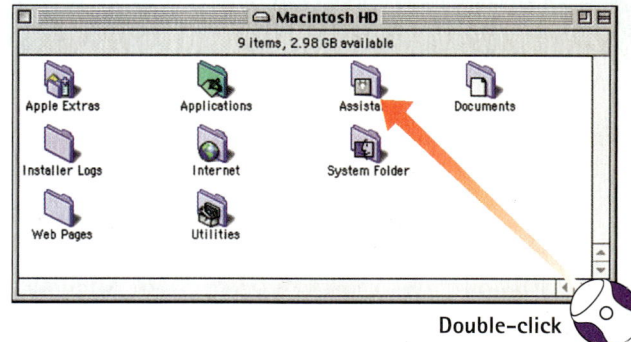

12 PART 1: HOW TO SET UP YOUR MAC

## 4 Run an Application

Inside the **Assistants** folder you will find two icons. In Task 2, you used an application labeled **Mac OS Setup Assistant** to set up your Mac. Click the **Mac OS Setup Assistant** icon twice to open it now and you'll find yourself back where you were then.

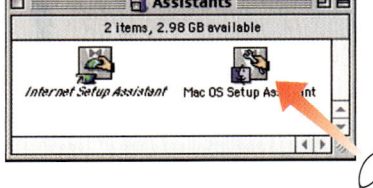

Double-click

## 5 Quit an Application

You make any changes you want. When you're finished, move the mouse over the word **File** in the menu that runs across the top of the screen. Hold down the mouse button, and a list will drop down. Move the mouse down the list until it is over the word **Quit**, and then let the button go. When a window appears asking whether you want to quit, click on the **Quit** button.

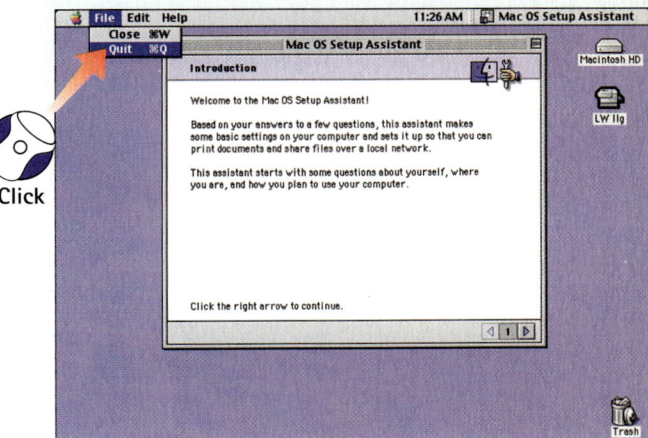
Click

## 6 Close a Window

If you are not careful, your desktop will become cluttered with open windows. It is easy to close those windows you do not need. In the upper-left corner of the **Assistants** window you have open is a small box. Click once on the small box to close the window.

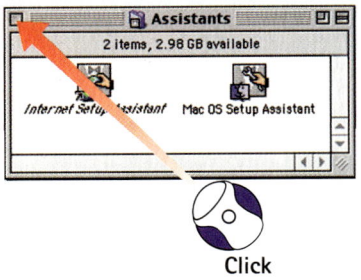
Click

## 7 Find Documents

Now it's time to fly solo. Open and close windows to your heart's content. Look for icons that resemble a sheet of paper with the corner turned down. Those icons represent documents. (Of course, not every document has a turned-down corner, but it is a good clue.) Double-clicking on anything that looks like the icons below opens the document with the application that created it.

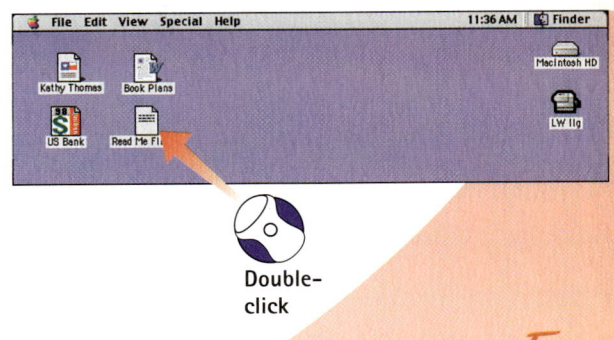
Double-click

*End*

How to Use Your Desktop

TASK 4

# How to Use Tutorials

You're new to the world of Mac computing, but wouldn't it be nice if there was a way that someone could stand over you as you learn your way around? Well, in addition to the instructions you'll read in this book, Apple has assembled an online tutorial for you.

## Begin

### 1 Click on the Help Menu

Drag the mouse cursor to the **Help** menu, click the **button**, and choose **Tutorial**. The Mac OS tutor will come on-screen. You'll have two courses, each of which will take about 15 minutes of your time.

### 2 Start with Mouse Skills

Point your mouse at the **Mouse Skills** button and click on it. You'll see this startup screen.

### 3 Learn Mouse Skills

As you complete each step of the Mouse Skills tutorial, press **Return** on your keyboard to move to the next step. You will be asked to click on items or click a **right** arrow to move on. Click the **Listen** button if you prefer a narration to a text screen.

14  PART 1: HOW TO SET UP YOUR MAC

## 4 Continue to Desktop Skills

You can click **back** or **left** arrows to repeat a step. When you're done, click the **Exit** button; then click **OK**, and you'll go back to the main screen where you can begin your Desktop Skills.

## 5 Learn Desktop Skills

As with the mouse tutorial, you'll be guided step-by-step through all parts of your Mac's desktop, so you'll learn how each function works. You'll click **right** arrows or press **Return** to move on.

Click

## 6 Finish Up

When you are finished with the online course, click the **Exit** button; then click **OK** on the next screen. You'll go back to the main screen, where you just click the **Quit** button to return to your Mac's regular desktop.

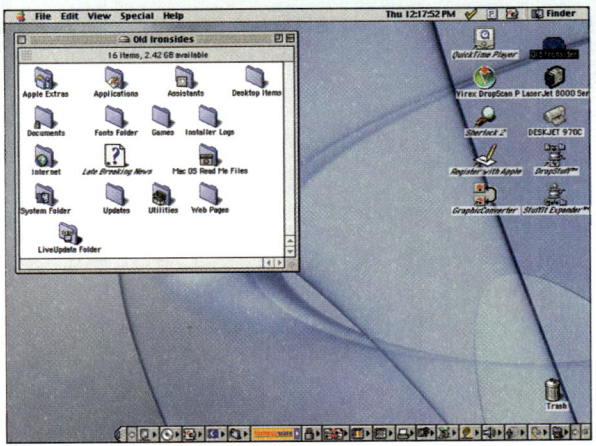

*End*

### How-To Hints

#### Tutorial Missing?

The Mac tutorial comes with brand-new consumer Macs, such as the iBook and iMac. If you don't see it in the Help menu, look for a folder called **Mac OS Tutorial** in the **Apple Extras** folder (double-click on each folder in succession; then double-click on the colorful icon called **Mac OS Tutorial** to start it). If it's not there, don't fret. You could restore it with your **Mac OS Restore** disk, but then you'd lose any new files or settings you've made. Instead, just follow the instructions in this book, and you'll soon master your Mac skills.

TASK 5

# How to Restart and Shut Down

When you finish watching TV, you can simply turn off the set. But your Mac is different. When you finish using it, you should never just turn off the power. Certain housekeeping steps must be taken before shutting down. If you do not take these steps, there might be problems the next time you turn on your Mac.

There are also times when you might want to restart your Mac. Restarting is almost like turning your Mac off and on. When you change how the computer operates in some ways, it must be restarted for those changes to take effect. Also, an application can occasionally create problems that can only be solved by restarting.

*Begin*

## *1* Use the Special Menu

The menu you see at the top of your screen depends on what application you are using. To shut down or restart, you must display the Mac OS menu by clicking anywhere in the desktop background. Then move your mouse to the menu and click on **Special**. The **Special** menu will open up.

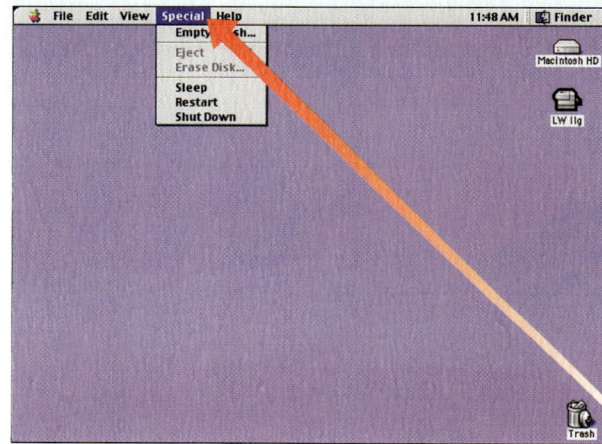

Click

## *2* Restart Your Mac

To restart your Mac, bring down the **Special** menu as described in Step 1 and then click on **Restart**. The computer will then behave much like it does when you first turn it on.

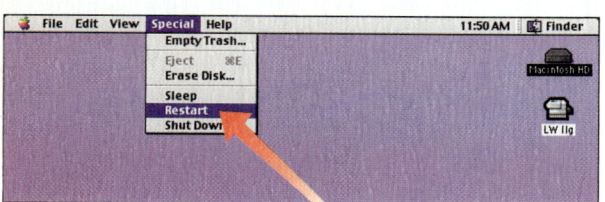

Click

## *3* Shut Down Your Mac

The procedure to shut down your Mac is almost the same as to restart it. The one difference is that you select **Shut Down** from the **Special** menu. All your applications will close and, after a few seconds for housekeeping chores, your Mac will turn itself off.

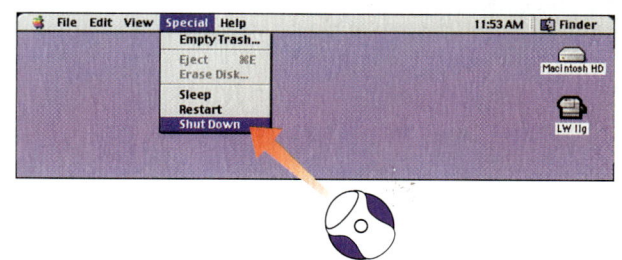

Click

16   PART 1: HOW TO SET UP YOUR MAC

## 4 Use the Keyboard

On a Mac, there are usually at least two ways to do anything. That is true of restarting and shutting down. Press the power button on your keyboard to find out. On most keyboards, the power button is in the upper-right and marked with a left-pointing arrow.

## 5 Make a Choice

When you press the power button on your keyboard, the following set of choices appears. To shut down your Mac, click on **Shut Down**.

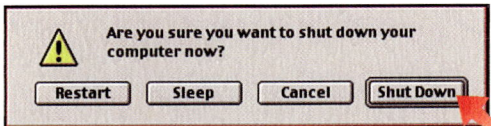

Click

*End*

---

## How-To Hints

### Don't Turn the Power Off Before You Shut Down
Your Mac is put through a few housecleaning chores before it's turned off, so your Mac is ready for your next computing session. If you just pull the plug, you stand the risk of causing damage to the hard drive's directory (or table of contents). While the risk is slight, it's always a good idea to follow the normal Shut Down process as described in this section.

### If You Don't Want to Shut Down
If you choose **Shut Down** from the **Special** menu you have to let it do its stuff. Then you can power up again. But if you use the keyboard or computer power switch, you can click the **Cancel** command, and you'll return back to your Mac's desktop.

### Why Do I Have to Save?
If you opened a document file and made a change to it, you'll be asked if you want to save the change. If you do, click **Save** so your Mac can continue its **Restart** or **Shut Down** process. If you don't save the changes, the document will not contain the changes you made.

### The Sleeping Mac
The **Sleep** feature puts your Mac into a low-power mode. When you do that, just press any key on the keyboard, and it'll come back up in a few seconds. It's a lot shorter than going through a full shutdown and startup process, and it's useful for an iBook or PowerBook. If you don't intend to use your Mac for a while, though, you can save some electricity by shutting it down.

# Task

1. How to Navigate a Window 20

2. How to Organize Windows and Icons 22

3. How to Identify Desktop Icons 24

4. How to Change Folder Views 26

5. How to Use the Menu Bar 28

6. How to Use a Dialog Box and Contextual Menus 30

7. How to Make an Alias and Rename a File 32

8. How to Launch and Quit an Application 34

9. How to Trash a File 36

## PART 2

# Discovering the Mac OS

*T*he Mac operating system took personal computing from complicated, text-based instructions to point-and-click simplicity. Instead of having to enter instructions (and not always easy instructions) on the screen when performing a function, the Mac OS introduced the concept of using icons to represent real-world behavior.

For example, you do your office work on a desktop, and the background pattern you see on the screen after your Mac has started up is also called a desktop. The items on the desktop are displayed as icons, representing, for example, files, folders, and disks. When you want to organize your files, you put them in folders.

Actions are performed on your Mac's desktop with the keyboard and mouse. When you want to perform a function, you first select the icon you want to work on by clicking on it. Double-clicking on the icon opens it.

Throughout this book, I'll explain these functions in more detail. But in this section, I'll cover all the basics of the Mac and how to use the functions that will serve you regardless of what you ask your Mac to do.

## Task 1

# How to Navigate a Window

A window displays the contents of something. It may list the contents of a disk, a folder, or a document. Regardless of what's inside, you use it the same way.

## *Begin*

### 1 Open a Window

Double-click on the icon for your Macintosh hard drive (it may be called **Macintosh HD** or something else).

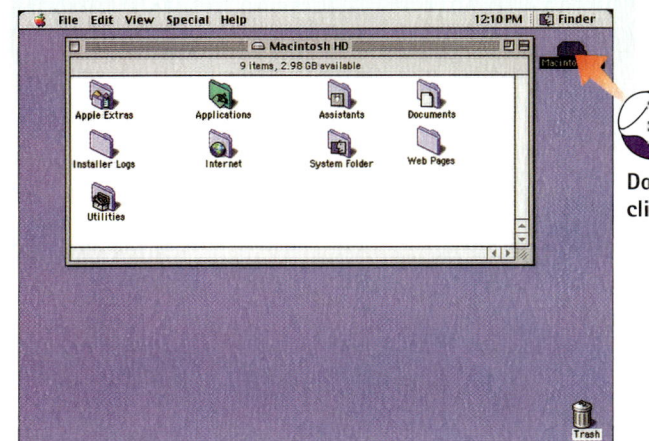

### 2 Scroll Through It

If the window is too small to display all the icons, you'll see a vertical or horizontal bar that you click and drag to see more. You can also use the arrows to move.

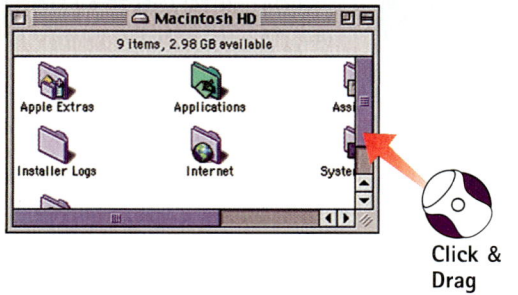

### 3 Expand It

Click the **Resize** box to make the window expand to show all the icons (or at least as many as will display on your desktop).

20    Part 2: Discovering the Mac OS

## 4 Reduce It

Click again on the **Resize** box to make it smaller.

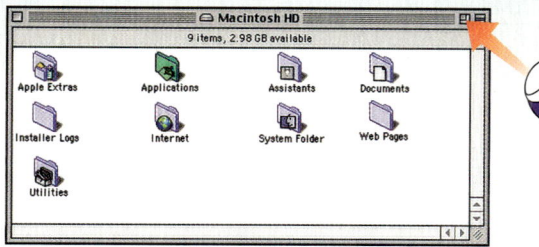
Click

## 5 Collapse It

Click on the **Collapse** box to reduce it to just the title; click again to restore it to its previous size. If this feature doesn't work, check Part 9 and read the instructions about changing the settings in the Appearance Control Panel.

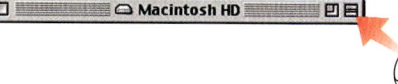

Click

## 6 Resize It

Click on the **Size** box and drag back and forth, or up and down, to change the size of a window.

Click & Drag

## 7 Close It

Click on the **Close** box in the upper left corner to close the window.

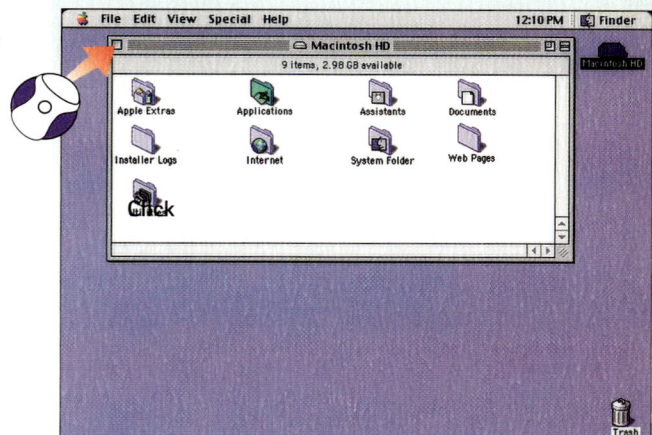

*End*

# How-To Hints

### Use the Option Key
The Option key on your Mac's keyboard adds some extra features. For example, if you have several windows open, holding down the **Option** key when you close one window will close all the other open windows, in most cases.

### When You Close a Document Window
Closing a window that displays the contents of a document, such as a word-processing document, doesn't actually close the program; in most cases, it just closes the file. To close a program, go to the **File** menu and select **Quit**.

### Change an Icon's Name
You can change the name of your hard drive and other icons simply by clicking on the name. After it is selected, you can type in the new name.

## Task 2

# How to Organize Windows and Icons

The ability to move windows and icons around can make for a rather messy desktop, just like the one in a regular office. But you can make things look neat with just a few Mac tricks.

## Begin

### 1 Sort Them

Go to the **View** menu on your desktop and choose **Clean Up**. Your windows and icons will organize themselves.

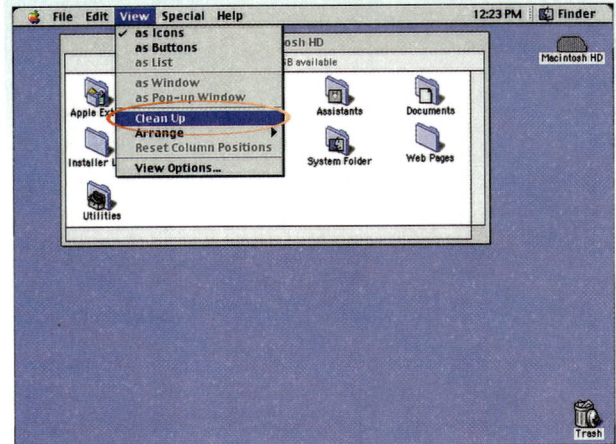

### 2 Arrange Them

Go to the **View** menu, choose **Arrange**, and pick your option from the sub-menu. Choosing by Name will arrange the icons in alphabetical order.

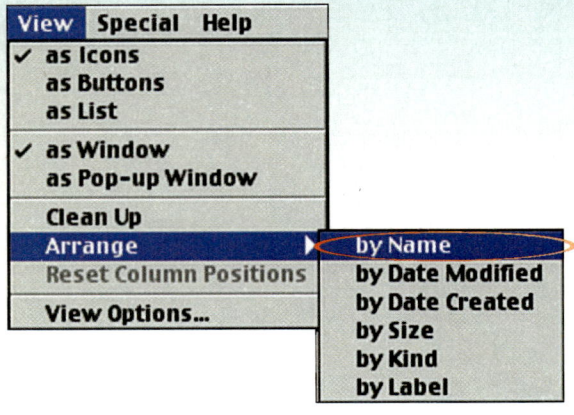

### 3 Line Them Up

Go to the View menu again and choose **View Options.** When a window is displayed choose **Always snap to grid**. They'll be lined up neatly.

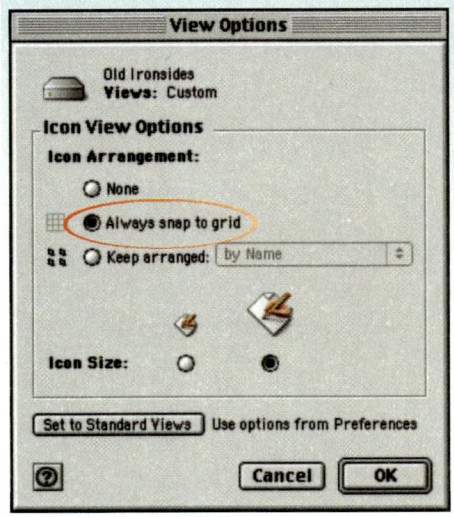

22  PART 2: DISCOVERING THE MAC OS

## 4 Change Grid Spacing

If you want icons to be closer together, choose **Preferences** from the **Edit** menu. Under **Grid Spacing**, click the **Tight** button.

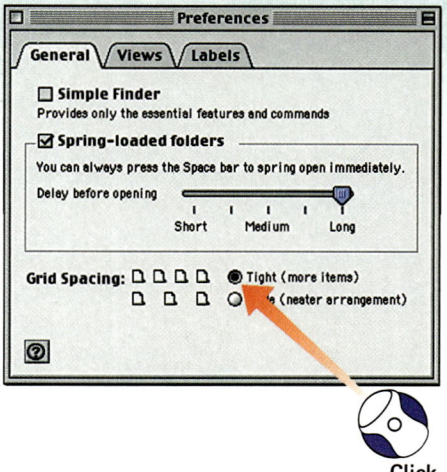

## 5 Print Desktop

To see a printed copy of the contents of your desktop, choose **Print Desktop** from the **File** menu.

Click

## 6 Print Window

If you've opened a window, the command becomes **Print Window**, and you'll see a copy of the contents of the directory window.

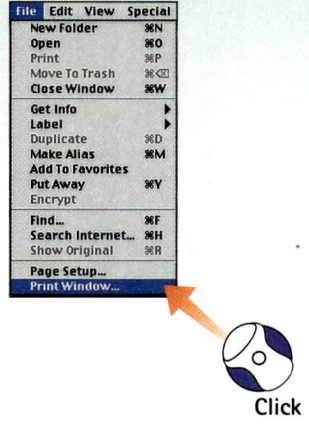
Click

*End*

## How-To Hints

### Make New Folders

To make a brand new folder, just choose **New Folder** (or type ⌘+N) from the File menu. It'll create an empty folder, labeled untitled. You can click on the word "untitled" and then type whatever name you want for the folder. After a new folder is created, you can put files and folders in it to organize your desktop.

### See Layout of Folders Within Folders

If you open a folder that's within another folder, hold down the ⌘ (Apple) key; then click on the folder's title to see a list of the folders in which that folder is placed. Click on any of these to move to that folder.

## TASK 3

# How to Identify Desktop Icons

There are several types of desktop icons, depending on what they represent. Here's how to identify them.

## *Begin*

### *1* Disk Icon

A disk icon will usually look something like a hard drive. When you double-click on it, it shows folders and files on the disk (although not folders within other folders).

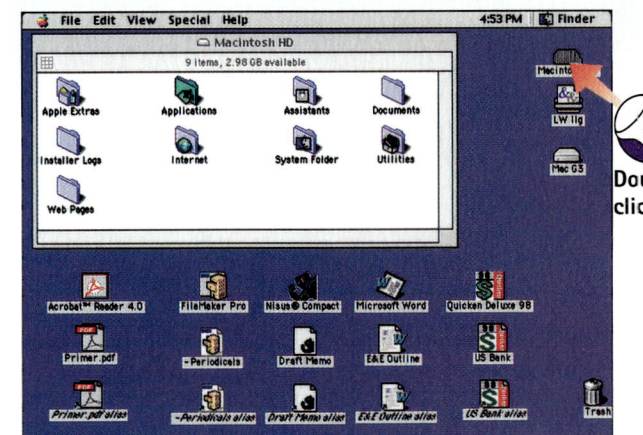

### *2* Printer Icon

Many of the printers you use will display a desktop icon when you install the software they need. (Some won't, so don't be concerned if you don't see one.) When you double-click on it, a new window appears showing what is being printed.

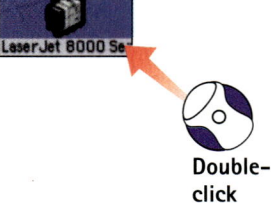

Double-click

### *3* Folder Icon

The folder icon resembles a physical file folder and performs a similar function. Some folder icons have special extra icons to show a special function, such as the Applications Folder. When you double-click on it, a new window will open showing the contents of that folder.

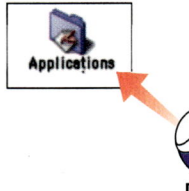

Double-click

## 4 Application Icon

The actual applications (programs) you use to create a document each have unique icons designed by their programmers to set them apart. It looks much like a product's unique logo. When you double-click on it the application runs.

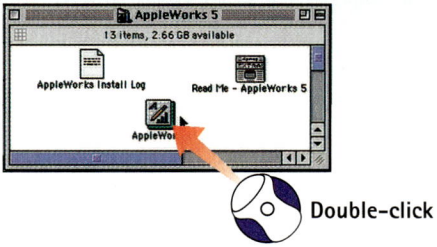
Double-click

## 5 Document Icon

This icon represents a file you create with one of your programs. When you double-click on it, the application that created the documents open it for you to view.

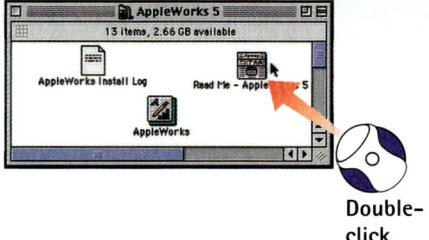
Double-click

## 6 Alias Icon

The little arrow at the left and an italicized label shows that the icon is an **alias**. An alias is a pointer or reference to the original file. You'll learn how to make an alias later in this section. For now just remember that double-clicking on an alias has the same result as double-clicking on the file to which it points.

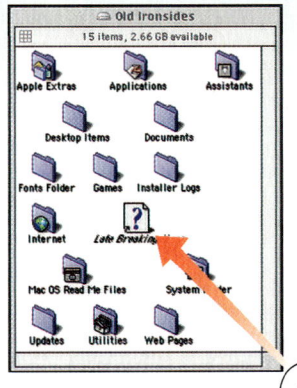
Double-click

## 7 Trash Icon

When you want to remove a file from your Mac, you put it in the **Trash**. Then you use the **Empty Trash** feature on the Special menu to get rid of it. Double-clicking on the trash will open it up and let you move items out of the trash.

Double-click

*End*

## How-To Hints

### Use the Tab Key to Navigate

You don't have to use a mouse for everything. You can also use keyboard commands for some functions. For example, if you have a number of icons on your desktop, just click on one to select it, and then press the **Tab** key to move from one to the other. Usually, it's alphabetical, but you can change the sort order, as you'll learn in the next section.

HOW TO IDENTIFY DESKTOP ICONS   25

TASK 4

# How to Change Folder Views

Normally, your Mac's desktop and disks and folder lists are shown as icons. But you can change the style in which they're displayed. This is especially useful if you have lots of icons in a disk or folder window.

## *Begin*

### 1 Check the View

Open a disk or folder window by double-clicking on it.

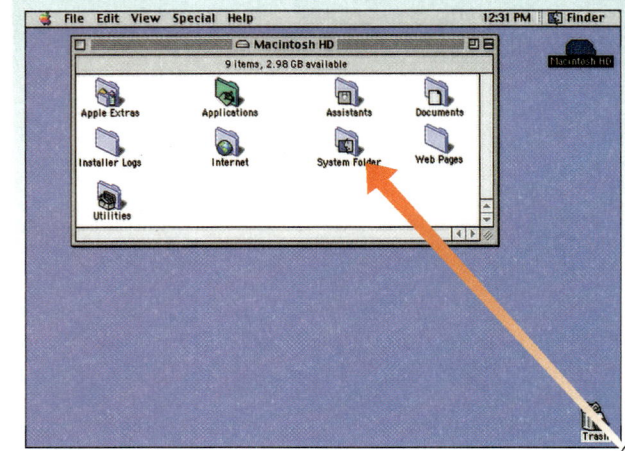

Double-click

### 2 View as List

Go to the **Views** menu and choose **as List**. In addition to changing the way a directory is viewed, you can select **Sort List** to change the way the items are sorted (the normal sort routine is by **Name**, and it is in alphabetical order).

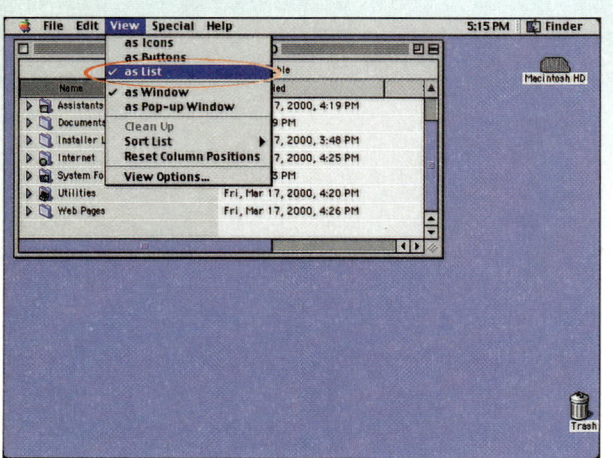

### 3 View as Button

You can also enlarge the icons and make them buttons that you can activate with just a single click by choosing **as Buttons** instead from the **View** menu.

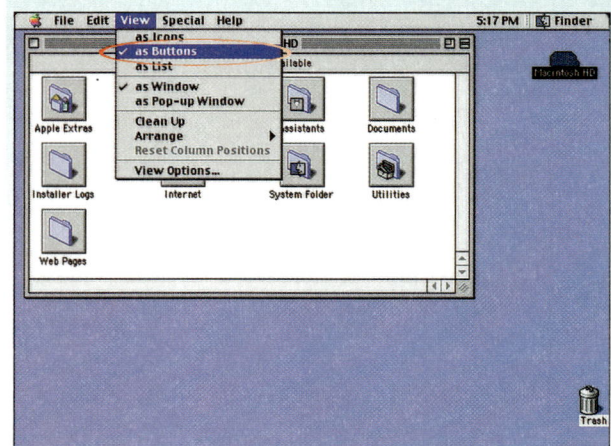

26   PART 2: DISCOVERING THE MAC OS

## 4 View as Pop-Up Window

This option moves the window (Macintosh HD, in this case) to the bottom of your screen, with just the title showing. Just open a folder and drag it to the bottom of the screen to produce a pop-up window.

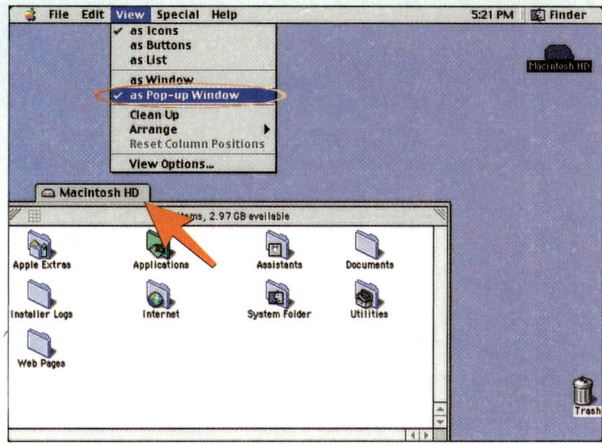

## 5 Open a Pop-Up Window

Click on the title of a pop-up window to see the contents. Click the title again to put it back at the bottom of your Mac's display.

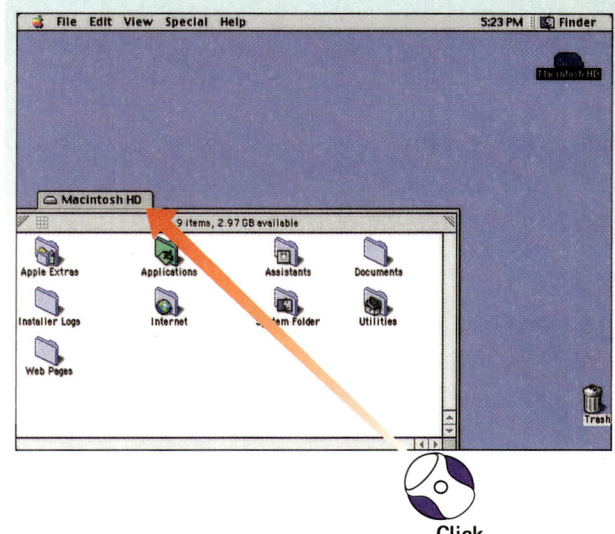

## 6 Change It Back

Return to the **View** menu and restore the settings the way you like.

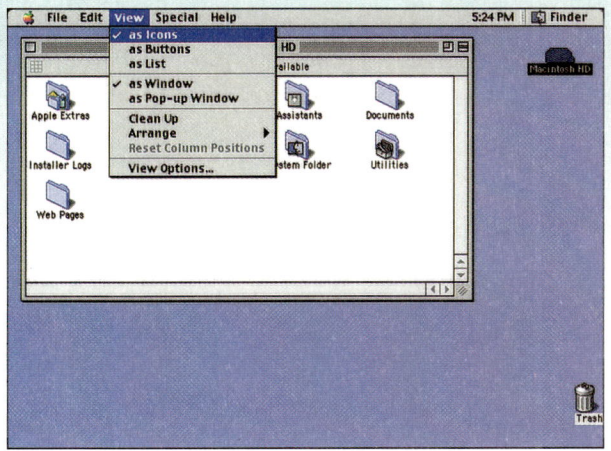

*End*

# How-To Hints

## You Can't View Desktop Items in List Form

The desktop is the exception. You are limited to Icon or Button view when you change views for desktop icons. You can't do List view on the desktop. Button view might be a nice thing to try, especially if you're still learning your double-click skills.

## Be Careful About Moving Folders Around

It's so easy to move icons around that you may put the wrong thing in the wrong place. It's a good idea not to move programs into other folders, especially the System Folder. If you move a program to the wrong place, you may have problems using certain programs or even affect the way your Mac runs. That's because many programs depend on a lot of support files in the same folder to run.

## Task 5

# How to Use the Menu Bar

At the top of your Mac's desktop and on virtually every application you work in is a menu bar. The menu bar lets you call up commands that relate to a particular application. To activate a menu bar command, simply click on a label and then choose the function from the pop-down menu.

## *Begin*

### *1* Check the File Menu

The **File** menu includes commands that let you apply actions to files, such as opening and printing them.

### *2* Check the Edit Menu

The **Edit** menu lets you change the contents of a window, such as copying, selecting, and cutting (deleting) and pasting.

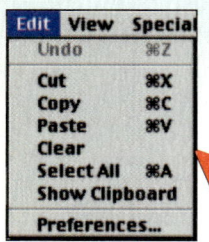

### *3* Check the View Menu

As explained in the previous section, the **View** menu changes the way icons are displayed. The **View as List** option, for example, is useful because it displays item titles rather than icons. This is a terrific way to reduce clutter in a folder list.

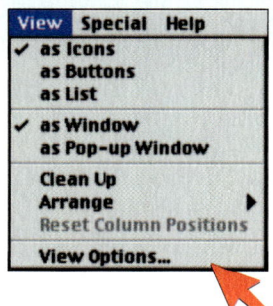

28   PART 2: DISCOVERING THE MAC OS

## 4 Check the Special Menu

The **Special** menu offers important functions, such as emptying the trash, ejecting a disk, erasing or restarting, and shutting down.

## 5 Check the Help Menu

The **Help** menu provides online instructions about how to use the Mac or an application.

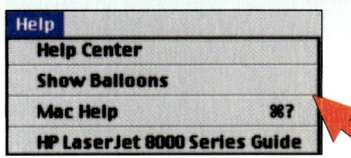

## 6 Check the Apple Menu

The **Apple** menu (located under the Apple symbol) lets you learn about your computer, and it can also call up some special programs. These include the **Chooser** (to select a printer) and **Sherlock 2** (to find things on your Mac or the Internet). The **Control Panels** feature lets you access applications that change the look and feel of your Mac.

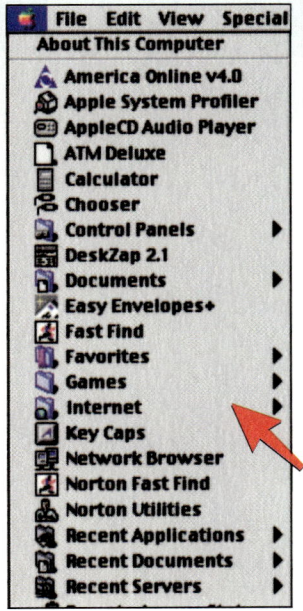

### How-To Hints

#### Programs Have Different Menu Bar Functions

Although basic functions in the Edit and File menus are similar, the menu bar changes when you use an application on your Mac. Some add a Window menu, while others add a Tool menu. In those menus, you'll find a special set of commands grouped under the labels.

#### Menus Stick

When you just click on a menu and release the mouse button, the menu will just stick there for 15 seconds. A sticky menu may be a little more comfortable for you, since it gives you time to look over the list of command functions without having to constantly hold down the mouse button.

*End*

How to Use the Menu Bar  29

TASK 6

# How to Use a Dialog Box and Contextual Menus

A dialog box is a window that enables you to enter information. Contextual menus are special pop-up menus whose choices depend on the situation. In this task, you learn about both.

## Begin

### 1 Display a Dialog Box

A menu option that will bring up a dialog box has three dots (an ellipsis) following the command. For an example, click once on the desktop, click again on **Edit** in the menu, and then click on **Preferences...** A **Preferences** dialog box will appear.

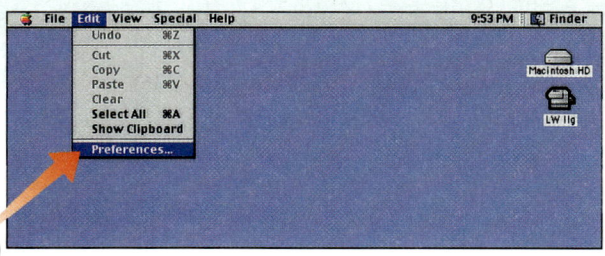

Click

### 2 Enter Information

Dialog boxes differ from box to box. This one has three folder tabs that enable you to see different screens. Click on the **Labels** tab. Your Mac enables you to mark folders and files with colors. Click on one of the colored boxes and a **Color Picker** appears, letting you change the selected color. Click on a box with a name and you can change what that color means for you. Aren't Macs great?

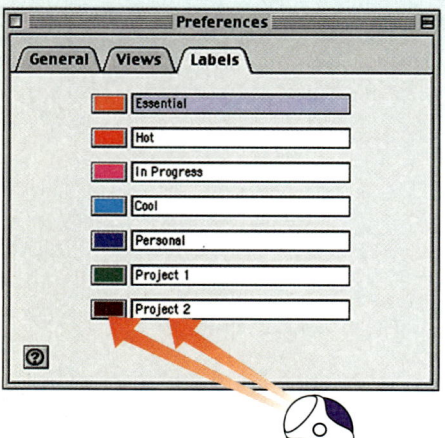
Click

### 3 Use a Pop-Up List

Now click on the **Views** tab. A new screen will appear. At the top right is a box with two arrows. Click on it and a pop-up list will appear. Select **List view**.

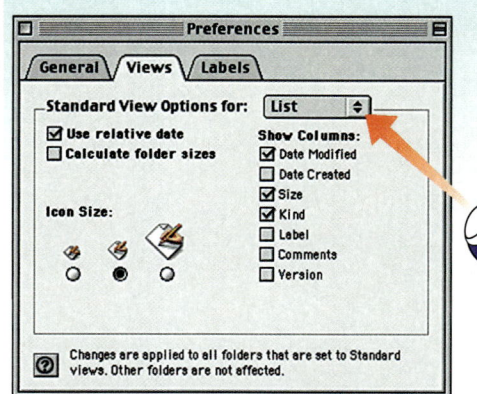

Click

30  PART 2: DISCOVERING THE MAC OS

## 4 Use Check Boxes

Notice that the screen has small squares and that some have check marks in them. Clicking in an empty check box adds a check and turns on that function. Clicking in the check box again turns off the function. If you check the **Use relative date** box, your Mac will change numeric dates to an easier-to-spot **Yesterday** or **Today**.

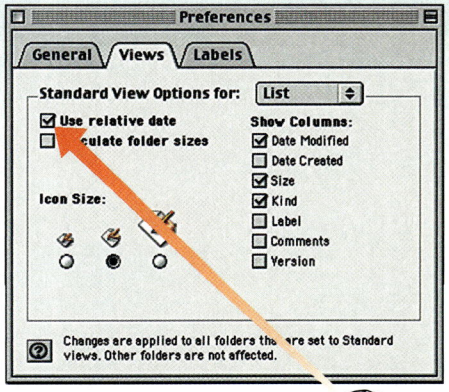

Click

## 5 Use Radio Buttons

At the bottom of the screen are three small circles. These are called radio buttons and they're different from check boxes because only one radio button can be selected (with a dot) at a time. Click on the radio button for the icon size you'd like to see in list views.

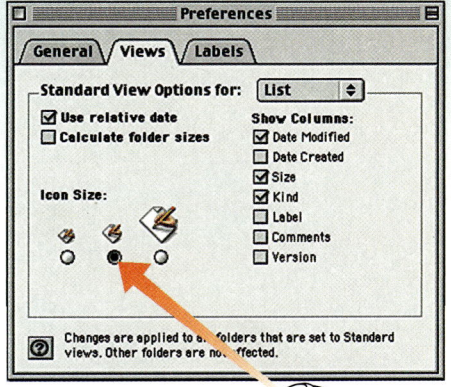

Click

## 6 Adjust Controls

Click on the General tab. In the middle of the new screen is an adjustable control (like on some stereos). If you put your mouse pointer over it you can drag the control to a new position. In this case you are adjusting the time before a Spring-loaded folder opens.

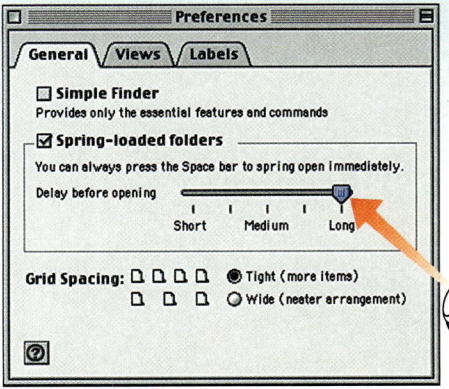

Click & Drag

## 7 Use Context Menus

Context text menus appear when you hold down the control key and hold down the mouse button. Whatever you select from the menu is applied to what is under the mouse arrow. To see how it works, hold down the control key, click once on a folder, then select Label followed by Cool from the two menus that drop down.

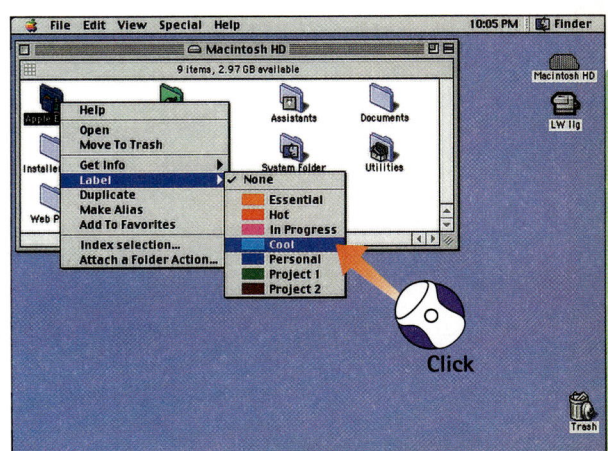
Click

*End*

How to Use a Dialog Box and Contextual Menus   **31**

## Task 7

# How to Make an Alias and Rename a File

Wouldn't it be nice if you could have quick access to a file or folder, even if it was buried many folders deep on your Mac? Well, you can do that with an alias. And they're easy to make.

## Begin

### 1 Select an Icon

If you want to make an alias of something, first select the item. I'm making an alias of the Documents folder because I use it often.

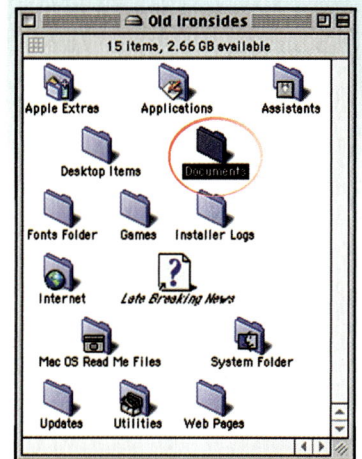

### 2 Make the Alias

Go to the **File** menu and choose **Make Alias**. A second copy of the file, with the name "alias" added, will be created. The alias acts as the original.

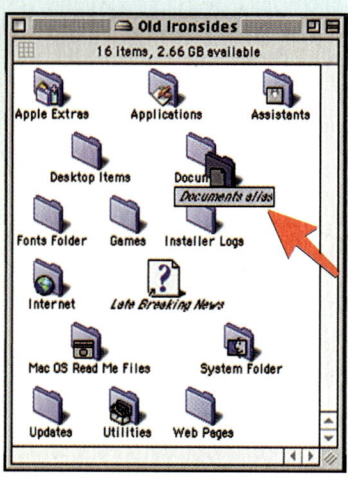

### 3 Rename a File

Click once on an icon. Watch the title get highlighted.

## 4 Rename It

Type the new name for the alias. You can use any characters, numbers, or punctuation except the colon (:). When you're done, click anywhere outside the text to save your change. In this case, we have named the alias **Work Papers**.

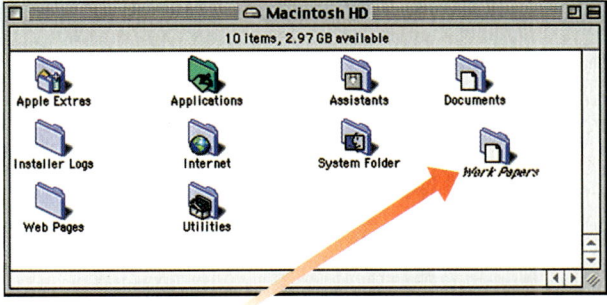

## 5 Move the Alias

An alias sitting next to the original would be pointless. In this case, we will move the alias to the desktop. Click on the alias icon and, holding the mouse down, drag the alias icon from its original folder to the desktop. When you have the alias where you want it, release the mouse button.

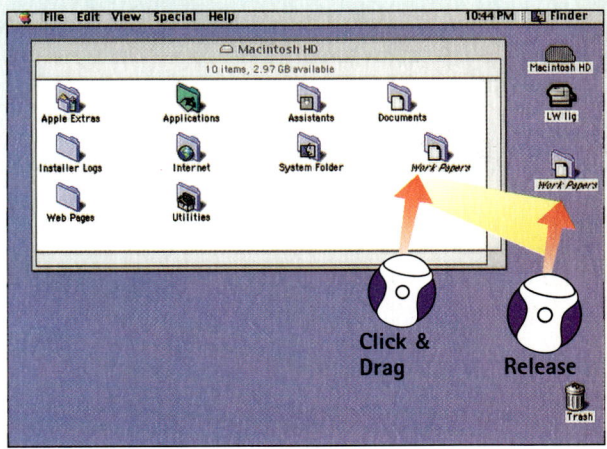

*End*

# How-To Hints

### Can't Rename File?

If file sharing is on (see Part 13, "Networking Your Mac," for more information), you cannot rename an icon on any shared item. The only solution is to turn off the sharing feature before you give it a new name.

### Be Careful What You Rename

Don't rename programs or any files in a program folder, nor should you rename System Folder items. When you change those names, it's always possible that the files will cease to function. Of course, if you make a mistake, you can always change it back.

TASK 8

# How to Launch and Quit an Application

The same double-click method you use to open a disk or folder directory can be used to open an application.

## Begin

### 1 Double-Click on the Icon

Double-click the program's icon or alias.

Double-click

### 2 Viewing the Splash Screen

The application will open, usually with a little introductory screen identifying its name, sometimes referred to as the splash screen.

### 3 New Document Opens

When you launch an application, it will usually open a new blank document, or give you a choice of what to do (as in the AppleWorks example below).

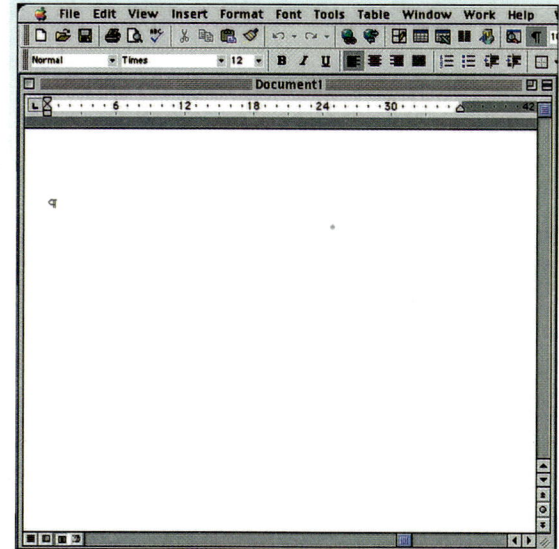

34  PART 2: DISCOVERING THE MAC OS

## 4 Quit the Application

When you're finished working in an application and want to close it, choose **Quit** from the **File** menu.

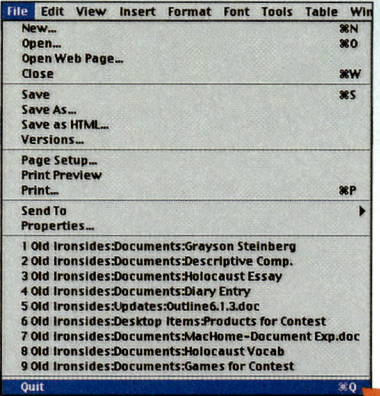

Click

## 5 Save First

If you have made changes in a file, but haven't saved those changes, you'll have the choice to do it now before the application closes.

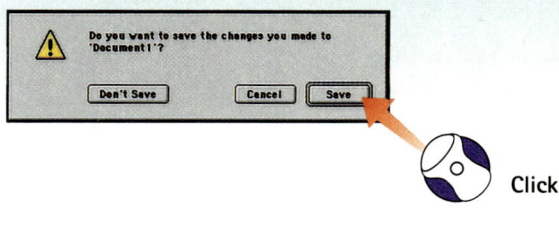

Click

*End*

---

# How-To Hints

### Where's the Blank Document?
Not all Mac programs open a blank document when you launch an application. If you just see your Mac's desktop, choose **New** from the **File** menu to open an empty document.

### Placing an Alias
Put an alias anywhere where it's convenient, for example, on your desktop or in a folder. You can also open the System Folder icon and place the alias icon in the folder labeled **Apple Menu Items**. When it goes there, it'll automatically show up in the **Apple** menu. Neat!

TASK 9

# How to Trash a File

Over time, you're likely to come across files and folders you just don't need any longer. You can easily remove those files with a few simple steps. But first make sure that you really don't want the files, as it's a lot more difficult (often impossible) to get back a file you have gotten rid of by mistake.

## Begin

### 1 Select the Icon

Locate the icon of the file or folder you want to delete. Click on it.

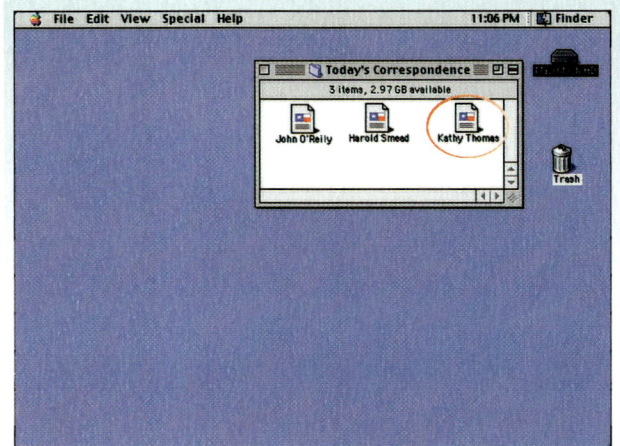

### 2 Drag to the Trash

Drag the file or folder to the **Trash** icon.

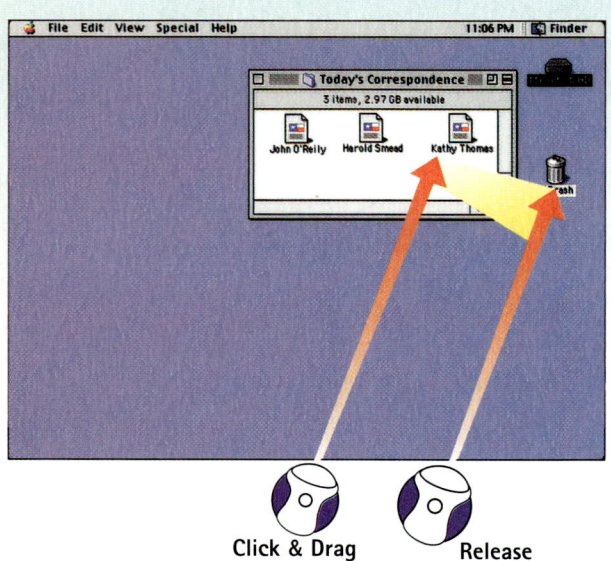

### 3 Notice the Trash Can Swells

The icon of the **Trash** will swell slightly to show there's something inside.

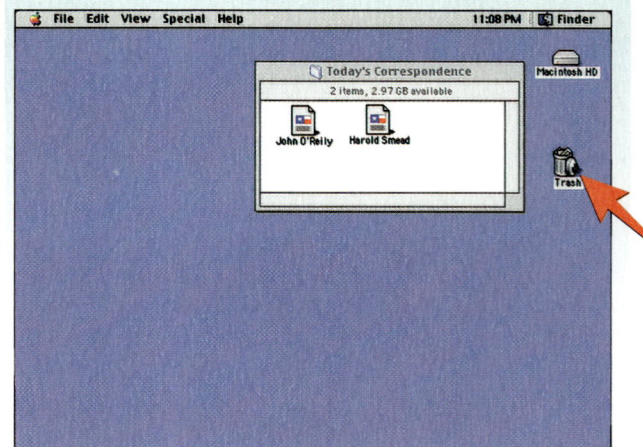

## 4 Take It Out of the Trash

If you've decided not to get rid of the icon after all, simply double-click on the **Trash** icon. Remove the item from the folder window that appears by dragging it out of the Trash and back to another location like the desktop.

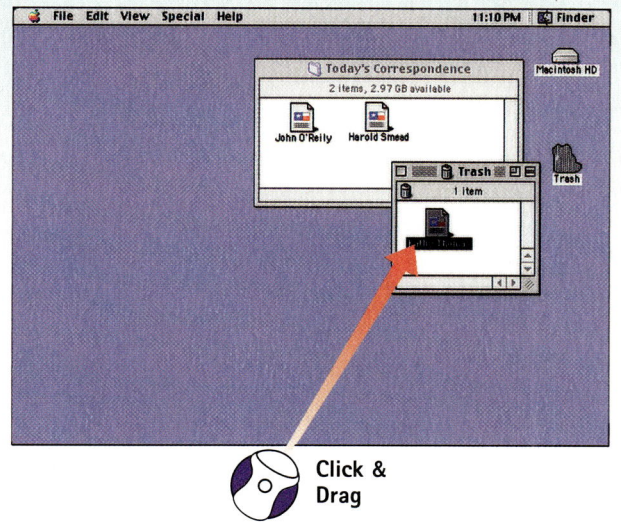

Click & Drag

## 5 Empty the Trash

When you're ready to actually delete the file, go to the **Special** menu and click **Empty Trash** (the command is only available when there's something in the Trash). The file or folder will then be deleted.

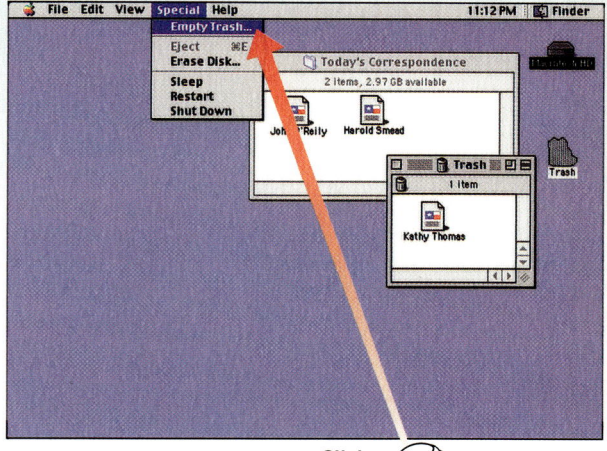

Click

*End*

## How-To Hints

### Is There No Going Back?

Sometimes, you make a mistake. You trash a file by mistake. It has happened to most Mac users at one time or another. The only possible solution to the problem is to run a special program that can "unerase" files. Such programs include MicroMat's TechTool Pro and Symantec's Norton Utilities. But you need to install the programs first to get the best possible protection against this problem. In the meantime, the best protection against losing a file you need is to make a backup (a second copy) on another disk. That way you have a spare if you lose the original.

### Locked Files

If a file is marked as "locked," you can't just empty the trash. But if you hold down the **Option** key, it will empty anyway. The Option key adds a lot of extra shortcuts to your Mac. For example, when you hold down Option and then click on another program from the application menu, all other applications are hidden. This clears up desktop clutter. Feel free to experiment with it to see all it can do for you.

# Task

1. How to Use the Standard Open Dialog Box 40

2. How to Use the New Open Dialog Box 42

3. How to Use the Standard Save As Dialog Box 44

4. How to Use the New Save As Dialog Box 46

5. How to Find a Place to Save Your File 48

# PART 3

# Opening and Saving Stuff

When you double-click on a document's icon to open it, the Mac OS launches the application that made the file and then opens the document itself. That you now know. But what do you do if you want to open a second document in an application while you're still working on the first? Do you go back to the desktop, locate the new file, and double-click again?

That will work, but often there's an easier way, one that doesn't require you to leave the application you are in to open another document. This way involves the use of an Open dialog box or, more accurately, the old and new types of Open dialog boxes. The one you use depends on the application. (Don't worry, they're not all that different.) Both will enable you to find and open another document in seconds without leaving an application.

You face much the same situation when you want to save a new version of a document without destroying the old version. If you use the Save command in the File menu, your old version will be written over and that's the last thing you want. The solution is to use the Save As command and make the changes you want in—you guessed it—either the old or new version of the Save As dialog box.

In this part, we'll explore how to use these four boxes as well as look at how to create folders to store all the things you'll create on your Mac. ●

TASK 1

# How to Use the Standard Open Dialog Box

The Mac is easy to use because most applications use the same sets of dialog boxes. In this task, you'll look at a dialog box that opens a new document.

*Begin*

## 1 Open an Application

Look on your hard disk for a folder called **Apple Extras**. Open **Apple Extras** and look for a folder called **Map Control Panel**; open it. Inside **Map Control Panel** is an icon labeled **Map Control Panel Read Me**. Double-click on the icon to open the document with SimpleText, the application that created the document.

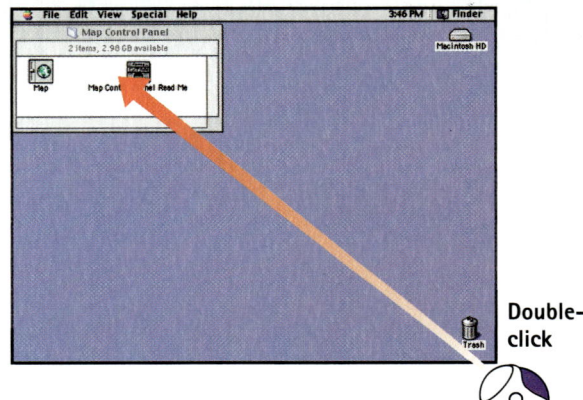

Double-click

## 2 Display the Open Dialog Box

Click on the Close box to close the document you are in. From the **File** menu, select **Open**. The **Open** dialog box will appear.

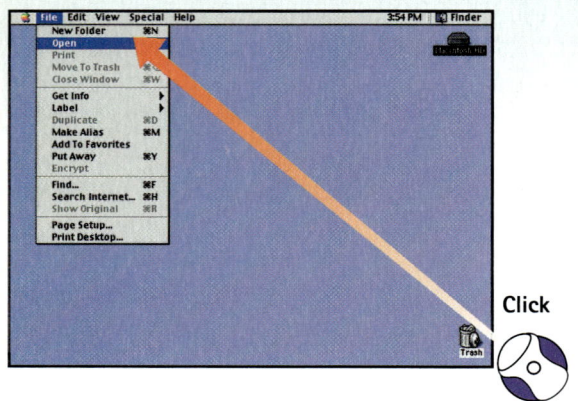

Click

## 3 Open a File

Notice that you are looking at the folder and document you just closed. To reopen the document, click once on its name and then click on the **Open** button. The document will open again. You can also just double-click on the document name.

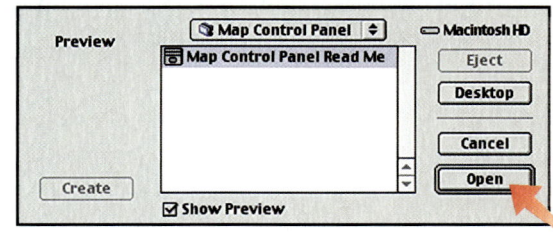

Click

40   PART 3: OPENING AND SAVING STUFF

## 4 Look Higher Up

If the **Open** dialog box does not display the document you want, you must use the navigation parts of the box to display the contents of other folders. Use **Open** in the **File** menu to display the **Open** dialog box again. Click once on the pull-down menu at the top of the box, and then click on **Apple Extras** (this will place you closer to the hard disk icon).

Click

## 5 Look Lower Down

When you clicked on **Apple Extras**, it displayed the contents of that folder. Use the scroll bar on the right to move down until you can see the **Map Control Panel** folder. When you find it, double-click on it to redisplay the **Map Control Panel Read Me** document. In Step 4, you moved up the folder structure; now, you have moved down the folder structure.

Double-click

## 6 Change the Hard Drive

You might also want to look on a different hard drive or on your desktop. To do that, click once on the pull-down list at the top of the Open box, and then click on **Desktop**. A list of everything on your desktop will appear.

Click

*End*

## How-To Hints

### Sometimes the Dialog Box Layout Is Different

There are two types of Open dialog boxes on a Mac. The second type is covered in the next task. In addition, the actual design of an Open dialog box depends on the program you're using. Some programs add preview images and extra pop-up menus to support extra features.

### Do It Via Keyboard!

Whenever you see a button in a dialog box that's surrounded by a thick rectangle, it's the default button. You can press the **Return** or **Enter** key on your Mac's keyboard to open it as a shortcut.

## Task 2

# How to Use the New Open Dialog Box

Beginning with Mac OS 8.5, a new Open dialog box came out, using technology Apple calls Navigation Services. While not all programs work with this new style yet, it has some neat features you'll want to use. The steps in this section apply to any program that uses this Open dialog box style, such as Microsoft's Outlook Express 5. If the program isn't developed to support the feature, you'll get the old style dialog box (you won't know until you try).

## Begin

### 1 Go to the File Menu

To bring up the new-style **Open** dialog box, choose **Open** from the **File** menu.

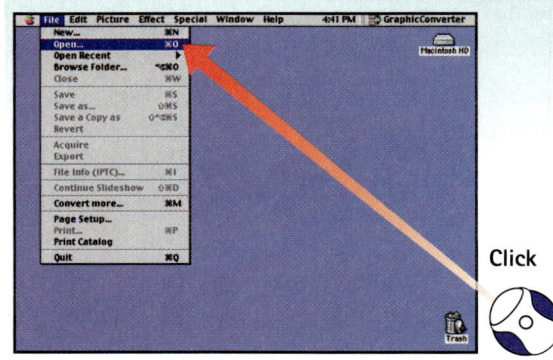

### 2 Change the Folder

If the folder shown isn't displaying the file for which you are searching, click on the folder pop-up menu in the upper left and choose the folder to which you want to go.

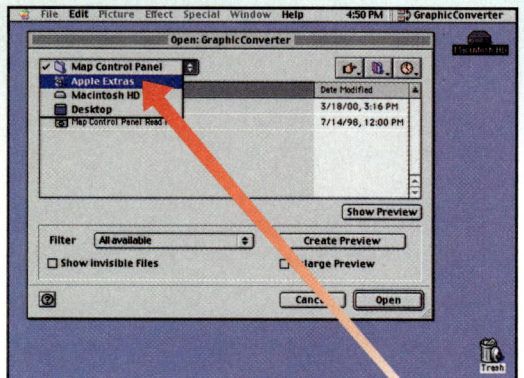

### 3 Change the Drive or Network

If you have other drives connected to your Mac and want to open a file on the another drive (or networked computer), click the **Shortcuts** icon (a button with a hand pointing right) to bring up the list of available drives.

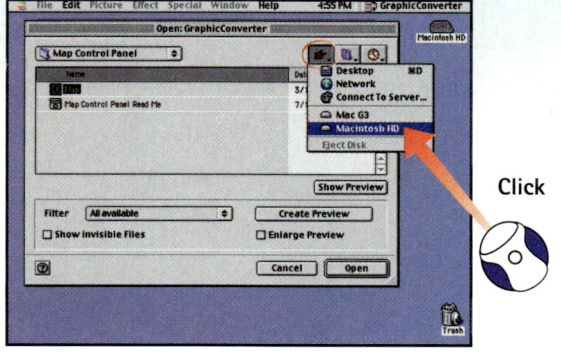

42  Part 3: Opening and Saving Stuff

## 4 Select the File

After you've located the file in the **Open** dialog box, click once on it to select it and then click the **Open** button.

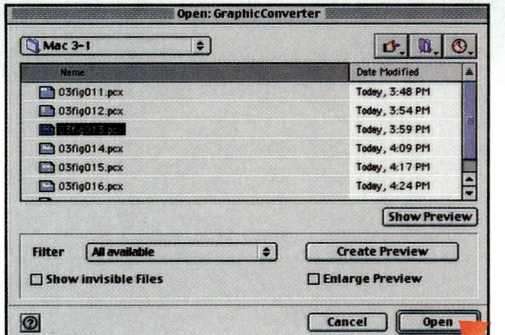

Click

## 5 Preview a Document

Some applications will let you see a preview of a document before you open it. To show a preview, click once on document, and then click the Show Preview button.

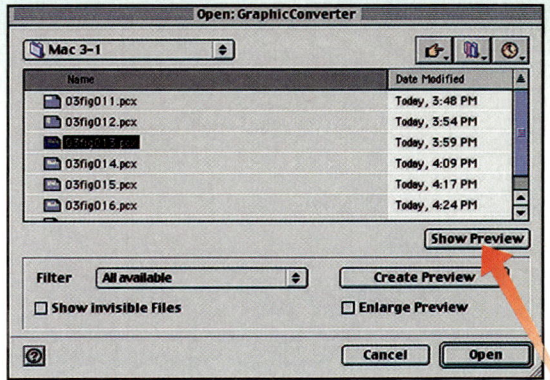

Click

*End*

# How-To Hints

## Add Favorites

The new style **Open** and **Save** dialog boxes let you store a list of Favorites for fast access to a folder or disk from the menu. Just select the item you want to make a favorite, click the **Favorites** icon (the button with a folder with a ribbon hanging down that is at the right of the Shortcuts icon), and choose **Add to Favorites** to store it.

## Recent Files Are Listed

The third icon (one that looks like a clock) in the new **Open** and **Save** dialog boxes is a list of recent files. As you open files in a program, they'll be added to the list.

HOW TO USE THE NEW OPEN DIALOG BOX

**TASK 3**

# How to Use the Standard Save As Dialog Box

The counterpart to the Open dialog box is the one you use to save a file. The first time you save a file, it brings up the Save As dialog box, so you can name your file and save it the very first time. After a document has been named and saved for the very first time, you just have to click Save to save further updates to the file, so you don't have to name or rename it again.

*Begin*

## 1 Go to the File Menu

Within an application, bring up the **Save As** dialog box by choosing **Save As** from the **File** menu.

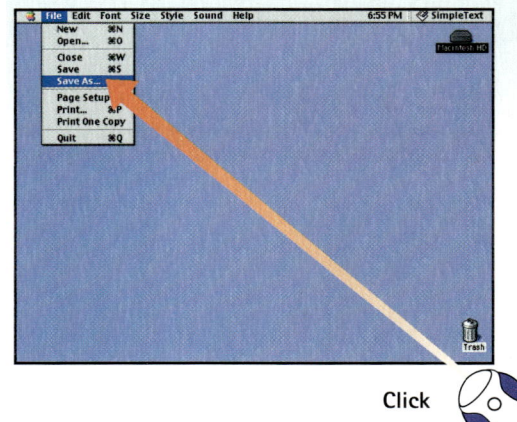

## 2 Change the Folder

If you want to save the file in another folder, click the folder pop-up menu in the upper left and locate the folder where you want to place your file.

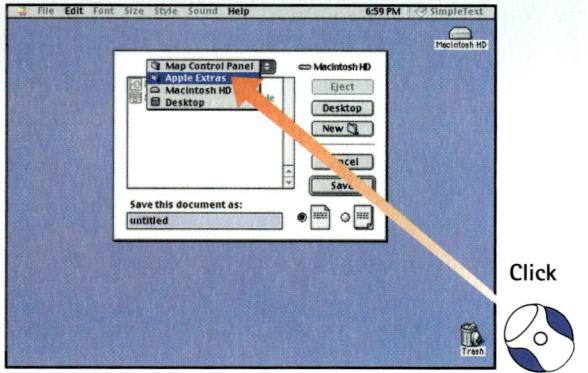

## 3 Change the Drive

If you have other hardrives connected to your Mac and want to put the file on another drive, click the Desktop button to view your desktop. Then click on the drive you want.

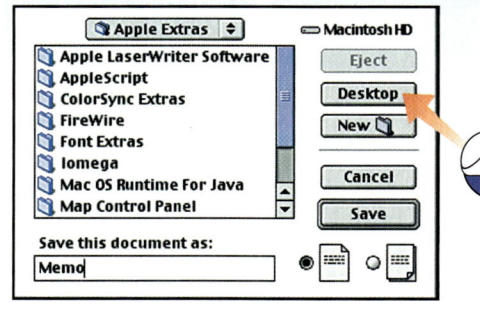

**44** PART 3: OPENING AND SAVING STUFF

## 4 Name the File

After you've located a place to put your file, click in the **Save this document as:** box and give the file a name. If another name is there, it'll be selected, and you can change it as you prefer. Click on the **Save** button to save the document.

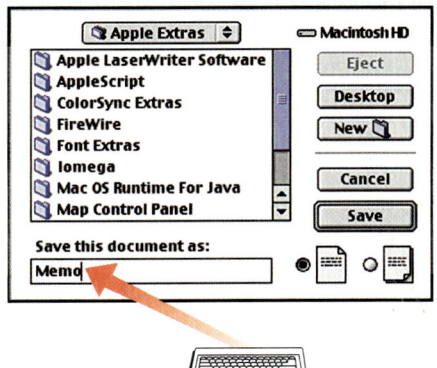

## 5 Make a New Folder

Should you want to put your file in a new folder, click the **New** button (with a folder icon).

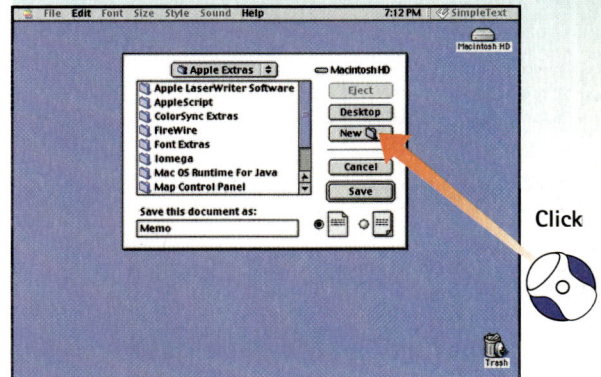

Click

## 6 Naming the Folder

Name your folder in the **Save this document as:** box that appears. Then click **Create** to make the folder.

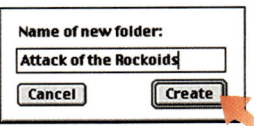

Click

*End*

# How-To Hints

## Watch for a Replace Warning

If there's another file with the same name as the one you've created in the folder, you'll get a warning dialog box, asking if you want to replace the file or cancel the operation. If you replace the file, the other one is removed and the new one is stored in its place. If you don't want to do this, click **Cancel**, and you'll be back in the **Save As** dialog box, where you can rename the file to something different.

## Save Often

As you change your document, you should use the **Save** command from the **File** menu often. That way all the modifications will be included. This is especially helpful if your Mac crashes (stops working) for any reason, so you don't lose anything in the file.

## Task 4

# How to Use the New Save As Dialog Box

The latest versions of the Mac operating system have a new Save As dialog box which some applications use. Here's how it works.

## Begin

### 1 Go to the File Menu

Within an application, bring up the **Save As** dialog box by choosing **Save As** from the **File** menu.

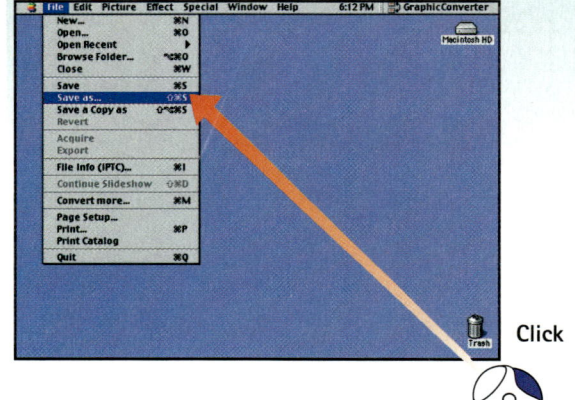

### 2 Change the Folder

If you want to save the file in another folder, click the folder pop-up menu and locate the folder in which you want to place your file.

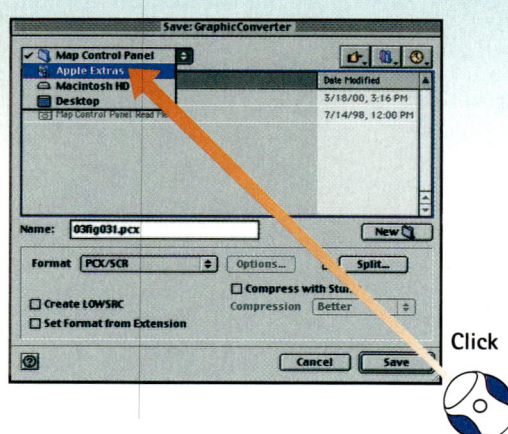

### 3 Change the Drive or Network

If you have other drives connected to your Mac and want to open a file on another drive (or networked computer), click the **Shortcuts** icon to bring up a list of available drives.

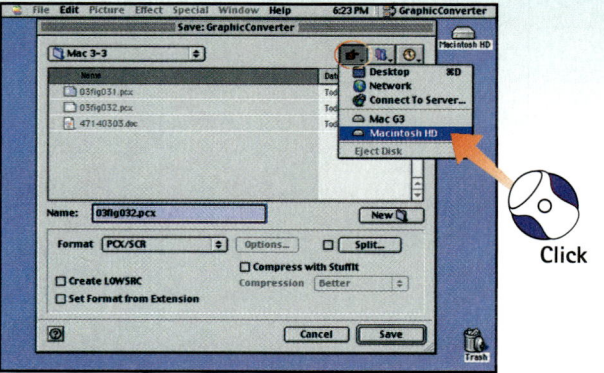

46    PART 3: OPENING AND SAVING STUFF

## 4 Name the File

After you've located a place to put your file, click in the text box next to **Name** and give the file a name.

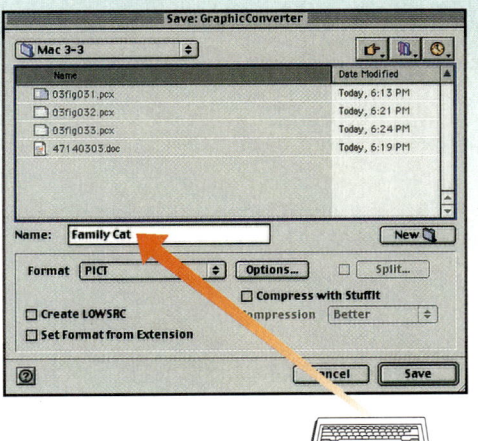

## 5 Make a New Folder

Should you want to put your file in a new folder, click the **New** button.

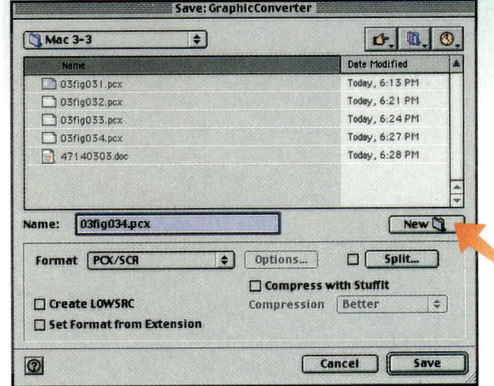

Click

## 6 Naming the Folder

Name your folder in the box that appears. Then click **Create** to make the folder.

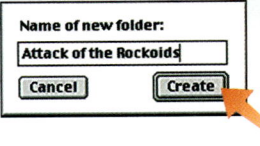

Click

*End*

# How-To Hints

## Need Help?

The new **Open** and **Save As** dialog boxes have a convenient **Help** icon (the one with a question mark). If you have a question about a specific feature, click the **Help** icon to bring up further information.

## Changing Your Mind

After you bring up a dialog box, you aren't forced to stick with your decision. If you'd rather not open or save a file at this time, click the **Cancel** button to close the box without changing or opening anything. You can also use two convenient keyboard shortcuts to do the same thing, ⌘+**.** (period), or just press the **Esc** key.

TASK 5

# How to Find a Place to Save Your File

After you've created a new document, the question arises as to where to put it. What's the best place on your hard drive to put your new files so you can easily find them without having to do a special search?

Here's a useful technique that'll make it easy to have all your files in convenient places.

## Begin

### 1 Go to the Desktop

Click on your Mac's desktop, which takes you to the Finder or Finder desktop (you can call it either).

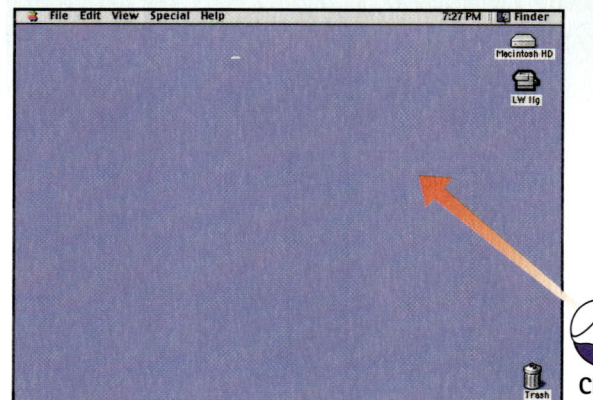

Click

### 2 Make a New Folder

Choose **New Folder** from the **File** menu. A new folder, called "untitled" will be placed on your drive's file directory.

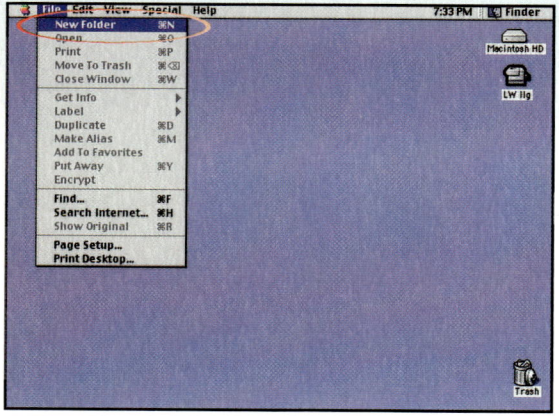

### 3 Open the Drive

Double-click on the hard drive icon (if the list of files isn't shown).

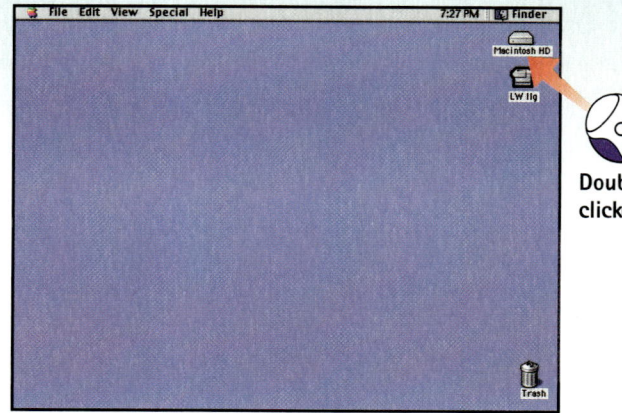

Double-click

48  PART 3: OPENING AND SAVING STUFF

## 4 Name the Folder

Click on the folder's name (untitled), type in the word Letters, and then press **Return**.

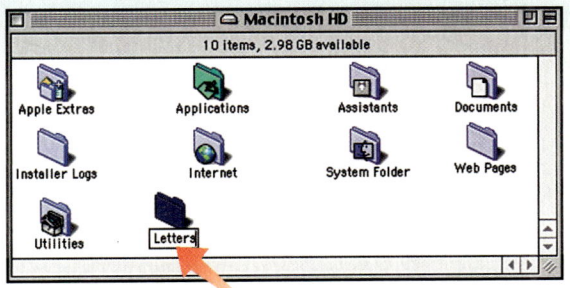

## 5 Open the Folder

Double-click the Letters folder to see what's inside; right now it's empty until you save files to it.

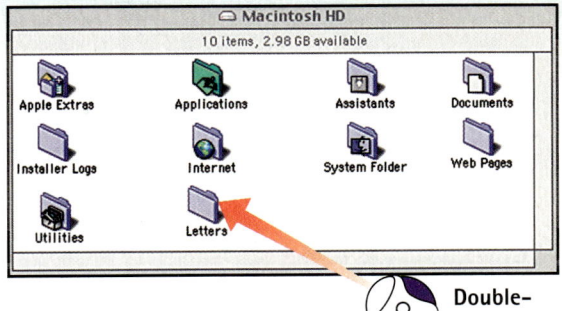

Double-click

*End*

# How-To Hints

## Subdivide the Documents Folder

If you create a lot of documents, you may find it easier to divide them by category. So, following the steps described above on making a new folder, open the **Documents** folder and use the **New Folder** command from the **File** menu to make additional folders. You can name each one with something that'll help identify the contents. You can have a folder for letters, another for business plans, or another for financial records. Use whatever label is convenient for you.

## If You Make a Mistake in the Label

If you write the wrong name for a folder, no problem. Just click on the title, and then put the cursor over the area that you want to change. Or just type the new name while the folder's title is highlighted, and it'll replace the name with the new one.

HOW TO FIND A PLACE TO SAVE YOUR FILE

# *Task*

1. How to Use Sherlock 2 to Find a File  52

2. How to Use Sherlock 2 to Find a File's Text  54

3. How to Use Sherlock 2 to Search the Internet  56

4. How to Select, Copy, and Move Folders and Files  58

# PART 4

# Finding and Moving Files

*T*his is a situation every Mac user encounters.

You created a new document. Or you copied a file from another drive or from the Internet. Now you need to work with them, but there's one problem: Where are the files? How do you find them? Where did you put them?

Or perhaps you are looking for some information about a subject, or the best price on some merchandise before you buy it. The Internet is positively huge, millions of sites, hundreds of search sites. How do you find what you want?

Or you just want to move an item from one place to another, somewhere on your hard drive or another drive. Do you want to just send it to a new location, or make a copy, leaving the original where it is?

We'll cover these subjects next.

## TASK 1

# How to Use Sherlock 2 to Find a File

Sherlock 2 is Mac OS 9's multifunction file search utility. From a single window, you can locate files on your Mac's drive or anywhere on the Internet.

## Begin

### 1 Launch Sherlock 2

Go to the Apple menu and select **Sherlock 2**.

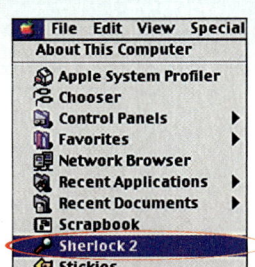

### 2 Choose an Option

Click on the **File Names** button.

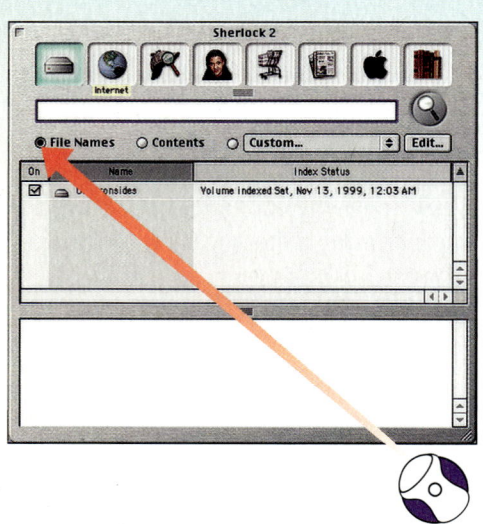

**Click**

### 3 Select a Drive

Click the **checkbox** next to the name of the drive you want to search.

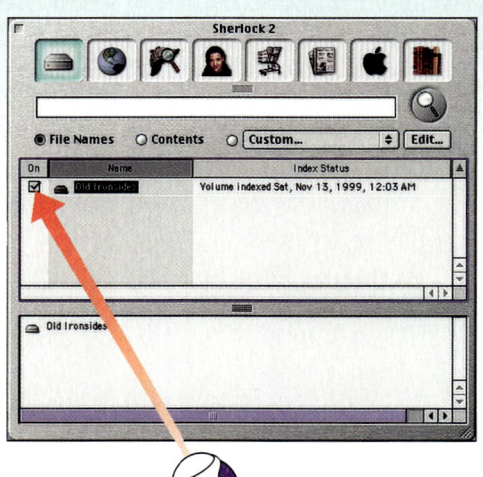

**Click**

## 4 Make a Request

Click on the **text entry** field and enter some of the characters in the name of the file you're trying to find; then click the **magnifying glass** icon.

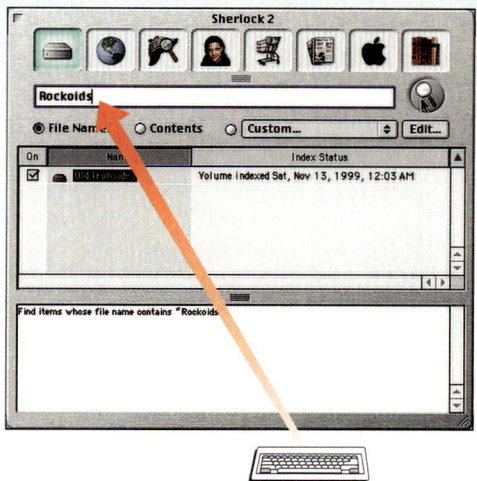

## 5 Check the List

If files matching your request are on your drive, you'll see the listing in the Sherlock 2 screen. They are ranked by relevance, or how closely they match your search request.

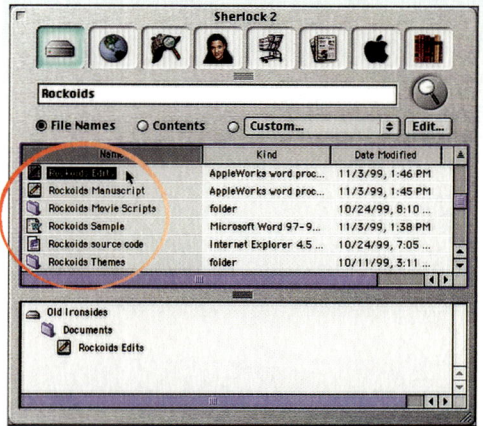

## 6 Open the File

Check through the list for your file. If you find it, just double-click on its **name** to launch the item you selected.

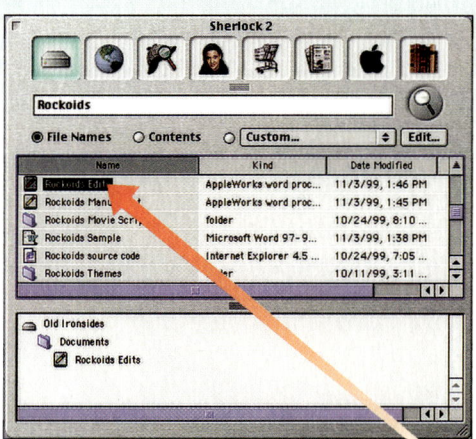

Double-click

*End*

## How-To Hints

### Can't Find the File?

If your first request for information about the file doesn't bring a satisfactory result, you can try again. Perhaps you misspelled the file's name, or you need to fine-tune your search to include more of the file's name.

### Forget to Check a Drive?

No problem, just start the search again, after checking the checkbox for the drive you want to include in your next search request.

## Task 2

# How to Use Sherlock 2 to Find a File's Text

In addition to being able to locate a file by its name, Sherlock 2 can actually check the text inside a file to find the contents you want.

## Begin

### 1 Launch Sherlock 2

Go to the Apple menu and select **Sherlock 2**.

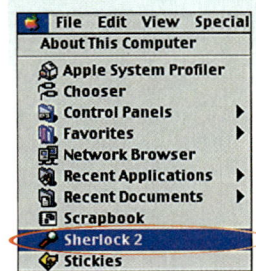

### 2 Index Your Drive

Click on the **Find** menu and choose **Index Volumes**. Then click on the **drive's name** (or **Shift+click** all drives listed) and select **Create Index**. When you index a drive, it records "pointers" for the text in your files, and it can take anywhere from a few minutes to a few hours to do, so be patient.

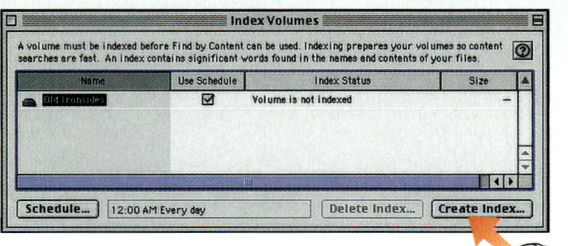

Click

### 3 Choose Your Search Option

After the drive is indexed, click on the main **Sherlock 2** screen and then click on **Contents**.

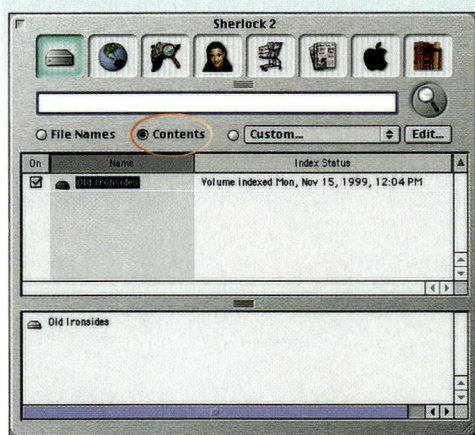

54   PART 4: FINDING AND MOVING FILES

## 4 Make a Request

Click on the **text entry** field, enter the **contents** of the file you're trying to find, and click the **magnifying glass** icon.

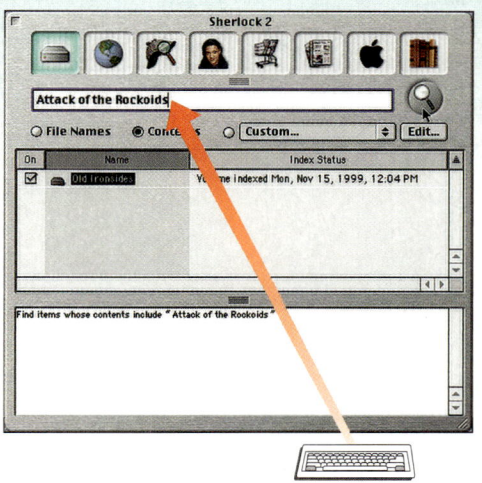

## 5 Check the List

If files with text matching your request are on your drive, you'll see the listing in the Sherlock 2 screen. They will be ranked by relevance to your request.

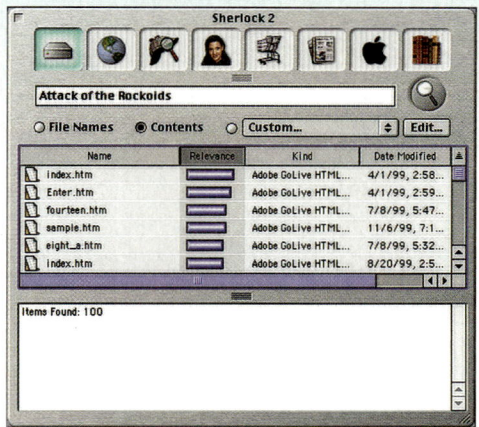

## 6 Open the File

Check through the list for your file. If you find it, just double-click on its **name** to launch the application and then the document.

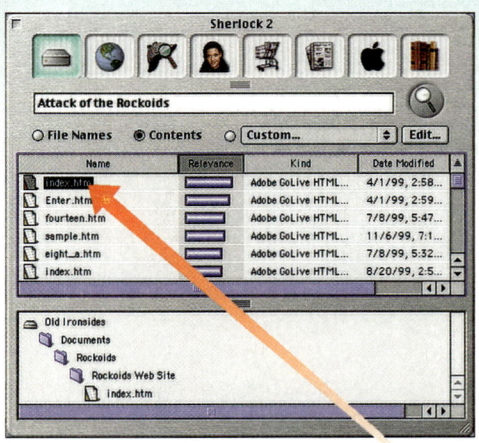

Double-click

*End*

# How-To Hints

### Can't Find the File?
Sherlock 2 will match up your text exactly. If you misspell a word, you won't get an accurate result. So, it's not a bad idea to make your request again if you don't get the files you want.

### When to Index a Drive
You cannot search the contents of the files on your Mac's drive unless Sherlock 2 indexes it first. Indexing can be a time-consuming process, so you'll probably want to schedule the session at a time when you're not using your Mac. You can also use the Schedule feature in the Index Volumes screen to have it update regularly, so the changes you make to your files will be recorded (updating doesn't take nearly as long as the initial indexing process).

## Task 3

# How to Use Sherlock 2 to Search the Internet

You are not restricted to finding material on your Mac's drive. In fact, you can search for material on the Internet as well. Sherlock 2 doesn't require knowledge of special search techniques. You make a plain English request, and Sherlock 2 will translate the request and send it to the Internet so you get the information you want. Of course, you need an Internet or AOL account to use this feature.

## Begin

### 1 Launch Sherlock 2

Go to the **Apple** menu and select **Sherlock 2**.

### 2 Choose an Option

Click on the **Internet Globe** or any of the **six channel** icons to the right of it. In addition to searching for a site, you can search the Internet for people, merchandise, the latest news, Apple Computer's large information database, and reference works.

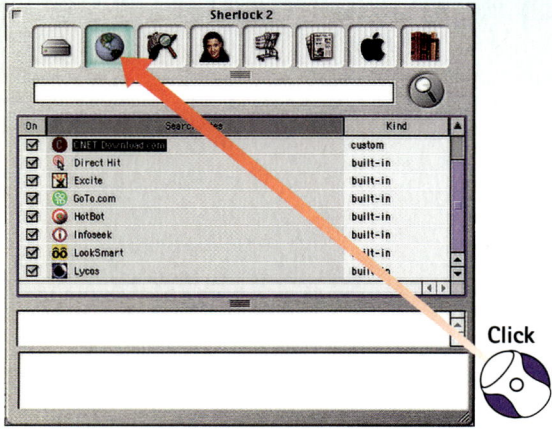

### 3 Make Your Request

Before you make a request, click the **checkboxes** next to the sites listed, if they're not checked, to expand your search. Type a **word**, or words, describing the information you want in the text box; then click the **magnifying glass** icon to start your search.

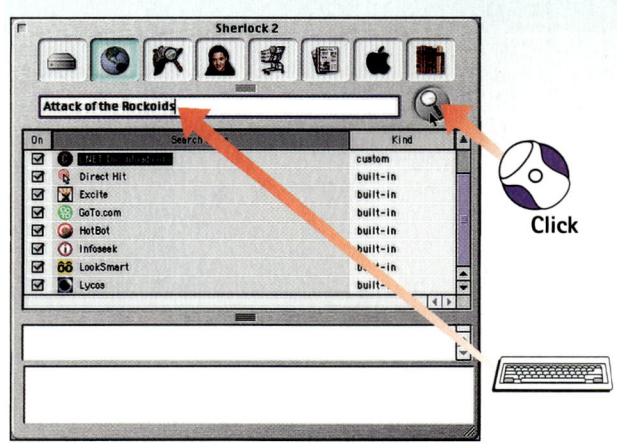

56    Part 4: Finding and Moving Files

## 4 Check the List

Over the next minute or two, your Internet service will be called up, you'll be logged in, and then Sherlock 2 will search the Internet to fill your request, which will appear ranked by relevance.

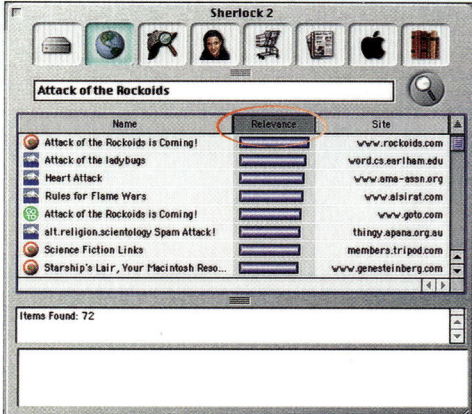

## 5 Select the Page

Locate and select the item you want, and you'll see a brief description of the contents of the Internet site at the lower pane of the Sherlock 2 window.

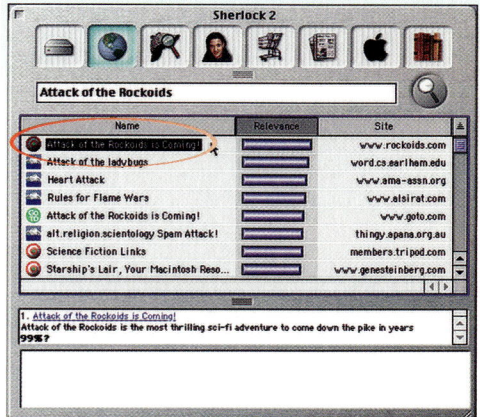

## 6 Open the Page

When you find the Web site that matches your information request, click on the **link**, and the page will open in your Web browser's window.

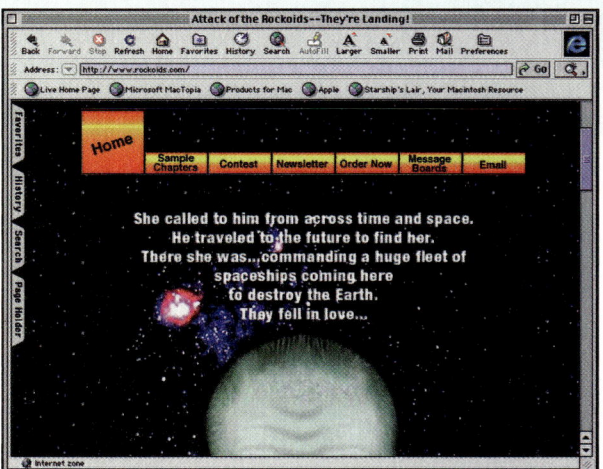

*End*

# How-To Hints

### Create Your Own Channels

You're not restricted to the Sherlock 2 Channels that Apple gives you. To make one of your own, just open **Sherlock 2**. Then choose **New Channel** from the **Channels** menu and give it a name. Then you can click on the **Channel type** menu and pick a channel type. On the basis of what you pick, you'll see a list of plug-ins that you can attach to the channel. Just **OK** all your changes to make your personal channel active.

### AOL Customers Should Log On First

Sherlock 2 can't log you onto AOL before it does a search request. If you're an AOL member, first connect to the service, and then make your Internet search request through Sherlock 2.

### Getting Internet Access

Internet access can really open up a whole new world for you. And many services have budget plans for limited use, such as just a few hours a month. You'll want to check a Mac magazine or your local newspaper for listings of Internet services that serve your city. Or just check one of those AOL or EarthLink CDs that are so widely distributed.

## Task 4

# How to Select, Copy, and Move Folders and Files

You have lots and lots of files on your hard drive, and you want to open them all at the same time, or move them to another location.

Perhaps you just want to make a copy and keep the original.

We'll cover these subjects here.

## *Begin*

### *1* Click on an Icon

To select an icon, just click once on it. Don't click twice, or you'll open the icon.

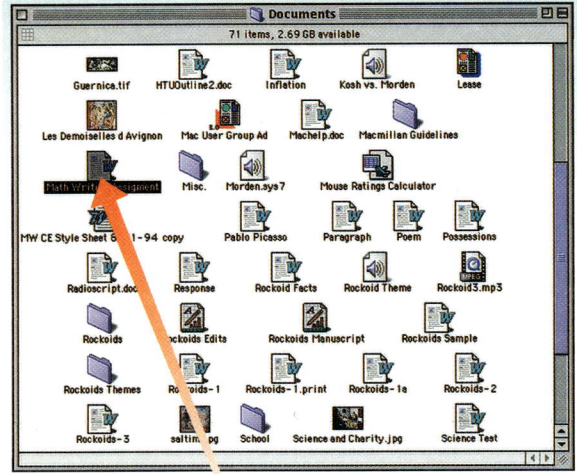

 Click

### *2* Shift+Click

If you want to select more than a single item, hold down the **Shift** key and then click once on each item.

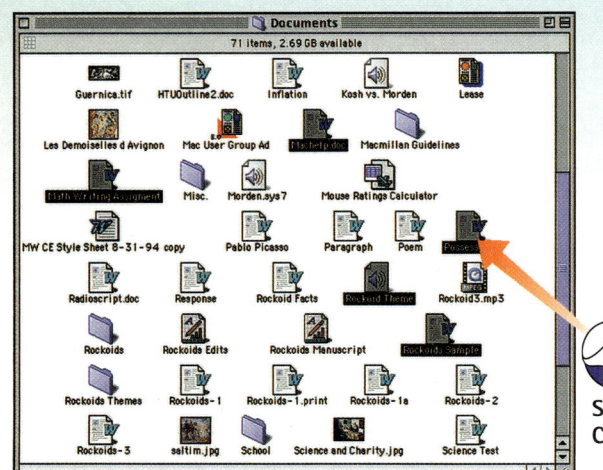

 Shift+ Click

### *3* Drag to New Location

Move the cursor to another folder on your hard drive or to another drive's icon. When you copy to another drive's icon, it will make a duplicate of the original. When you drag it to another folder on the same drive, you just move the original. When a copy is being made, you'll also see a progress bar showing the copy status.

**58**  PART 4: FINDING AND MOVING FILES

## 4 Make a Duplicate

If you just want to make a copy of the original items, keeping the original in place, hold down the **Option** key when you drag the icons to a new location.

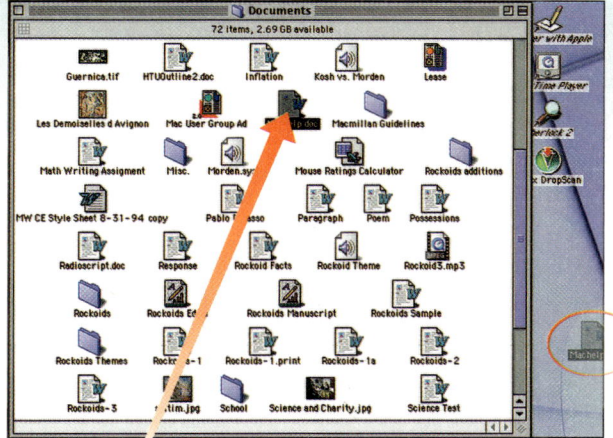

Option+Click & Drag

## 5 Make a Copy in the Same Folder

If you just want to make a duplicate and keep it in the same place as the original, select the icons and then type ⌘+**D**. This action will copy the file, but add the word "copy" to the file's name, so it can stay in the same folder (you can't have two copies of identically named items in the same location without one replacing the other).

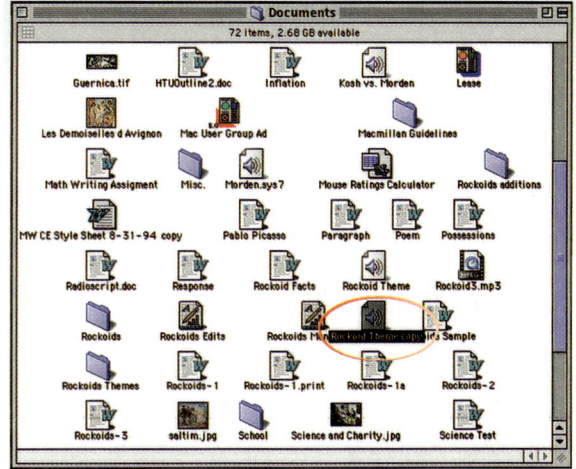

*End*

---

## How-To Hints

### If You Get a "Replace" Warning

If you try to move icons to a folder that contains items of the same name, you'll get a warning (called an "alert box") indicating that one or more files has the same name as the ones you're trying to move. If it's one file, you'll see a message as to whether the duplicate is older or newer than the one you're replacing it with. If this happens, stop what you're doing. Open the folder to which you want to move the icons and check them to make sure you aren't replacing something you need.

### Use List View

A good way to check an icon to make sure whether it's newer or older than one with a duplicate name is to use the View menu's **List** option. It will affect any open folder. You cannot use this feature for items on your Mac's desktop, though.

## Task

1. How to Create a New Document and Enter and Select Text  62

2. How to Move, Copy, and Paste Text  64

3. How to Undo and Redo an Action  66

4. How to Drag Items from One Place to Another  68

5. How to Export and Import Data Between Documents  70

PART 5

# Working with Documents

In this section, we'll explore how to create and edit documents. For this example, I'm using AppleWorks, Apple Computer's popular integrated program, which comes as standard equipment with the iMac and iBook.

AppleWorks is the quintessential word processing program for the Mac. It's easy to learn, easy to use, and packs enough power so that you can create professional quality documents in minutes.

What's more, it has features that used to be reserved for very expensive programs. In addition to being able to function as a word processor, AppleWorks will work as a spreadsheet program to handle financial calculations and a database program for your records and Address Books. You can also add illustrations, using the program's convenient paint and draw features.

After you learn the basics of using AppleWorks, you'll also be able to apply the same skills to using other Mac programs. That's because the Macintosh operating system provides a reasonably uniform set of tools that work in many programs. You will discover that this similarity saves you time and prevents confusion. If you understand one piece of software on a Mac, you know something about all the others.

## Task 1

# How to Create a New Document and Enter and Select Text

In just seconds, you can create a brand new document in AppleWorks. Once the document is open, you can begin to enter text, so you can write a letter, a memo, or a novel. After you've entered your text, you can select portions of it so you can begin to edit your document and make it look the way you want.

## *Begin*

### *1* Launch the Program

To launch AppleWorks, locate and double-click on its icon (it's usually located inside the **AppleWorks** folder in your Mac's **Applications** folder). After a few seconds, you'll see the program's introductory screen and then a dialog box in which you can select the kind of document you want to create.

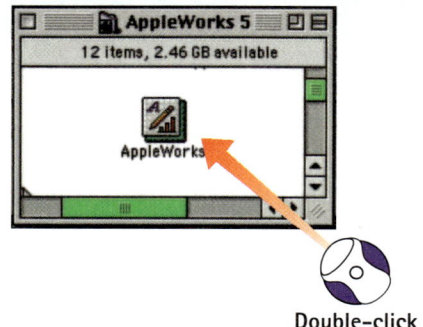
Double-click

### *2* Choose the Document Type

On the **New Document** dialog, select the kind of document you want to create. For this task, click on **Word Processing**.

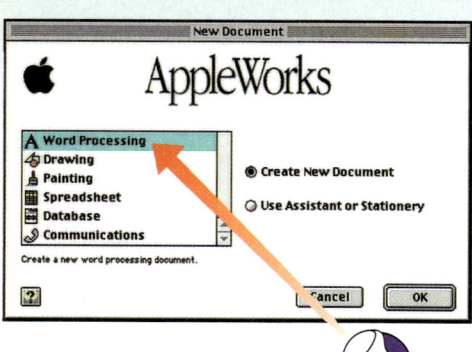
Click

### *3* Bring the Document Onscreen

After your document type is selected, click **OK** to bring your new blank document to the screen.

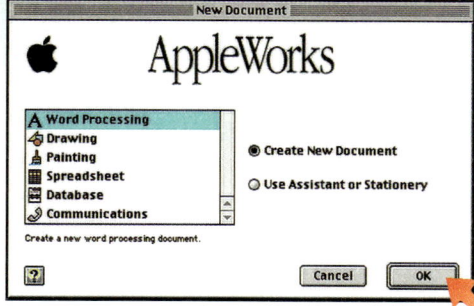
Click

**62** Part 5: Working with Documents

## 4 Enter Your Text

You'll notice your document window already has a blinking cursor at the upper left of a rectangular area in the document window. This is the text entry area. All you have to do now is to begin typing.

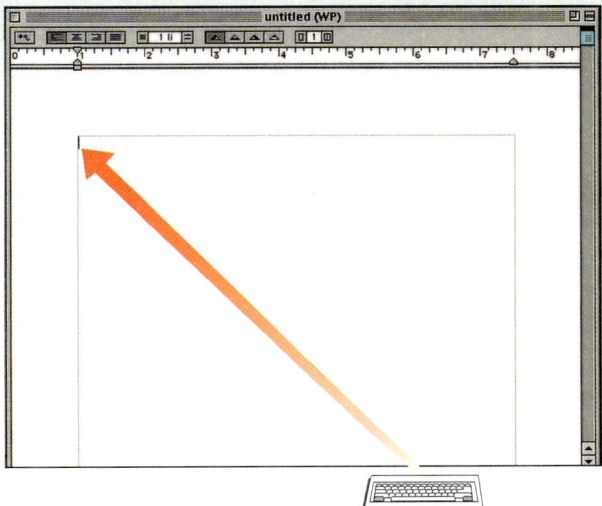

## 5 Select Your Text

After you've written your document, you may find areas you want to change or edit. Perhaps you want to use another word or fix a spelling error. To edit material, you'll have to select it first. Click on the beginning of the area you want to edit.

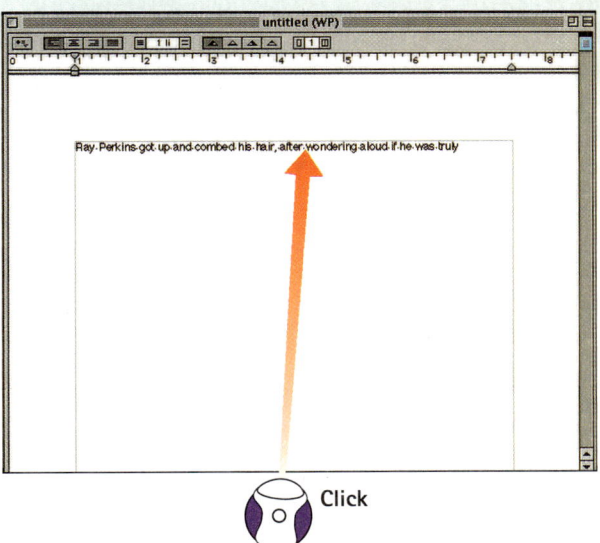

Click

## 6 End Your Selection

After you've clicked at the start of an area to edit, drag the mouse cursor across that area until you reach the end of the section you want to edit. Then release the mouse cursor. The area has now been selected.

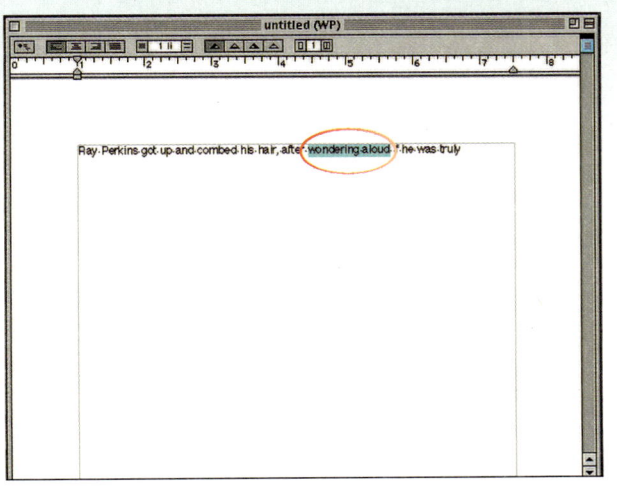

## How-To Hints

### Only Return After a Paragraph

Unlike a typewriter, you don't press the **Return** key after every line. It's unnecessary because AppleWorks will automatically break (or wrap) the words from line to line within your paragraph. You do, however, press **Return** at the end of a paragraph.

### Multiple Clicks Save Time

You don't have to just click and drag to select part of a file. If you want to select an entire word, quickly click twice on it. Click three times for a paragraph and four times to select the complete document. This clicking routine applies strictly to AppleWorks; other programs may produce different results from those extra clicks.

*End*

How to Create a New Document and Enter and Select Text

TASK 2

# How to Move, Copy, and Paste Text

Once you've created your document, you'll probably reach a point where you need to make some changes in the text. Perhaps you want to take a few words out and put them elsewhere. Or maybe the third paragraph fits better before the first. Fortunately, the Mac makes it easy for you to move text around your page.

## Begin

### 1 Select It

To move text from one place to another, first you need to click on the beginning of the text you want to move; then drag the cursor to the end to select it. Release the **Mouse** button.

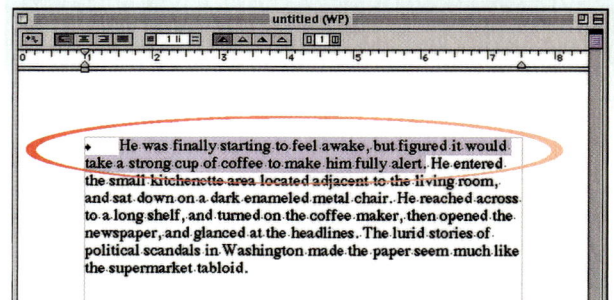

### 2 Cut It

Click on the **Edit** menu; then select **Cut**. This will remove the selected text from your document. Now move on to Step 4.

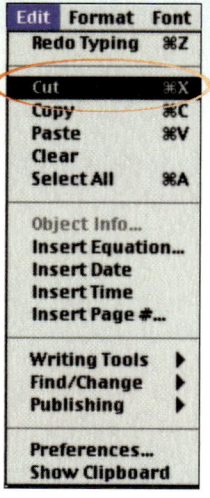

### 3 Or Copy It

If you just want to make a duplicate of your text to place elsewhere in your document, rather than remove it, choose **Copy** from the **Edit** menu.

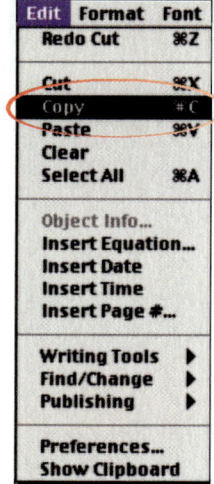

64   PART 5: WORKING WITH DOCUMENTS

### 4. Locate the Pasting Area

Scroll through your document and click at the place where you want to insert the text you cut or copied. In this example, I've placed the cursor after the word "tabloid."

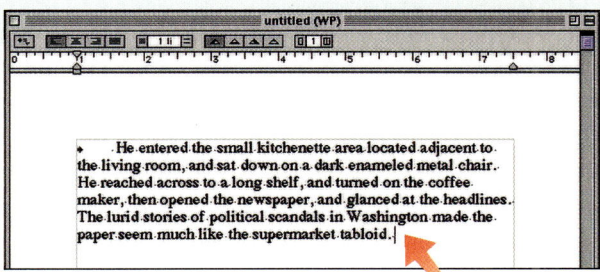

Click

### 5. Paste Your Text

Choose **Paste** from the **Edit** menu, and the text will magically appear in its new location.

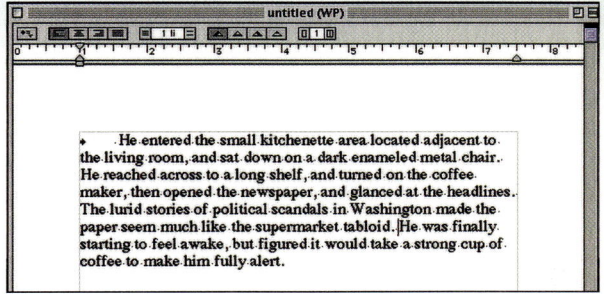

### 6. Or Drag It...

Instead of using the **Copy**, **Cut**, and **Paste** commands from the **Edit** menu, try this. Click on the document and drag the cursor to the end of the area you want to move; then release the mouse button.

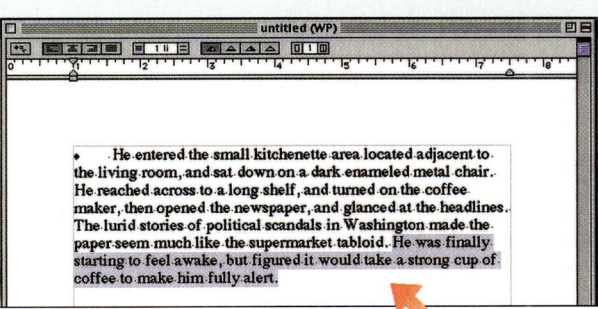

Click & Drag

### 7. ...And Drop It

Now click anywhere in the area you've selected and drag the mouse cursor to where you want the text placed in your document. The cursor will show a dotted rectangle. Release the mouse, and the text will drop into its new location. Neat!

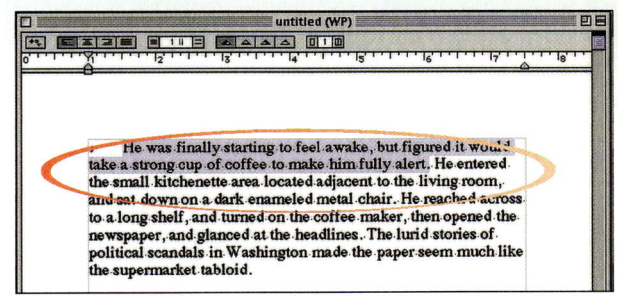

*End*

## How-To Hints

### Just Cut One at a Time
When you cut text from a document it goes in an area of memory on your Mac calls the clipboard. Only one thing can go there at a time. If you cut another item before pasting the first, you'll lose the first.

### Not All Programs Allow Drag-and-Drop Editing
The drag-and-drop text editing feature works in many programs, such as AppleWorks. Check your software's documentation to see if it supports drag-and-drop.

TASK 3

# How to Undo and Redo an Action

Did you make a mistake? Perhaps you removed or moved text and then decided you really didn't want the text to disappear or be placed in a particular part of your document. Is there no going back? Yes, there is a way to return things to the way they were, by following these steps.

## Begin

### 1 Undo It

If you change your mind, don't panic. If you haven't done anything else to your document, just choose **Undo** from the **Edit** menu, and your previous action will be cancelled. This menu selection switches from **Undo** to **Redo** (see next step), depending on what you did last.

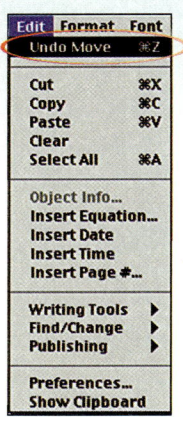

### 2 Redo It

If you find that you prefer to restore your change, just choose **Redo** from the **Edit** menu.

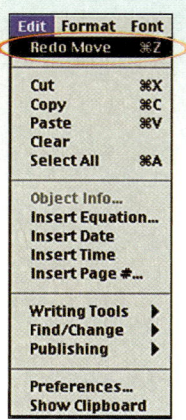

### 3 Revert a File

Applications such as AppleWorks give you another way to correct what you've done wrong. To restore a file to the condition it was in the last time you saved it, choose **Revert** from the **Edit** menu. The document will go back to the last saved

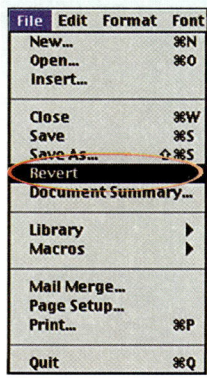

66    PART 5: WORKING WITH DOCUMENTS

## 4 Performing Multiple Undos

version.

Applications such as Microsoft Word believe that once isn't enough. They can do multiple Undos and Redos. Just choose **Undo** (the name of the action, such as typing or pasting, will be displayed) from the **Edit** menu for each step you want to go back.

## 5 Performing Multiple Redos

If you want to restore your changes in Microsoft Word, choose **Redo** (the name of the action, such as typing or pasting, will appear) from the **Edit** menu for each change you want to make.

*End*

## How-To Hints

### Revert Option Not There

AppleWorks and a number of other applications support the **Revert** feature. Microsoft Word doesn't. However, Word's multiple undo and redo capability is a worthy substitute, since it gives you the ability to repeat the process over and over again. Besides, you can get the same result as **Revert** by closing the document without saving it and opening your last saved version. **Revert** is just easier.

### Can't Undo?

If you see the **Can't Undo** option in the **Edit** menu, there's nothing you can do to get something back aside from manually making the change you want.

TASK 4

# How to Drag Items from One Place to Another

Most Mac applications take you way beyond copy, cut, and paste. You can actually move something from one document window to another in the same application simply by dragging and dropping across the two document windows.

In addition, if your Mac display is too small to show both documents, you can place the material on the desktop. Then it becomes a clipping.

*Begin*

### 1 Open the First Document

Open the first document that has the text you want to move.

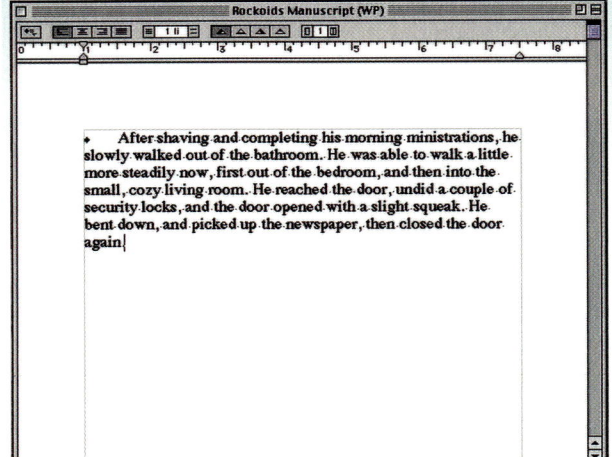

### 2 Open the Second Document

Now double-click on the second document file, which will open in the application window.

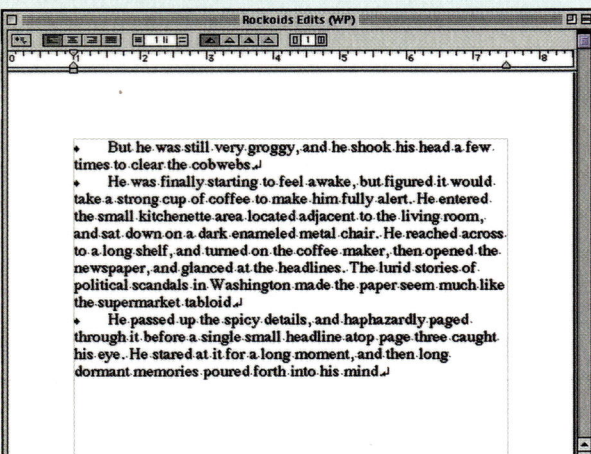

### 3 Position the Document Windows

Place the two document windows side by side (source at left, target document at right), so you can see them both. Scroll to the area on each document where you want to do your editing.

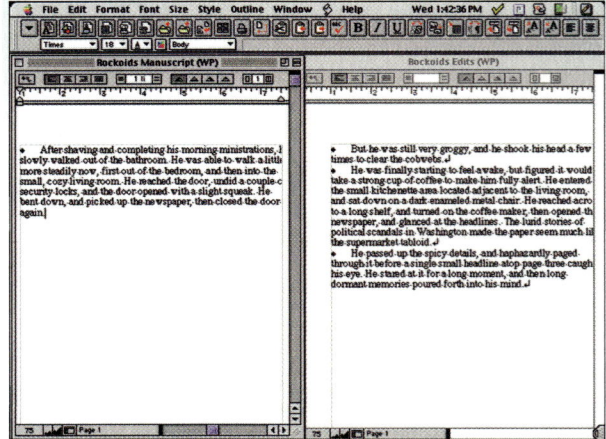

PART 5: WORKING WITH DOCUMENTS

## 4 Select It

Locate the material in the first document you want to move to another document. Click on the beginning of the material; then drag the cursor to the end of the passage and release the mouse button.

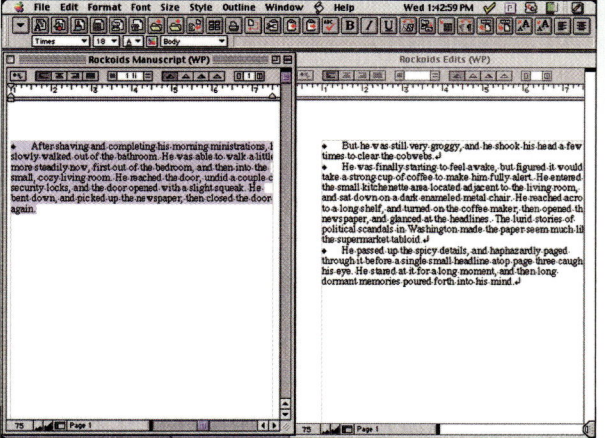

## 5 Move It

After the item is selected, just click on the item and drag the cursor right on over from the left document window to the one at the right; then release the mouse button.

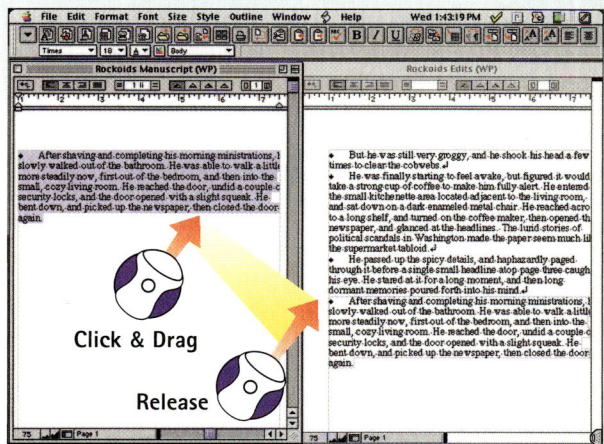

Click & Drag

Release

## 6 Drag to Desktop

If there's not enough room to show both document windows, you can drag the material you selected to the desktop. It will be saved as a text-clipping file.

## 7 Drag from Desktop

Bring up the second document window. Then click on the clipping file and drag it to the second document window, placing it where you want it. Then release the mouse button.

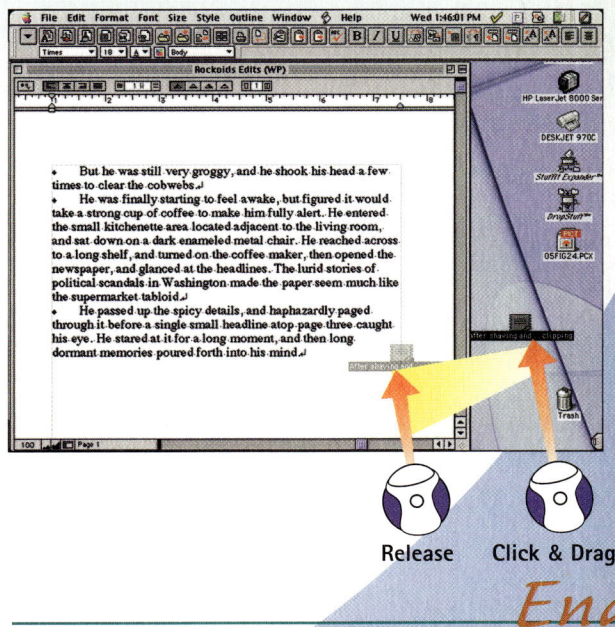

Release   Click & Drag

*End*

---

### How-To Hints

#### Don't Forget to Resize Document Windows

If each document window is too large to appear side by side, try using the **Zoom** or **View** option to reduce the size of the text; then move the size bar to make the window smaller. Otherwise, save the material as a clipping file before you move it to the second document.

How to Drag Items from One Place to Another

## Task 5

# How to Export and Import Data Between Documents

Not all applications let you transfer material between them by dragging and dropping. If you want to transfer an entire document between two different applications, such as a drawing program to a word processing program, exporting is usually the way to go.

## Begin

### 1 Open the Document

Double-click on the document that you want to send or export to another application.

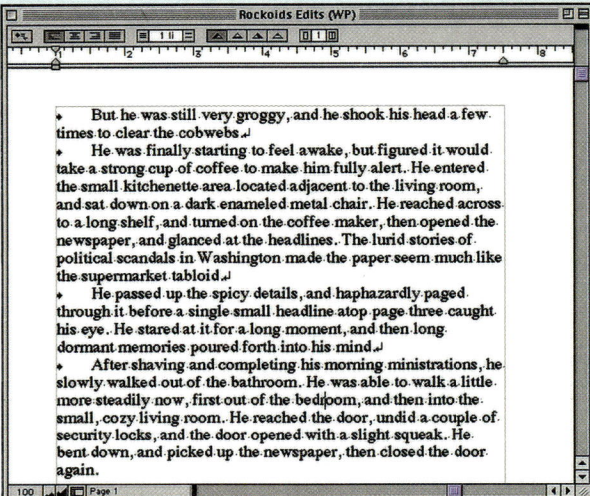

### 2 Export (Save As)

Convert the document to a form that it can be read by the other program, by choosing **Export** from the **File** menu. If the **Export** command isn't there, use **Save As** instead.

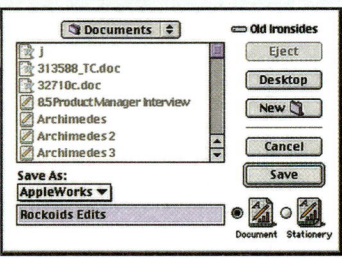

### 3 Choose the File Format

Look at the pop-up menu and choose the file format that matches the type of the document you're exporting to. If you want to insert your AppleWorks document in Word, save it in Word format. Click **Save** to complete the operation.

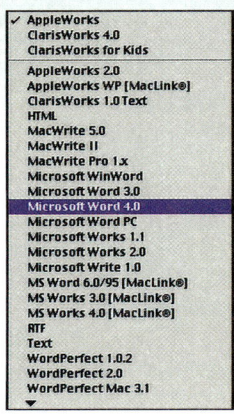

**70**  PART 5: WORKING WITH DOCUMENTS

## 4 Open the Other Document

After the file has been exported or saved in the proper fashion, double-click on the document in the other application where you want to place that file. Click the cursor where you want to put that file.

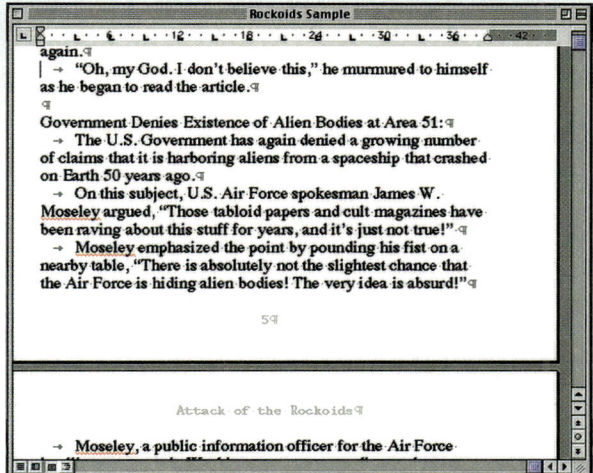

## 5 Import It

Go to the **File** or **Insert** menu (whichever applies) and choose the command that lets you insert the material. It can be called **Import, Insert,** or **Place,** depending on the program you're using. Locate the file you want to insert in the **Open** dialog box.

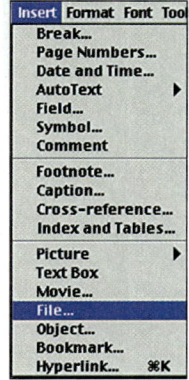

## 6 Place It Here

After the file is located, click the **Open** command to insert the material in your document where you positioned the cursor.

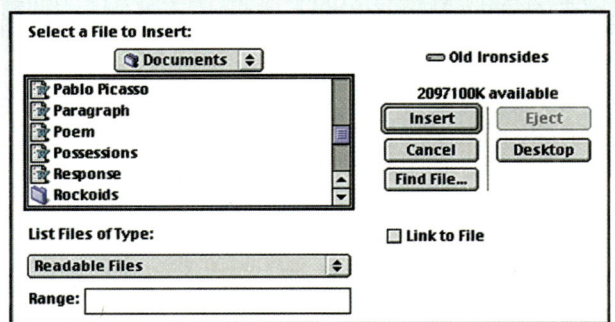

## How-To Hints

### Some Exported Files Are Easy to Open

When you export a file to open in another application, double-clicking on it will launch that application. This can help save you the Insert or Import process unless, of course, you want to merge the copy with another document you're working on.

### Not All Files Transfer Easily

Even if your application lets you export files to another application, don't expect the file transfer to be seamless. Typefaces, colors, and other formatting may drop out. If you have any problems, look at the manuals that came with your application.

### What If You Can't Export?

If your application won't let you Export, save the file as you normally would. Then launch the other application, click **Open** from the **File** menu, and see if you can locate the file. If you can, it will probably open just fine.

## Task

1. How to Run the Internet Assistant  74
2. How to Use a Web Browser  78
3. How to Search Online  82
4. How to Use an Email Program  86
5. How to Prepare and Send Email  90

## Part 6

# Getting Connected to the Internet

If you are like thousands of others, you bought your Mac for one reason: to get on the Internet. In fact, so many people who bought new Macs have gotten on the Internet (90 percent according to Apple reports), that some claim the *i* in iMac stands for *Internet*.

There is good reason for all this interest. Almost anything you might want to find is on the Internet. There's email to keep in contact with friends, news on every topic imaginable, as well as music and movie reviews. In many communities, you can even shop for groceries online.

In the following pages, we will look at the Internet Setup Assistant that came with your Mac. Have no fear: It is well written and takes you, step by step, through the process of setting up your Mac for the Internet. You'll find, however, that the questions you must answer require some very specific answers, answers that only your Internet provider is likely to know. So, you might want to go through this chapter, making note of all the questions you need answered. Then call your Internet provider and get an answer for each question before you begin the setup.

TASK 1

# How to Run the Internet Assistant

Earlier, you used the Mac OS Setup Assistant to tailor your Mac to your situation. In the tasks that follow, we will use the Internet Setup Assistant to do the same for your Internet account. If you have no interest in the Internet, you can skip this chapter. But, if you want to join the millions who have gone online with their Macs, read on.

## *Begin*

### *1* Launching Internet Setup Assistant

Double-click on your hard disk icon and, in the window that opens, look for a folder named **Assistants**. Double-click on it and another window will open. One of the icons should be labeled **Internet Setup Assistant**. Double-click on it and you are ready to go.

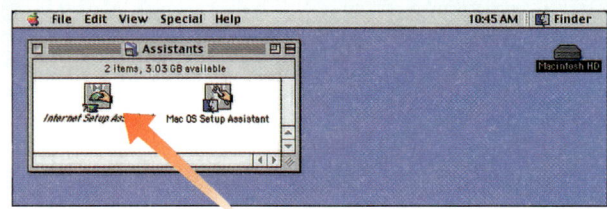

Double-click

### *2* Just Say Yes

The first question you'll be asked is whether you'd like to set up for the Internet. Do the obvious and click once on the **Yes** button.

Click

### *3* Set Up an Existing Account

At this point, we'll assume that you already have an Internet account, so when you are asked about this, click on the **Yes** button.

Click

## 4 The Technical Terminology

You'll then see a screen filled with technical terms. If the terms mean nothing to you, don't worry. It's the responsibility of your ISP (Internet Service Provider) or, on the job, your network administrator to know what these terms mean. Click the **right arrow** in the bottom right to move to the next screen.

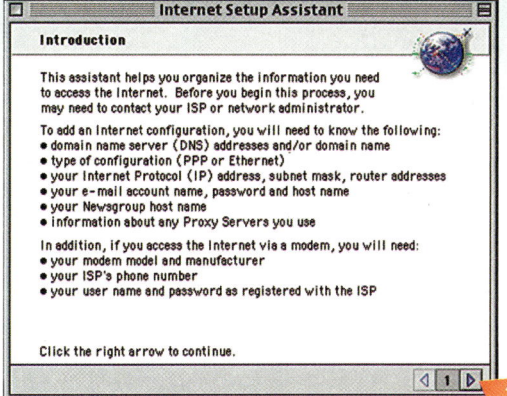

Click

## 5 Provide a Name

You might have several Internet accounts or you might log on to the same Internet service from different locations (if you use a laptop). To avoid confusion of your different configurations, you can give each a name. Enter the name in the box at the top and indicate how you will connect. Then click on the **right arrow**.

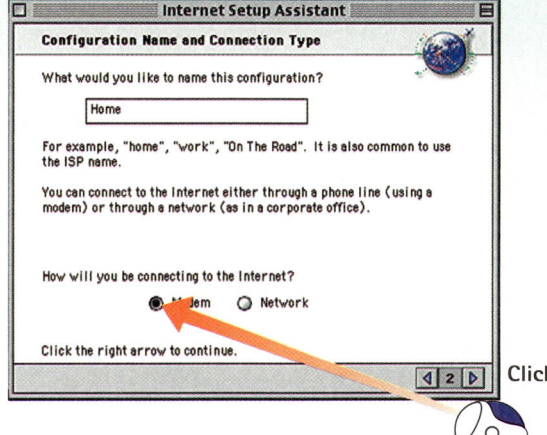

Click

## 6 Set Up Your Modem

Your modem talks through the phone lines to your Internet provider. In the drop-down menu, find the modem whose maker and model number seem closest to the modem you are using. Unless you know to do otherwise, leave the **Port** setting in its default. Finally, unless you have to use an old-fashioned dial phone, choose **Tone** from the two radio buttons. Then click on the **right arrow**.

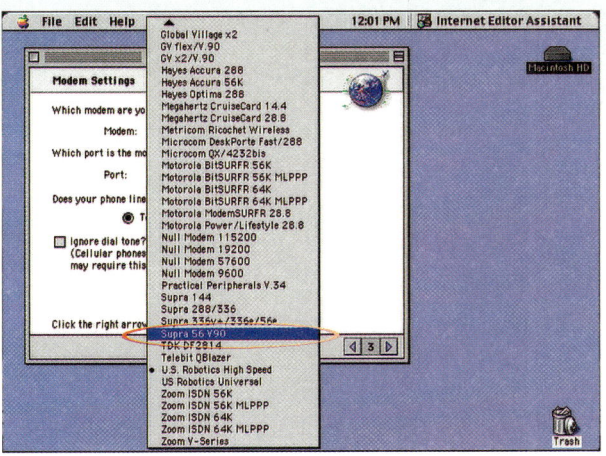

## 7 Set Up Your Internet Account

The next screen enables you to enter the phone number of your Internet provider; again, the phone number is something the ISP will provide to you. You also need to enter the unique name your provider has given you for your account. Enter your account password. When finished, click on the **right arrow**.

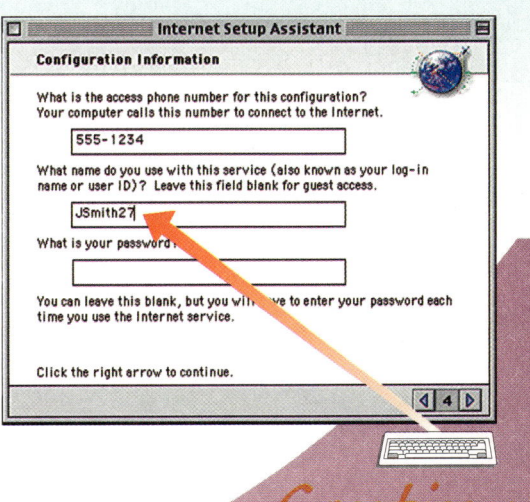

*Continues*

## How to Run the Internet Assistant Continued

### 8 Concerning Connect Scripts

Here's a question for your Internet provider: "Do you require me to PPP Connect Script?" If the answer is yes, you'll need to get a copy and install it exactly as a supplemental screen tells you. Assuming the answer is no, click on the right arrow.

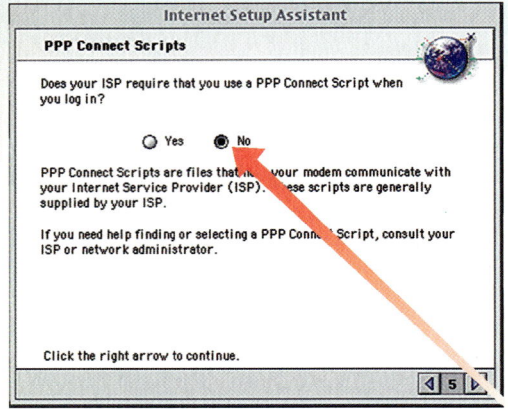

Click

### 9 Specify an IP Address

An IP address is a long number that's unique for each device on the Internet. Some Internet providers give each user their own number. If that is true, you should have been given that number and should answer Yes and enter it on a supplemental screen. If you have no such number, click on No and the right arrow.

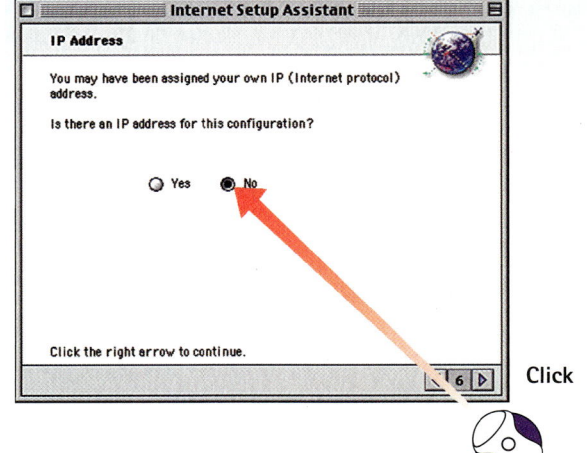
Click

### 10 Domain Name Servers

Though you need not wonder why, your access to the Internet depends on something called a Domain Server. Your Internet provider will give you the numberic address (or addresses) to enter in the large box and, perhaps, a name for the smaller box. Enter them and click on the right arrow.

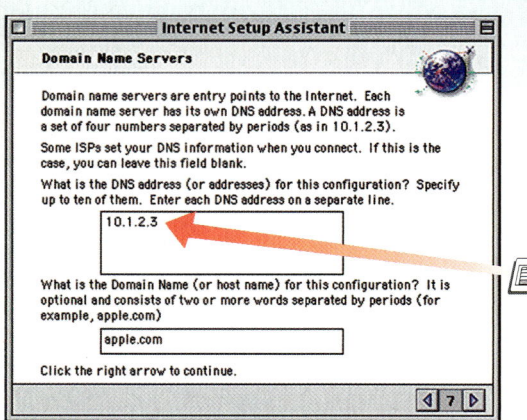

### 11 Set Up Your Email

Your Internet provider will give you an email address. Type your email address into the top box. Enter the password for your email account in the bottom box if you don't want to enter it every time you check your email. Then click the **right arrow**.

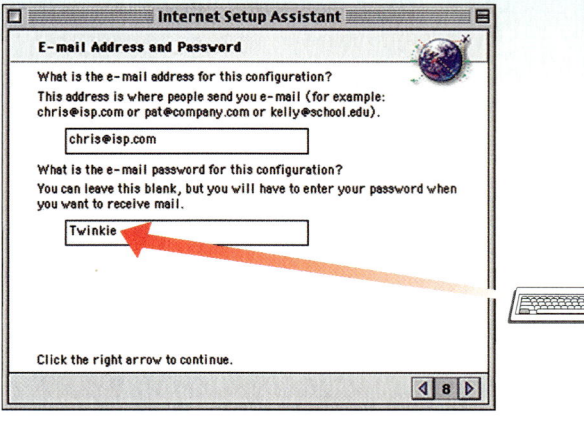

76   PART 6: GETTING CONNECTED TO THE INTERNET

## 12 More for Email

Your email software needs to know where go to get your email. Fill out these two fields with the information your provider specifies. Then click on the **right arrow**.

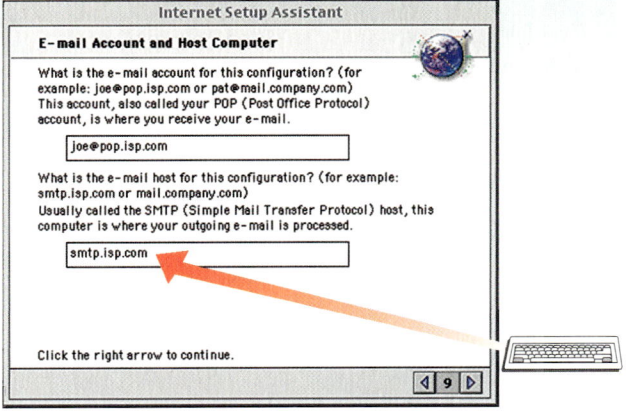

## 13 Use Newsgroups

After you are on the Internet, you might want to participate in newsgroups. To do that, you need access to a host computer. Your Internet provider should give you the name of a host computer, which you can enter here. Then click on the **right arrow**.

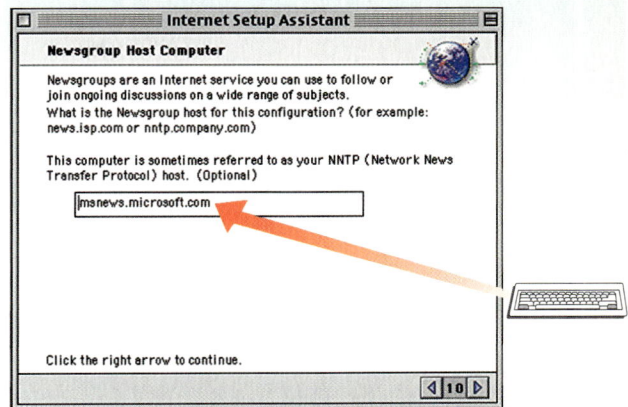

## 14 Proxy Servers

Large organizations often use proxy servers to provide added security. If that is the case with you, click on **Yes** and enter the information your network administrator gives you on a supplemental screen. If you are not using a proxy server, click on **No** and the **right arrow**.

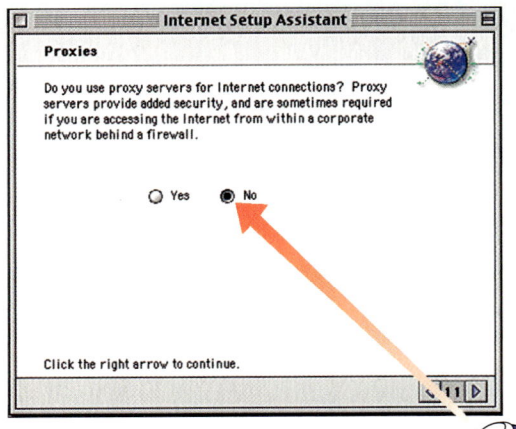

## 15 You're Done

Congratulations, you're now ready to go online. Check the **Connect when finished** box if you want to go online as soon as you exit Internet Setup Assistant. Click **Go Ahead** to save the changes and you are done.

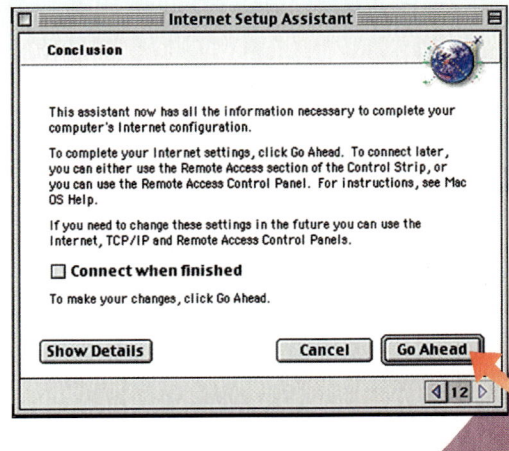

Click

*End*

How to Run the Internet Assistant    **77**

## Task 2

# How to Use a Web Browser

Joining an Internet service provider (and I'll call them ISPs from now on) is only the first step.

The second step is to actually connect to your service and take advantage of the many features available on the Internet. The main program used to access the Internet is a Web browser. A browser is a program that can retrieve pages from the World Wide Web and then display them in their original form (or a close approximation thereof) on your Mac.

## Begin

### 1 Open Remote Access

One way to connect to the Internet is through an application called **Remote Access**. Go to the Apple menu (that drops down from the Apple symbol on the left side of the screen), pull down the menu and select **Remote Access**.

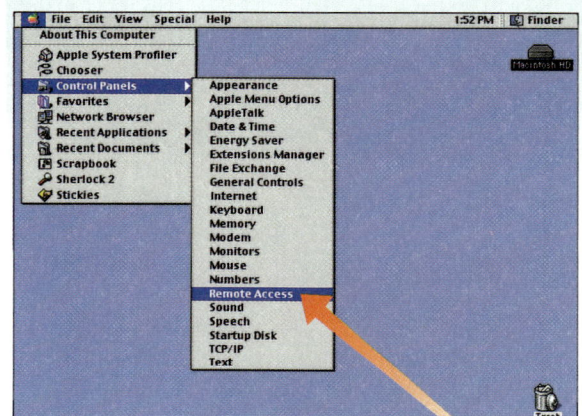

 Click

### 2 Make Your Connection

Click on the **Connect** button to log in to your ISP. Or choose the same option from the **Remote Access Control Strip** module. To log out, open **Remote Access** again and click on the **Disconnect** button.

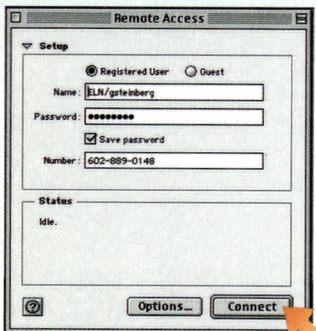

 Click

### 3 Open Your Web Browser

Locate the folder with your Internet browser and double-click on the browser icon. It should open within a short time. For this exercise, we will be using Microsoft's Internet Explorer. If your browser is set up to start out with an initial "home page," then it should appear. If not, skip to Step 5.

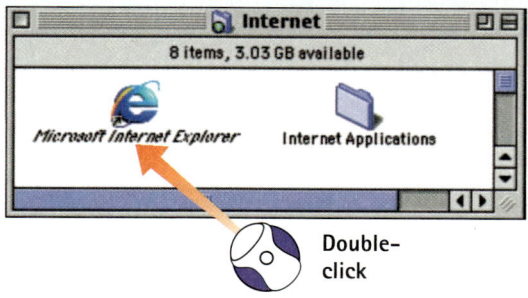

Double-click

PART 6: GETTING CONNECTED TO THE INTERNET

## 4 Entering a Web Page Address

There are several ways to go to a new web page. You may have seen an ad that gives the "dot com" address of a web site. You can go to there by typing that address into the **Address** area near the top of the browser screen. Here we have typed www.apple.com and pressed **Return**. (Explorer entered the rest for us.) Apple's corporate web site appears.

## 5 Saving a Favorite Site

Does this site look like one you'd like to visit again? If so, then go to the top of the screen, pull down the **Favorites,** and click on **Add Page to Favorites.** The address for Apple is easy, but some sites have such complicated addresses, you'll love this feature. To use it, simply drop down the **Favorites** menu and click on the site you want.

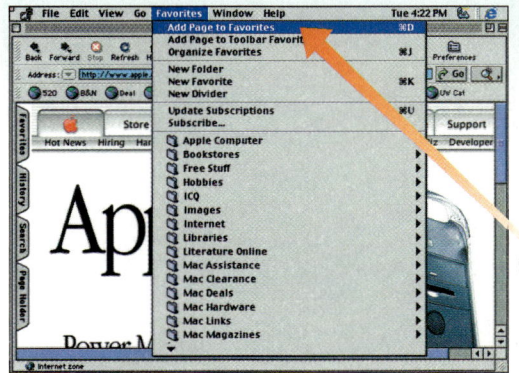

Click

## 6 Organizing Your Favorites

When you first put something in your **Favorites** list, it's placed at the bottom of the **Favorite** menu. Before long, you'll find that list getting very long. That's when you'll want to use an option on the **Favorites** menu called **Organize Favorites.** We won't go into here, but it allows you turn chaos into order by moving links around and organizing them into folders. You can also use clear in the **Edit** menu to get rid of a no-longer favorite link.

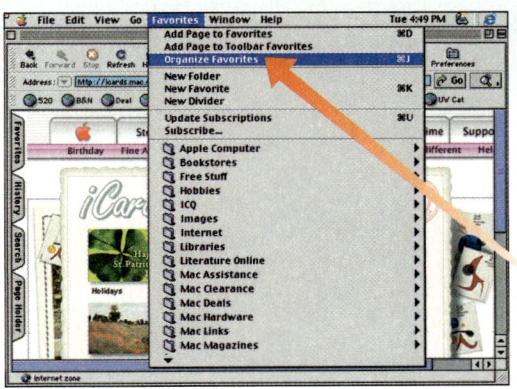

Click

## 7 Going from Page to Page

One of the best features of the web is the ability of one web page to point your way to another web page. This is done by "links" hidden behind images and text. If you see underlined text on a page, it's always linked to another page. In Explorer, the mouse pointer gives you a clue, it turns to a hand over a link. Simply click once to go to the linked page. For instance, clicking on the iCards folder tab in the page below will jump you to the page in Step 6.

Click

*Continues*

How to Use a Web Browser

*How to Use a Web Browser Continued*

## 8 Going Backward and Forward

Often you'll want to go back to a page you visited a few minutes earlier. With most browsers, that couldn't be easier. You simply clink on the arrow at the top left that's labeled **Back**. Going forward is equally easy, simply click on the Forward arrow.

Click

## 9 Refreshing or Stopping a Page

Sometimes a page will seem to take forever to display and you'll want to go on to other things. To stop a page from loading, click on the red **Stop** icon. At other times a page won't seem to display properly. To load a new copy of the current page, click on the **Refresh** icon.

Click

## 10 Printing a Page

So far, those who though computers would create a "paperless society" have been disappointed. When you see a page with information that is important enough to print and save, you can click on the **Print** icon or choose **Print** from the **File** menu. Just be advised that sometimes a page won't look the same in print as it looks on screen.

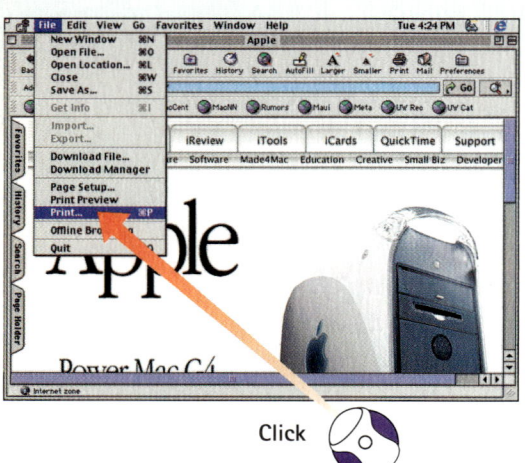
Click

## 11 Add Page to Favorites

Choose **Add Page to Favorites**, and the site you pick will be added to the search menu.

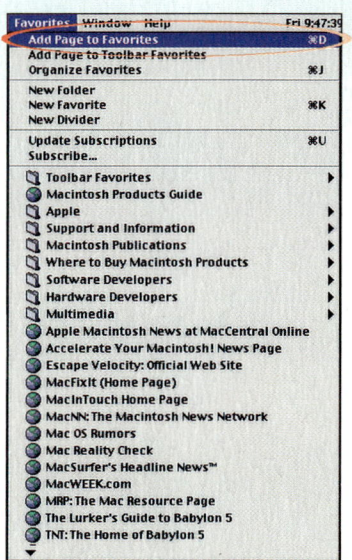

80   PART 6: GETTING CONNECTED TO THE INTERNET

## 12 Print the Page

If you'd like a printed copy of the Web page, click the **Print** icon, which brings up your **Print** dialog box. Press the **Print** button to get a paper copy.

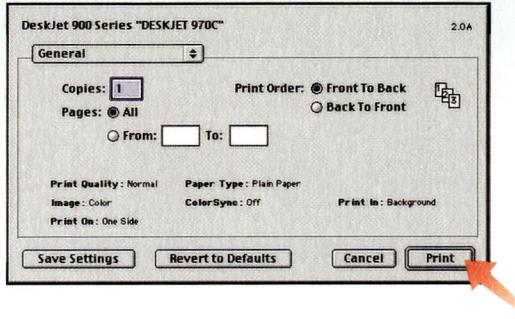

Click

## 13 Log Off

When your Internet session is over, return to the **Remote Access Control Panel** and click **Disconnect**. If you just want to exchange email first (see Task 4), you can stay connected.

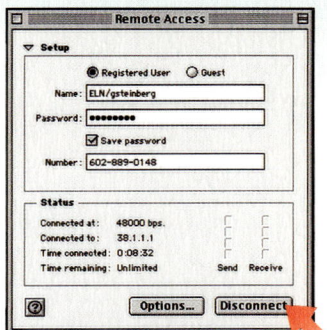

Click

*End*

## How-To Hints

### If You Join AOL

If you intend to join AOL, or you're already a member, you won't want to use the Internet Setup Assistant. Instead check the Internet folder, and look for another folder with the **America Online** label on it. If you don't have it, check your **System CD**, in a folder called **CD Extras**. If that doesn't produce a satisfactory result, you may copy the installer from another Mac, or check at your favorite computer store or in a magazine or newspaper. AOL CDs are everywhere, well almost.

### If Your Modem Won't Connect

Often a modem doesn't work simply because it's not plugged into a live telephone line. If it is correctly connected, check the documentation that came with the modem for further advice. If your Mac came with a built-in modem, Apple's **Help** menu can guide you through the setup process and some basic troubleshooting to help you deal with any serious problems.

### What About Netscape?

Another Web browser available on your Mac is Netscape. Most of the features you'll see with Netscape are the same, with a major exception. Netscape refers to its Favorites feature as Bookmarks, but you'll be able to set it up in pretty much the same fashion as described above.

### No Remote Access Control Panel?

For recent versions of the Mac operating system before Mac OS 8.5, it was called PPP but the way you connected to your ISP was the same.

TASK 3

# How to Search Online

The World Wide Web has millions of Web pages. How do you find the one you want when you don't even know its address? How can you find other information online? Rest easy—search engines and online databases will be our focus in this task. Just remember that the sites we look at are examples. You might find other sites that better suit your needs.

## Begin

### 1 Search the Web

To find Web pages on a topic that interests you, use a search engine. It uses software that goes around the Web, cataloging all it finds into a large database. Given the right keywords, the search engine will locate the very page you want. To get to a search engine, bring up your browser and type this in the **Address** box: **http://www.metacrawler.com/**. After pressing **Return**, you should see something like this.

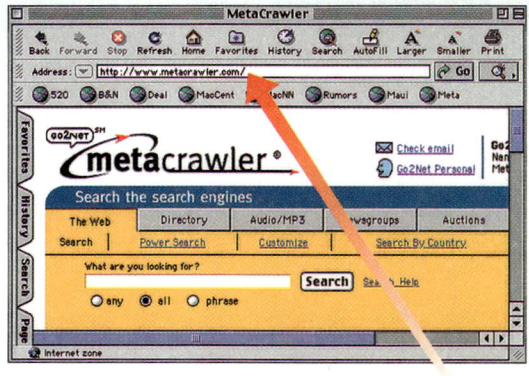

### 2 Look for Your Topic

Entering a topic is easy. Just type words that uniquely describe the topic into the text box and click Search. Be careful with your words. Try not to be too specific or vague. Use the right radio buttons, too. Choose **any** and the search engine will find Web pages with any of the words you enter—and that could be a lot. On the other hand, **all** will find only sites with all of the search words, whereas **phrase** will find only those sites with all the words in the order you specify. Here I've entered **iMac** and **style**, specifying that both be on the Web page. Then I clicked on the **Search** button.

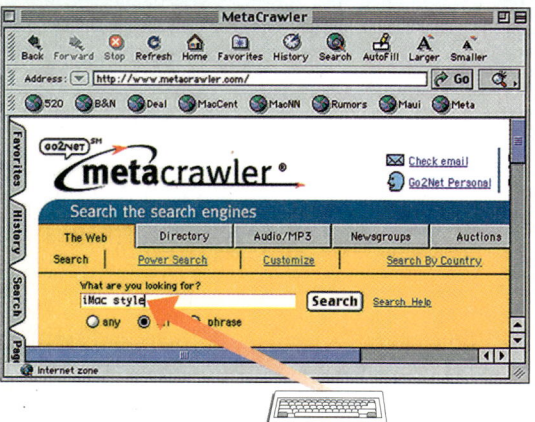

### 3 Use the Search Results

The results you get back depend on the search engine. MetaCrawler's will look like this. Browse though the list, and when you find something interesting, click on the underlined words to go to that page. (You can use **Back** to return to your search results.)

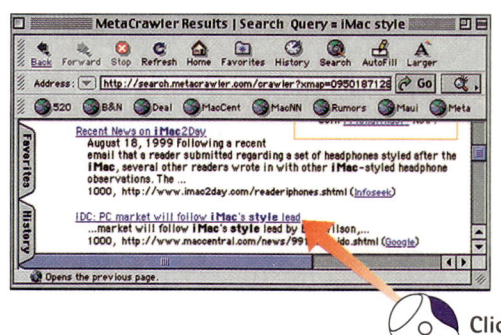

Click

82    PART 6: GETTING CONNECTED TO THE INTERNET

## 4 Search a Library

What if you're not for a Web page looking, but for a book on a topic that intrigues you. Would you like to search a library with over 12 million volumes? You can if you go to the Library of Congress at `http://www.loc.gov/library/`. The results will look like this. Click on the underlined **Library of Congress Online Catalog** to do a search. Or choose **Other Libraries Online Catalogs** for links to other libraries.

Click

## 5 Find Software

You can also download software from a Web site to your Mac and be using what you downloaded within minutes. For an example, enter `http://www5.zdnet.com/mac/download.html` in your browser's address box, press **Return**, and you will get this result.

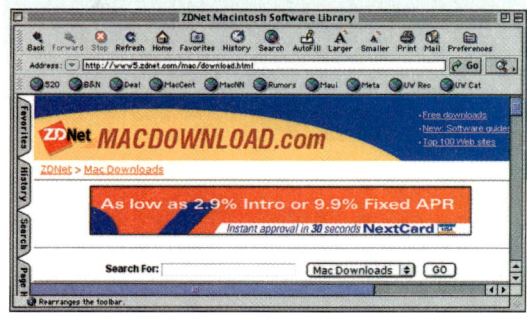

## 6 Search for Software

Type words that describe what sort of software you want to find into the **Search for:** box and click on the **Go** button. As with Web pages, pick your words carefully. I am looking for something to liven up my computer screen when I'm not using it, so I entered **screensaver**.

## 7 Choose the Software

Searching for **screensaver** gave these results. If you find something in the list that looks interesting, click on the underlined part. You'll be shown a Web page with more about that program and the option of downloading it. In this case, I'll click on **Chronos 2.0**.

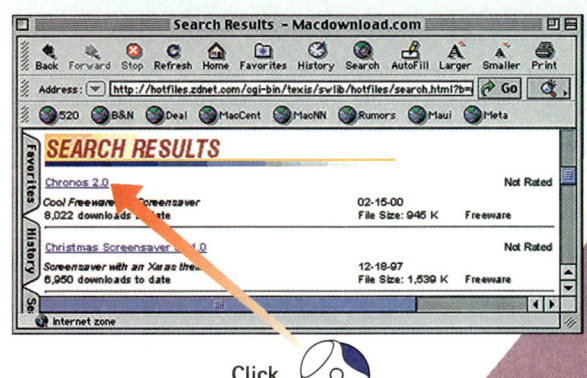

Click

*Continues*

HOW TO SEARCH ONLINE   83

## How to Search Online Continued

### 8 Download Software

We now get more information about the software. If you like it, click on the **Download** button and your browser will take care of the rest. This program happens to be free, but if you download shareware and you use it, be sure to pay the author.

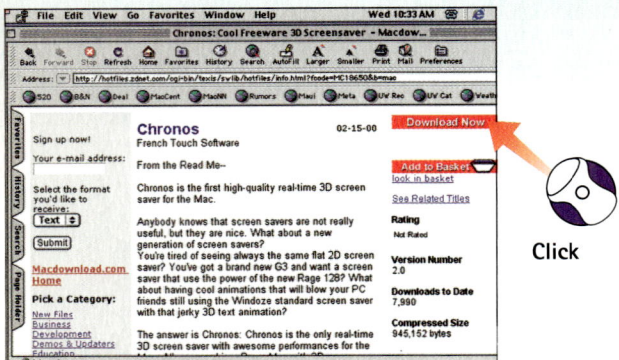

Click

### 9 Find a Phone Number

Are you looking for an old friend who's moved across the country? Then you might find him or her through an online phone directory operated by a phone company, such as the directory at **http://uswestdex.com/**. To look up your friend, click on the **People** tab.

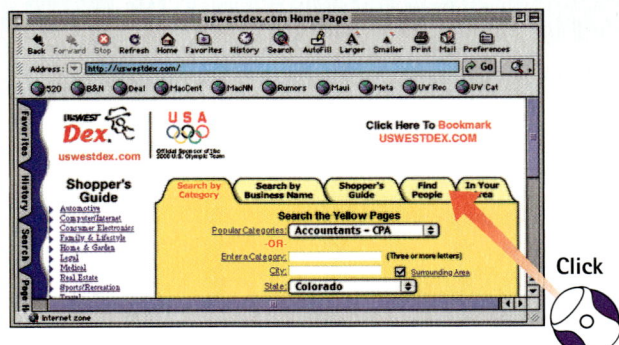

Click

### 10 Look for an Old Friend

You're now on a page that enables you to search phone directories by name and city. In this case, I'll spare you from seeing all the John Smiths in Seattle.

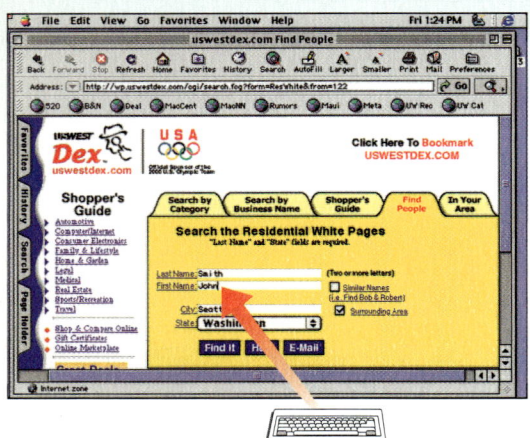

*End*

**84**   PART 6: GETTING CONNECTED TO THE INTERNET

## How-To Hints

### Web Search Hints
If you want to search for a phrase, put the request in quotes, such as "Mac software." When you see a list of matches to your request, there will usually be a sentence or two describing the site. Just click once on the site's title to bring it up and see if it has what you want.

### Site Not Available
If the site doesn't appear in a minute or two, you'll see a dialog that the browser cannot connect to it. If this happens, re-enter the site's address, making sure that every letter and number is correct. Even if it's correct, the site might not be available. It could be down for maintenance (which happens sometimes during the early morning), or the site may no longer be available. You might want to just try again later on.

## Task 4

# How to Use an Email Program

Aside from using a Web browser, sending and receiving electronic mail (or email) is probably the most popular Internet activity.

With email you stay in touch with family, friends, and business contacts. In fact, many folks do all of their business via email without ever actually meeting business associates face-to-face, or by telephone. It's the ultimate in telecommuting.

This book, for example, was written by using email. The manuscript and illustrations were emailed to the publisher, and corrections and updates were sent to the author and back to the publisher in the same fashion.

## Begin

### 1 Get Connected

In order to exchange email, you'll want to connect to your ISP. First, go to the **Apple Menu**, choose **Control Panels**, and then select **Remote Access** from the sub-menu.

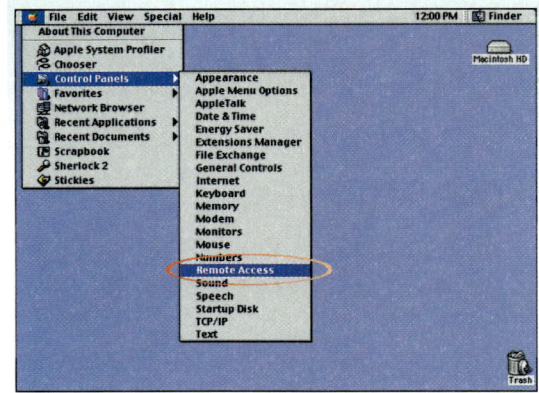

### 2 Log On

When the **Remote Access** window appears, click **Connect** to log in to your ISP.

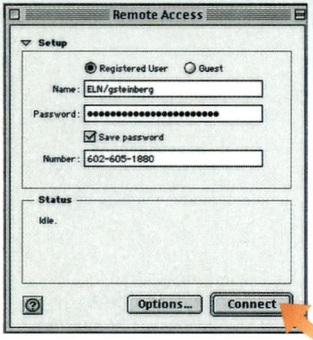

Click

### 3 Locate Your Email Software

Open the **Internet** folder and then open the folder containing your email software. For this example, I'm using Microsoft's Outlook Express version 5.0.

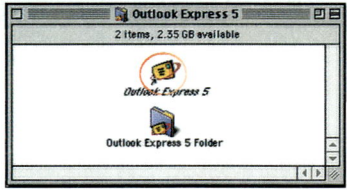

## 4 Launch the Program

Double-click on the **Outlook Express** icon to launch it. You'll see the program's main email window.

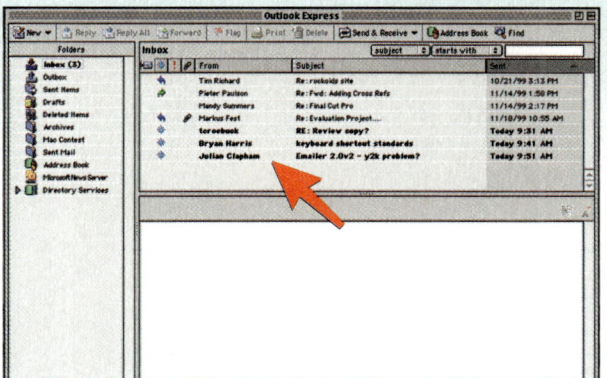

## 5 Check Mail

Click the **Send & Receive** button to send any email you've written and to check your mailbox for new messages.

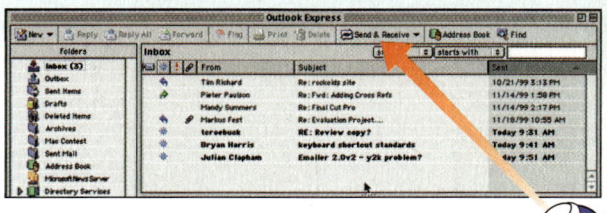

Click

## 6 New Mail Arrives

Your newest email will show up in your Inbox folder, and are usually highlighted in bold.

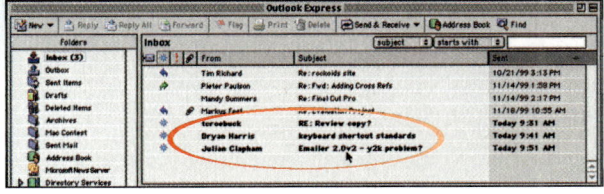

## 7 Read Your Mail

Click on a message's title to see its contents appear in the message pane below.

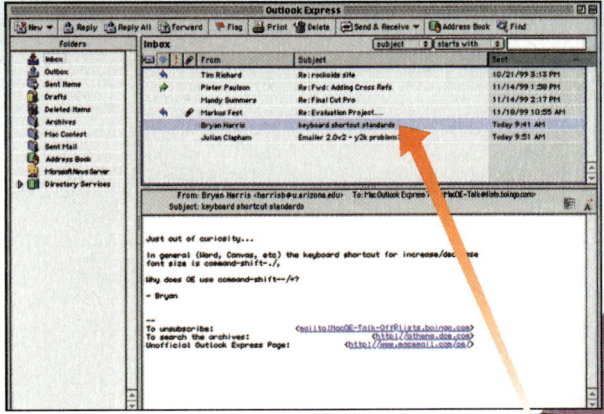

Click

*Continues*

HOW TO USE AN EMAIL PROGRAM   87

## Email Program Continued

### 8 Reply to Your Mail

To respond to the message, click the **Reply** button. (If the message went to multiple recipients, click **Reply All** to reply to all of them.)

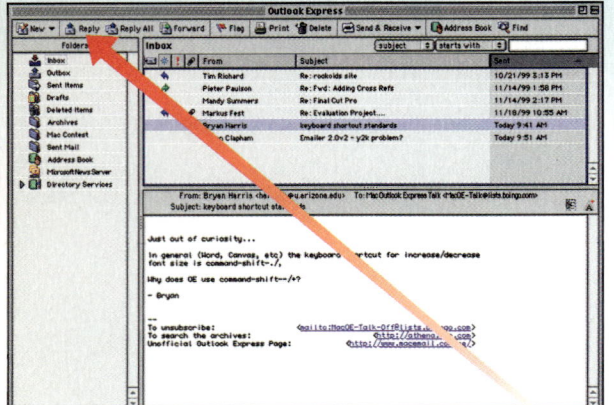

Click

### 9 Write Your Response

Click on the message window and then type the reply to the message. Check the next task for helpful information on writing email messages.

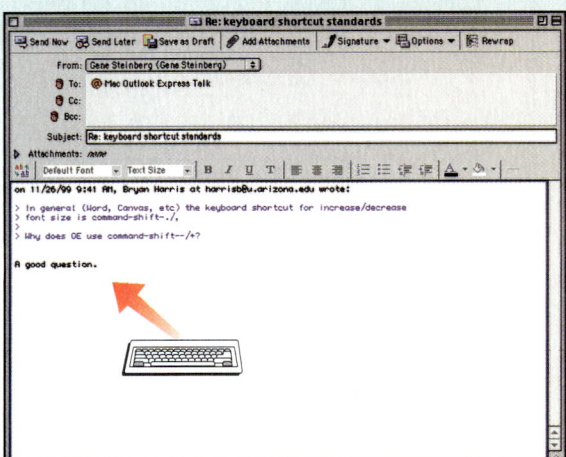

### 10 Forward the Message

If you'd like to forward a message to someone else, click the **Forward** button instead; then write your comment in the message window above the material you're forwarding.

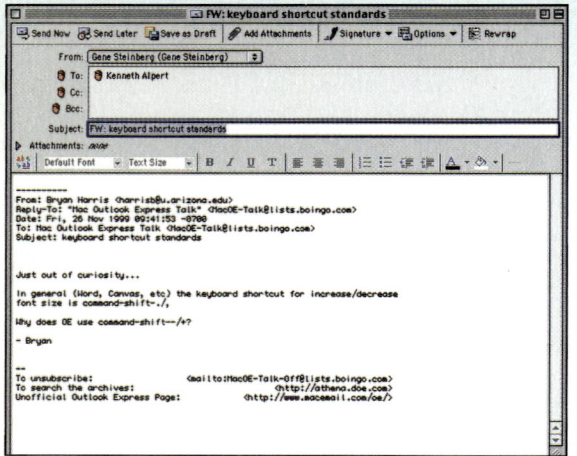

### 11 Send It

When your message is ready, click **Send Now** to speed it on its way. When you're finished sending email, quit the email program; then go to **Remote Access** and click the **Disconnect** button to end your session.

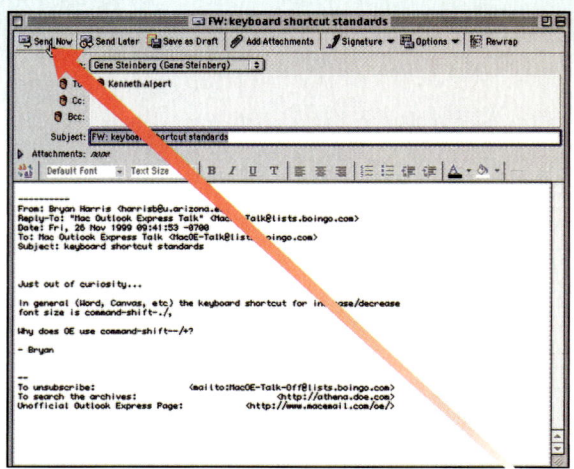

Click

88  PART 6: GETTING CONNECTED TO THE INTERNET

## 12 Use the Address Book

If you'd like to keep a record of your contacts, click the **Address Book** button, enter the information about the client, and click **Save** to store it.

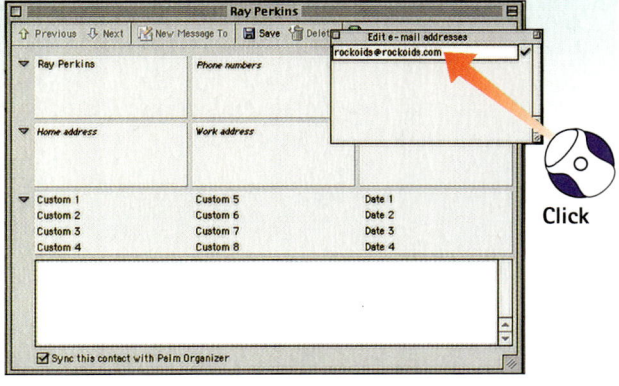

Click

## 13 Flag a Message

Sometimes you get a message that is so important that you don't want to forget it, but also one that you can't respond to immediately. Put a red flag next to the message by clicking once on the message in your **Inbox,** then clicking on the red **Flag** button.

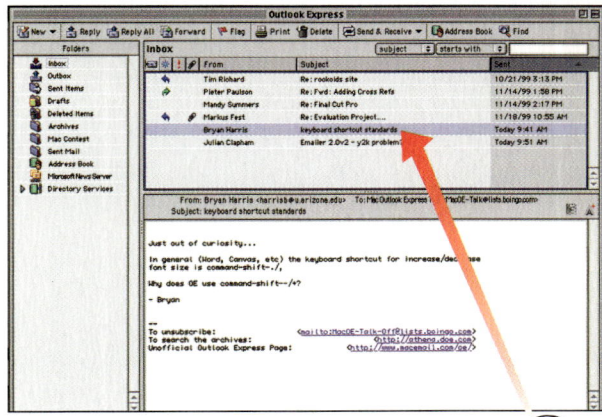

Click

*End*

## How-To Hints

### Watch Out for Junk Email!

Once you join an ISP, you may begin to receive unsolicited offers. They might contain get rich schemes, offers of super cheap prices on merchandise, and a few may contain links to Web sites that have pornography. If you get such messages, don't respond to them. Instead, use the Forward feature to send a copy to either **abuse@<enter name of service here>** or **postmaster@<enter name of service here>**. The name of the service will be the information that comes after the @ on the offensive email, such as **aol.com**, **earthlink.net**, or wherever it came from. The folks who run Internet services take a dim view of such material, and will investigate on your behalf. They are also able to recognize when the addresses have been faked (which is, by the way, a common occurrence). I have received junk mail supposedly from me, coming directly to me. Go figure!

### Don't Have Outlook Express 5?

The latest versions of Microsoft's Internet software are available from their popular MacTopia Web site. You can get there by pointing your browser to **http://www.microsoft.com/mac**.

### Other Email Software

Netscape Communicator has its own email program, which has features that are similar to Outlook Express. There are also retail email programs, such as Eudora and QuickMail Pro, that provide special features you may want to check out. But the basic steps in setting up and using an email program are similar to the ones described here (although labels may be slightly different).

TASK 5

# How to Prepare and Send Email

Now that you've gotten acquainted with how to handle email, you'll probably want to use the program to send messages.

Preparing an email message isn't all that different from preparing a regular written message that you send via the U.S. Postal Service.

## Begin

### 1 Open a New Mail Screen

Click the **New** button in Outlook Express to bring up a blank message screen.

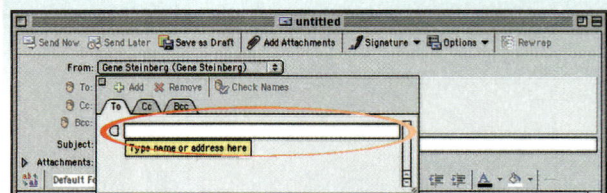

### 2 Address It

Type the exact address of your recipient in the **To** window. If you want to send a "carbon copy" to someone else, put it in the **Cc: window** instead. If you want someone to get a copy without any of the other recipients knowing, put their address in the **Bcc** (blind carbon copy) box. Use the **Tab** key to move from text box to text box.

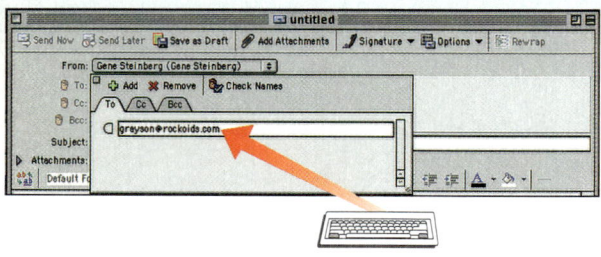

### 3 Give It a Topic

Enter a word or phrase in the **Subject** box that briefly describes the subject of your message, so the recipient knows what it's about.

## 4 Type Your Message

Write your message. Type **Return** twice after each paragraph for easier reading (it's not necessary to press Return at the end of a line as the email software will make the line breaks for you).

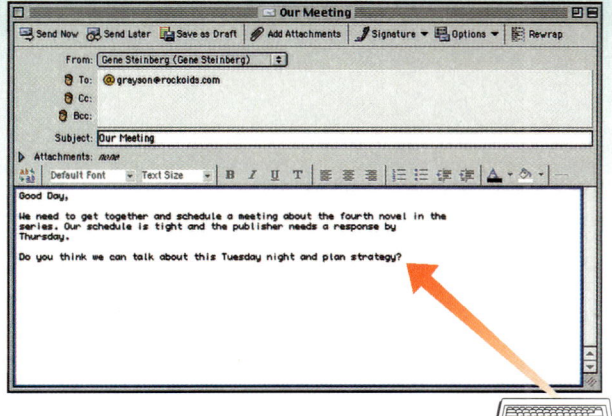

## 5 Sign It

Put your name at the bottom of the message, so the recipient knows who sent it. Sometimes an email address is very, very different from one's real name.

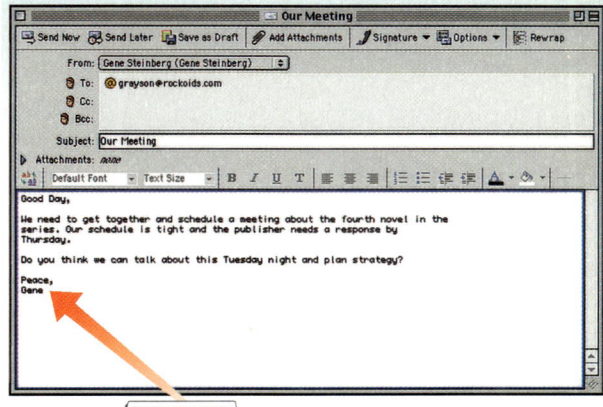

## 6 Send It

Click the **Send Now** button to speed it on its way.

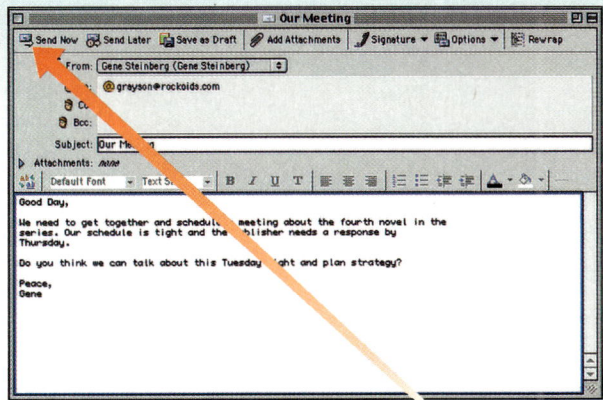

Click

*End*

# How-To Hints

### Wrong Addresses

As with a Web address, every character in an email address must be exact. Don't use spaces between words (except on AOL). On the Internet, if there's a space, use an underscore instead (_). If you get one character wrong, the message may go to the wrong person, or be returned as undeliverable.

### Email Isn't Instantaneous!

Sometimes it takes a little while for a message to get to its destination. Expect a delay of minutes or hours, depending on which service you're sending the message to and how busy the Internet network is

# Task

**1** **How to Identify and Use Extensions Folder Items  94**

**2** **How to Identify and Use the Contextual Menu Items and Control Strip Modules Folders  96**

**3** **How to Identify and Use Control Panels Folder Items  98**

**4** **How to Use the Preferences Folder  100**

**5** **How to Identify and Use Other System Folder Items  102**

# CHAPTER 7

# Exploring the System Folder

The System Folder is the heart and soul of the Mac operating system. Inside it are the software components that create the look and feel of your Mac. Without it, your Mac would just put up a blinking question mark when you started your computer (literally).

On the surface, the System Folder looks like an awfully complex place. It's filled with hundreds of files and, depending on the version of the Mac OS you have, may fill hundreds of megabytes of storage space on your hard drive.

It can seem daunting, a no man's land where touching and moving the wrong thing can cause serious problems to your Mac.

While it's true that moving certain files to the wrong place may affect performance, perhaps even preventing your Mac from starting properly, many of the items there are really designed to help you get the most value from your Mac. ●

Task 1

# How to Identify and Use Extensions Folder Items

The Extensions folder basically consists of two types of programs. One is the true extension, which adds features to your Mac. These features may range from the ability to share files with another Mac to the ability to use QuickTime.

The other components in your Extensions folder include drivers. They are used to communicate with, or "drive," a peripheral component, such as a printer or a removable drive. In addition, there are files called shared libraries, which are files that may be used by several programs.

In this section, you'll see some of the types of files you see in the Extensions folder and what they're used for.

*Begin*

### 1 Open the Extensions Folder

Double-click on the **System Folder** icon; then locate and double-click on the **Extensions** folder icon.

Double-click

### 2 System Extensions

Extensions are little files that add key features to the Mac. The **ATI Graphics Accelerator** extension shown here, for example, is used to provided speedier video display on many Macs.

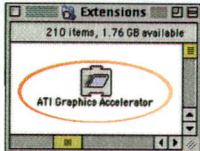

### 3 Drivers

Another important extension is a **driver**. A driver is an extension that allows your Mac to work with a device that is connected to your Mac, such as a printer, a scanner, an extra drive (such as a Zip or SuperDisk drive), or a digital camera (to cover a few possibilities). Shown here is one for a LaserWriter printer.

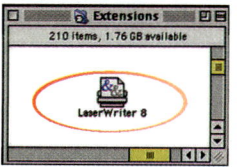

94    Part 7: Exploring the System Folder

## 4 Shared Libraries

A **shared library** is an extension that offers functions to various programs. Since it is shared, more than one program can use it. The example shown is for Microsoft's Internet programs, and is used both by Internet Explorer and Outlook Express.

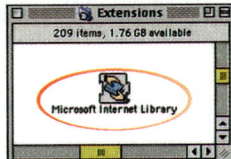

## 5 Network Extensions

Your Mac needs extensions to communicate with other computers and printers across a network, using a technology called **Open Transport**.

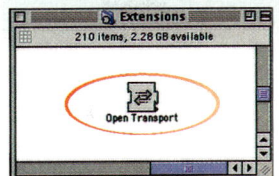

## 6 QuickTime

Another useful set of extensions is **QuickTime** (only one of these is shown here). QuickTime allows you to play audio and video files on your Mac and create your own videos using special programs (such as iMovie, which comes with the iMac DV series).

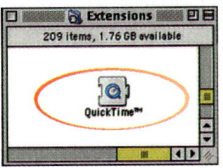

# How-To Hints

### What Can I Throw Out?

Many of the components in your Extensions folder are needed by some programs in order for them to run. For example, items with the name Microsoft are needed by Microsoft's software, including their Internet programs and even AOL, to work. If you take them out by mistake, these programs won't work properly (although many Microsoft programs will launch special installers that will replace the items). The most likely candidates to toss are printer drivers you don't need. Most of these are clearly labeled as to which printer they belong to.

### What Do They Do?

Some files in the Extensions folder aren't labeled very clearly, so you don't really have an obvious indication of what they do. An example is **High Sierra File Access**, which is required for your Mac to use certain CD-ROMs. If the extension comes from Apple, the Extensions Manager Control Panel can display what its purpose is when you click on an item. For other programs, the information isn't available. There's also a neat program called **Conflict Catcher** from Casady & Greene, which also manages extensions. It adds the capability to run a test for software conflicts, and it also has a big database that it uses to tell you what many of those strangely named extensions are needed for.

How to Identify and Use Extensions Folder Items  95

## Task 2

# How to Identify and Use the Contextual Menu Items and Control Strip Modules Folders

Two more folders in your System Folder have especially valuable components. The Contextual Menu is a little pop-up menu that appears when you click on an item on your Mac's desktop and hold down the Control key. If you're migrating from the Windows platform, you'll remember a similar feature accessed via a right-mouse click.

A Control Strip is the little floating bar that appears at the bottom of your screen. The items that appear on the Control Strip, such as the File Sharing icon or the various display-related icons, require that the actual programs be placed in the Control Strip Modules folder.

## Begin

### 1 Contextual Menu

To look at a **Contextual Menu**, click on an **item** on your Mac's desktop and press the **Control** key.

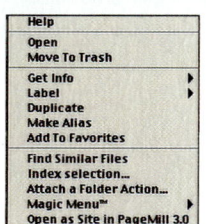

### 2 Check the Folder

Double-click on the **System Folder** icon; then double-click on the **Contextual Menu Items** folder.

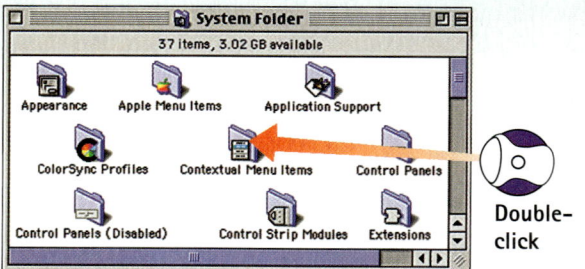

### 3 Check the Files

When you double-click on many **System Folder** components, you'll see a message as to where they belong.

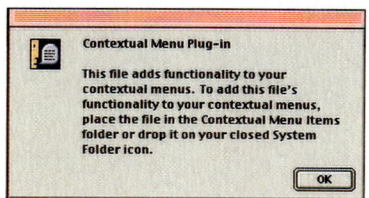

## 4 Look at Your Control Strip

The Control Strip consists of handy icons that perform various functions on your Mac. These include changing file sharing, monitor settings, printer settings, sound levels, and more.

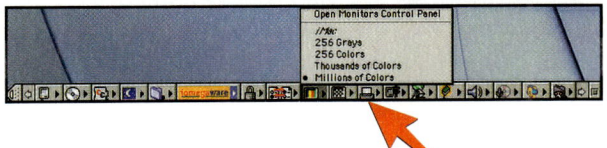

## 5 Check the Folder

Double-click on the **System Folder** to open it; then double-click on the **Control Strip Modules** folder.

Double-click

## 6 Look at the Files

Notice that each Control Strip module is generally clearly labeled as to what it does.

*End*

# How-To Hints

## What Is the (Disabled) Folder?

When you turn off various System Folder components, using Extensions Manager, they are simply moved to a folder with the name of the original folder, plus the word (Disabled), such as Extensions (Disabled). When they're put in that folder, they won't load when you restart your Mac.

## When There Are No Contextual Menus in a Program

Not all programs support Apple's Contextual Menus feature. Very old programs were made before the feature was introduced. And some software publishers have decided they don't need it anyway, and haven't changed their programs to support it. This is nothing to be concerned about, although when it's not there, you may miss its presence.

If there are control strip modules that you don't need, you can shorten the strip by removing their files from the Control Strip Modules folder. You may want to create a folder labeled CSM (disabled) and store them there. The changes will take effect when you restart.

## Task 3

# How to Identify and Use Control Panels Folder Items

Control Panels are much different from other components in your System Folder. For one thing, they actually do something when you double-click on their icons. That's why they are in the Control Panels folder because they are used to activate and adjust different features of an application or the Mac OS.

An example of a Control Panel is the Mouse Control Panel, which controls the speed of the mouse cursor and how fast you need to double-click for it to work. By using Control Panels, you can also change your Mac's desktop appearance, your network settings, display settings, sound levels, and the drive from which your Mac boots, to name just a few of the features. Even the ability to display a submenu of Control Panels from the Apple menu is performed by a Control Panel called Apple Menu Options.

## Begin

### 1 Open the Control Panels Folder

Pull down the **Apple** menu in the upper left corner of your screen, select **Control Panels** and a list will appear that lets you select a control panel. In this case, select **Appearances**.

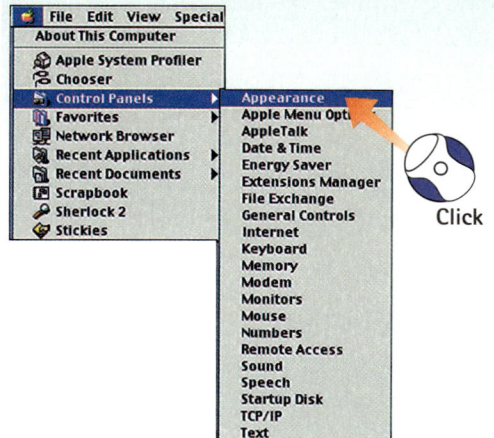

### 2 Changing Your Mac's Desktop

The **Appearance Control Panel** sets the desktop display of your Mac and how directories and titles are displayed.

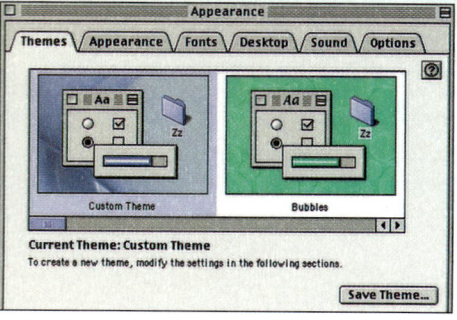

### 3 Desktop Pictures

Click on the **Desktop** folder tab and then on the rectangle on the left that represents your screen. Clicking on **Place Picture** will bring up an **Open** dialog box and enable you to choose a picture to liven up your desktop. Look around and find a picture you like. Clicking on the **Set Desktop** button will then place that picture on your desktop.

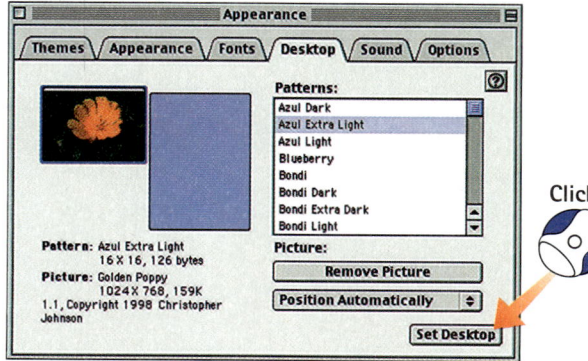

98  Part 7: Exploring the System Folder

## 4 Changing Internet Settings

The **Internet Control Panel** is used to control your Internet settings. You can set how you are identified when you send email and what home page to display when you visit the World Wide Web. Most of the critical settings, though, are done when you install software for your Internet Service Provider (ISP).

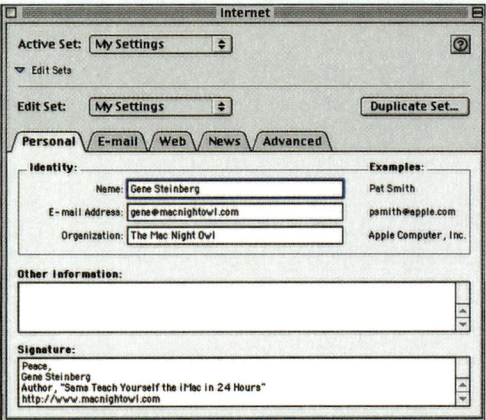

## 5 Changing Display Settings

The **Monitors Control Panel** is used to control color depth (number of colors on your screen) and resolution. The second setting controls how big text and other objects appear on your screen.

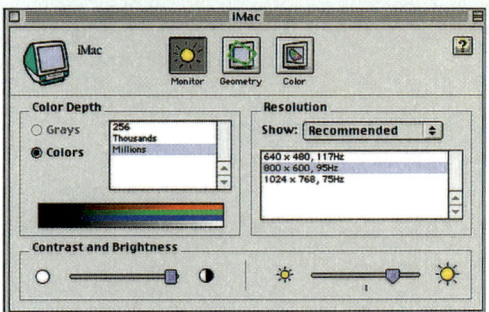

## 6 Updating Apple's Software

**Software Update** is a feature that was first introduced with Mac OS 9. It lets you automatically dial up Apple via your ISP and receive new software updates (if any are available).

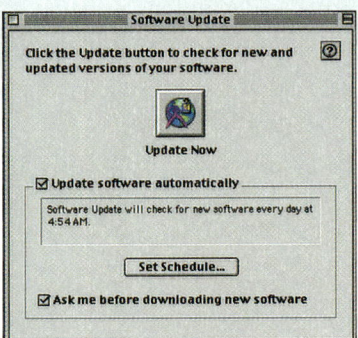

### How-To Hints

#### Moving the Location of the Control Strip

To see if your Mac can use this feature (and older Macs can't), check the Control Strip Control Panel. Then make sure that the strip is activated. Once it's there, you can easily put it somewhere else. Just hold down the **Option** key, click on the **curved edge**, and **drag it** anywhere on your Mac's desktop.

#### What About the Rest?

Feel free to double-click on any **Control Panel** to see what it does. So long as you don't change a setting, there's nothing to be concerned about. Many of the Control Panels will have a little **Help** icon. When you click on it, you'll learn more about its functions and how to use it.

*End*

TASK 4

# How to Use the Preferences Folder

A preference is a setting you make in a particular application to change the way it runs. As soon as you open many applications for the first time, they'll create a preference file. Normally, this file goes into the Preferences folder, located inside the System Folder. On some occasions, though, the file turns up right in the actual applications folder. It doesn't matter where the application places the file, as long as the application works properly.

## Begin

### 1 Open the Folder

Double-click on the **System Folder icon**; then double-click on the **Preferences folder icon**.

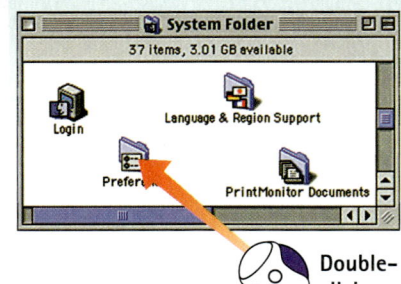

Double-click

### 2 Check the Contents

Most preferences are clearly labeled as to which program they work in.

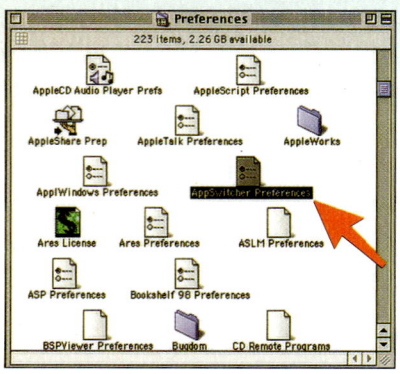

### 3 Check a Preference

If you want to set preferences for **AppleWorks**, for example, open up the application. Then click on the **Edit** menu and select **Preferences**. You can set up preferences for other programs in a similar fashion. (For Microsoft's programs it may appear in the **Tools** menu; for others in the **Edit** menu.)

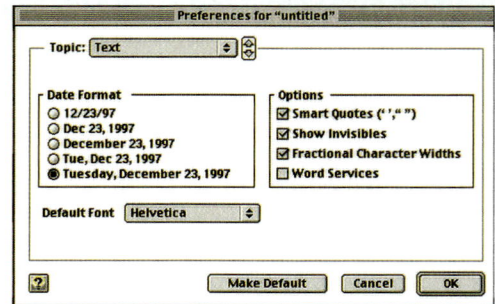

100   PART 7: EXPLORING THE SYSTEM FOLDER

## 4 Change a Preference

To get an idea what preferences do, pull down the menu labeled **Default Font** and change it to something else. Then click the **OK** button to store your setting.

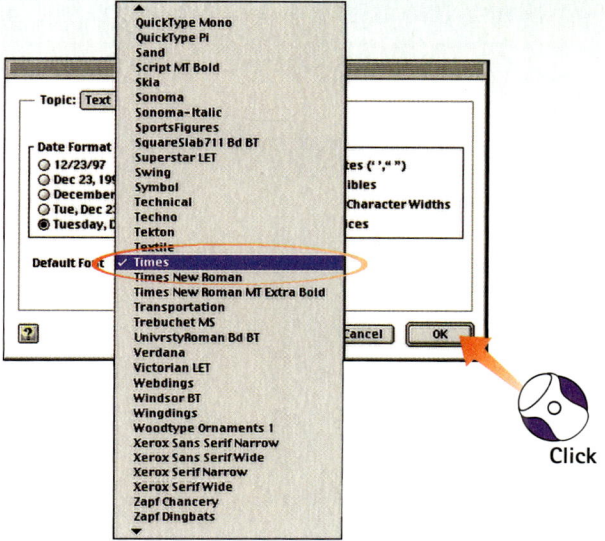

Click

## 5 See the Effect

Now, when you type something in your document, the default font (the one you used before you picked a font) will be changed.

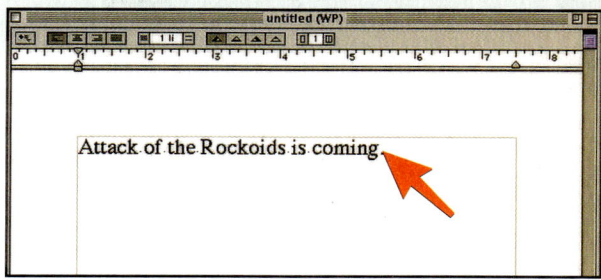

## 6 Change It Back

Open the **Preferences** dialog box again and change the font to something else. When you open a new document, you should find the font has changed again.

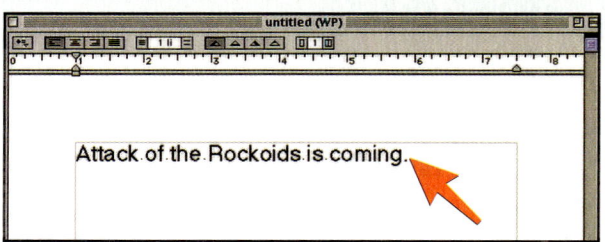

*End*

## How-To Hints

### When You Can't Find a Preference File

Some programs don't create separate preference files. They store the information in the application itself. This is a choice made by the people who wrote the software and is nothing to be concerned about.

### No Preference Settings

If you have gone through every conceivable menu and cannot find a **Preferences** or **Settings** command, don't fret. Not all programs have such settings. Again, this is the choice of the designers of the program, and if the feature doesn't seem available, first check the documentation or **Help** menu. If there's nothing about it, then there's nothing to be concerned over.

## Task 5

# How to Identify and Use Other System Folder Items

The folders described so far contain many of the key System Folder components, but not all of them. There are some very important items that aren't placed in those folders, but actually sit directly in the System Folder.

## Begin

### 1 Open the System Folder

Double-click on the **System Folder** icon to open it.

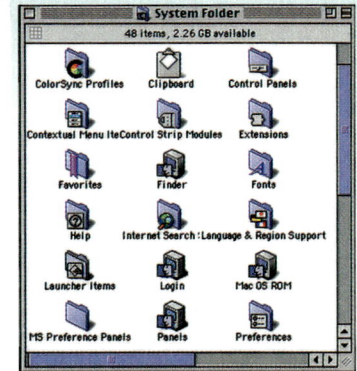

### 2 Finder

The Finder is actually an application that launches when you start your Mac. It controls the desktop display, and also helps you manage all the desktop functions, such as moving and copying files, folders, and disks.

### 3 Fonts Folder

Double-click on the **Fonts** folder to open it. The Fonts folder contains the fonts used in your documents, and it is also used to display system directories, title bars, and dialogs.

Double-click

102 PART 7: EXPLORING THE SYSTEM FOLDER

## 4 Mac OS ROM

Some of the newest Macs use the Mac OS ROM file to store key system software components needed to make your Mac run. Older Macs stored all this stuff in a computer chip, also called a ROM.

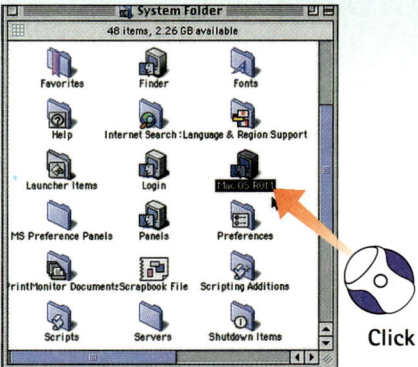
Click

## 5 System

The core features of your System software are contained in this file, plus keyboard layouts and system sounds.

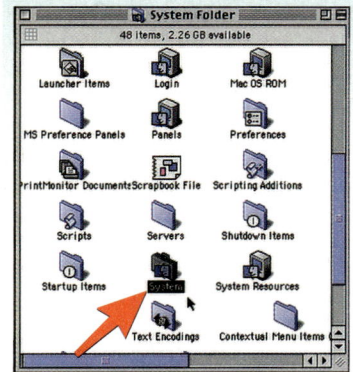

## 6 Open the System File

Just double-click on the **System File** to display the list of contents. The **Kind** column describes what type system resource each item is. Chime, for instance, is a sound your Mac can make.

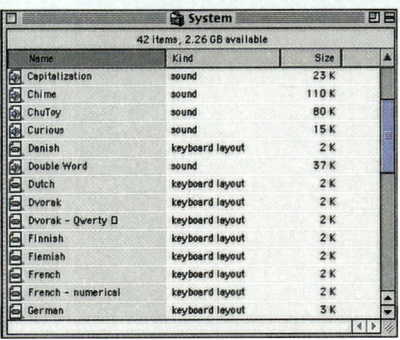

*End*

## How-To Hints

### How Do You Install This Stuff?

Most system add-ons come with an installer application, a program that puts the right files in the right places. But if you want to add such items as a font, a keyboard layout, or a system sound, just drag the item to the closed System Folder icon. The Finder will put up a message as to where it goes. You click **OK**, and the smart Mac OS Finder will place the files in the right place (well, usually).

### What's a System Resources or System Enabler File?

Some Macs use additional components, called System Resources or System Enablers, to allow them to run properly. If you see such files, you should leave them alone. If you remove them by mistake, your Mac may refuse to boot properly.

# Task

**1** How to Use the Installer  106

**2** How to Use ReadMe Files  108

**3** How to Set Up Application Preferences  110

**4** How to Give an Application More Memory  112

**5** How to Remove Applications  114

PART 8

# Installing and Removing Applications

*I*t seems intimidating. You have a new application, all on a CD, which is capable of holding hundreds and hundreds of megabytes of files. And now you're ready to install it on your Mac. What do you do?

Are there secrets to putting a new application on your hard drive and making sure it works the way you want? What about those preferences settings? Do you need to worry about them?

In this part, we'll explore the process of setting up new software and how to make it run in the best possible manner once it's installed.

And, if you need to remove an application, I'll tell you how to make sure that everything is gone—or at least the parts of the application that will affect the way your Mac runs.

TASK 1

# How to Use the Installer

In the old days of Mac computing, you installed an application simply by dragging a folder to your hard drive. But today, applications are big and complex, and they consist of a number of components that go into different places on your Mac's drive. So you need to run an Installer instead.

*Begin*

### **1** Put the CD in the Drive

Get the application's **Installer CD** and place it in your **Mac's drive**.

### **2** Launch the Installer Program

Locate an icon with the word **"Installer"** on it and then double-click on the **icon**. I'm using the installer for **AppleWorks**, Apple Computer's popular integrated word processor/spreadsheet/database and drawing software. (The program was once called ClarisWorks, which explains why the CD in the previous picture has a different label on it.)

Click

### **3** Select a Location for the Installation

Normally, an application will be placed on your startup drive. If you have another drive on which you want to place the software, pick it from the introductory screen.

**106**  PART 8: INSTALLING AND REMOVING APPLICATIONS

## 4 Agree to Software License

Most application installers require that you accept the publisher's software license as part of the installation process. If you don't accept the license, you can't install the software.

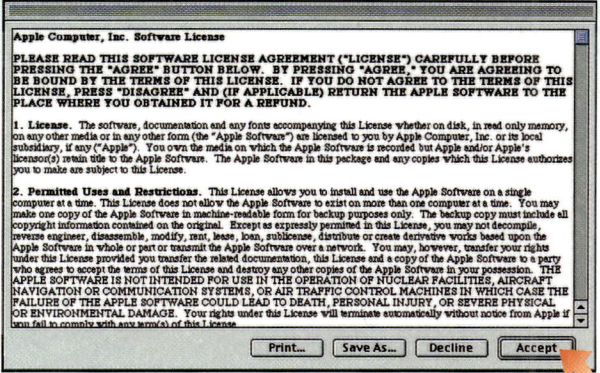

Click

## 5 Choose Your Installation Options

Some installers let you customize the installation, in case you want to only add components of the application. Look for an **"i"** icon on the **Installer screen** to explain what the various options do.

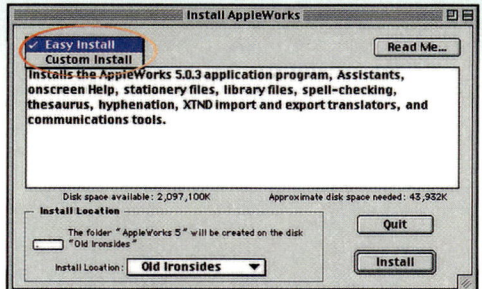

## 6 Restart Your Mac

Many installers place items in your System Folder that will not work until you restart your Mac, so at the very end of the process you'll see a **Restart** prompt. Otherwise, you'll see a **Quit** prompt.

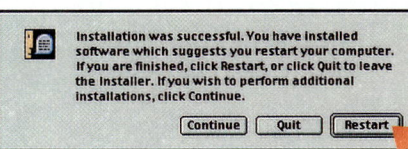

Click

*End*

# How-To Hints

### Not All Software Has an Installer

All new Microsoft programs can work without an installer. Just drag the program's folder to your Mac's drive. The first time you launch the program, a **"First Run"** installer will run, which will place any extra needed files in your Mac's System Folder before the program actually launches. Microsoft Office does have an installer option if you decide you don't want to install all the applications in the package.

### Software Comes on Floppies

If you have a new Mac without a floppy drive, and the software comes in floppy form, don't despair. Contact the publisher and see if they have a CD version. If not, you might consider getting an external floppy drive or SuperDisk drive.

### Disable Virus Software!

Virus detection software can interrupt a software installation or cause an incomplete installation. Disable any virus software you have before an installation. **Symantec's Norton Anti-Virus** will normally offer to turn itself off when it detects that you're running an installer. **OK** that message.

HOW TO USE THE INSTALLER    107

## Task 2

# How to Use ReadMe Files

It's a fact of the software business that there's no way to make an application 100% compatible with all other programs. Fortunately, most companies will include a list of known problems and solutions in a text file called **ReadMe**. They will also discuss errors in the printed documentation and new features that weren't mentioned elsewhere.

## Begin

### 1 Look for the ReadMe

Check the **installation one of the application's folders** for a file with a name like "Read Me" or "Read Me First." Double-click on it.

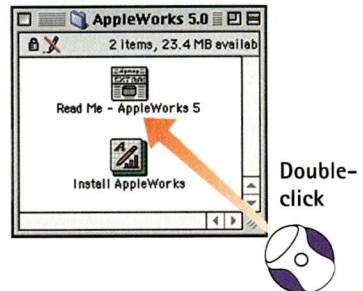

Double-click

### 2 Opening the File

Usually an Apple-written application called SimpleText will open the file.

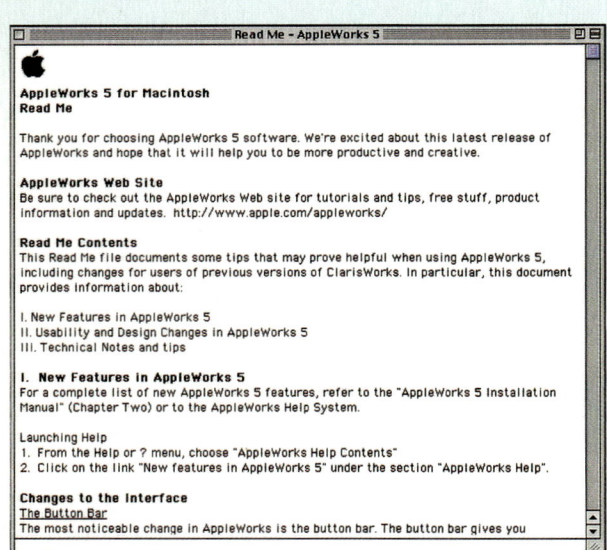

### 3 Read It

While not everything you see may be related to your particular installation, you should at least scan the file to see what's important.

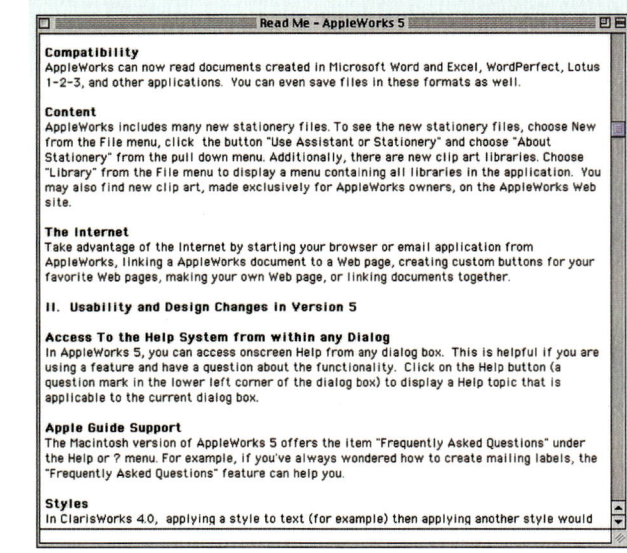

## 4 Print a Copy

It's a good idea to make a printed copy so you can refer to it later if you have a problem with your new software. To print a copy, choose **Print One Copy** from the **File** menu.

## 5 Keep It with the Program's Disk

Take the printout of the ReadMe file and place it in the same location as the installation CD. That way you can find it quickly if you need to refer to it later.

*End*

## How-To Hints

### If You're Unable to Read ReadMe

Most ReadMe files are created in **SimpleText** format, a text program that comes installed on your Mac. But some may require **Adobe Acrobat Reader** instead. Acrobat is a program that lets you read so-called electronic documents. If you don't see a copy on your Mac's drive, check the software CD, or look on your Mac OS CD.

### What If the ReadMe Says You're Not Compatible?

If the ReadMe says something you're using won't work with the new application, then you should follow the company's recommendations. If you don't, you risk performance problems or system crashes. You may want to contact the publisher of each application to see if they have an update that fixes the conflict. Sometimes, the brand new software you buy in a box at the dealer has been updated already; it can take a while for a new version to get out to all the dealers. And some updates are only available from the publisher or on the Internet.

HOW TO USE README FILES    109

## Task 3

# How to Set Up Application Preferences

When you install a new application, it is set up the way the publisher expects it to be used by most people. But that doesn't mean you need to use it that way. Most applications have a **Preferences** option (usually available from the **Edit** menu) that lets you change the way it runs to meet your needs.

## *Begin*

### *1* Open the Preferences Dialog

Choose **Preferences** from the **Edit** (or other) menu.

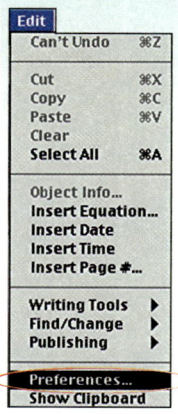

### *2* Choose an Option

Look at the **Preferences** dialog and see if the checkboxes and other options make the application run the way you want.

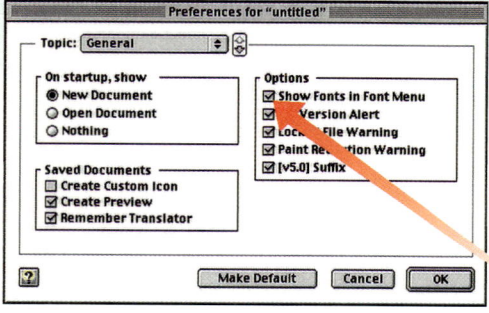

Click

### *3* Change the Preference

A application may give you the option to display your list of fonts in **WYSIWYG** style, which means the typefaces will appear in their true form, not just a generic face. Whatever option you choose, click the **checkbox** that activates the change and see if you like the way it runs.

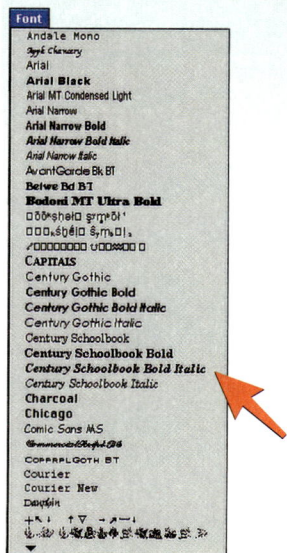

**110** Part 8: Installing and Removing Applications

## 4 See How It Works

Once you make the change, you'll want to work with the application and see if it now runs the way you like.

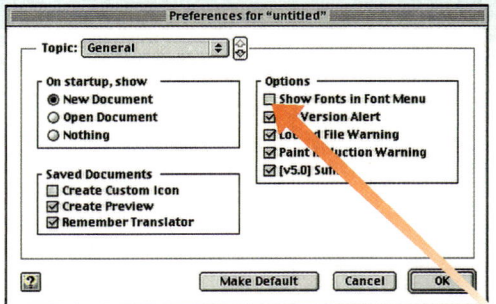

Click

## 5 Change It Back

You don't like the change? No problem. Bring up the **Preferences** dialog box from the **Edit** menu and change it back.

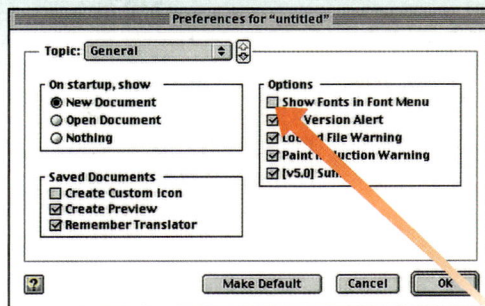

Click

*End*

# How-To Hints

## No Preferences

Not all Preferences settings are in the **Edit** menu. Publishers may have their own ideas of where it should be found. You'll also want to check the **File** menu and, if available, the **Tools** menu, for this option.

## Is There a Quick Way to Go Back?

Yes, there are two ways. One is to look for a **Defaults** option in the **Preferences** dialog. The other is to trash the actual settings file that an application makes. You'll usually find that in the **Preferences** folder, located inside the **System Folder**. Don't worry. If an application can't find its preferences file in the proper place it will simply create a new one with the default settings.

## Task 4

# How to Give an Application More Memory

When you launch an application, it takes up a portion of your Mac's random access memory (RAM). The maker will set memory requirements that work well in most situations. However, if you want to work with large documents or want to have several documents open at once, you might find an application works faster if you give it more memory. (In some cases, an application can't even handle a particular document or task without more memory.) There's nothing difficult about giving an application more memory; it is as easy as typing numbers.

## Begin

### 1 Click on the Applications Icon

Find the icon for the application whose memory requirements you want to change and click once to select it. (Do not double-click because that will open the application.)

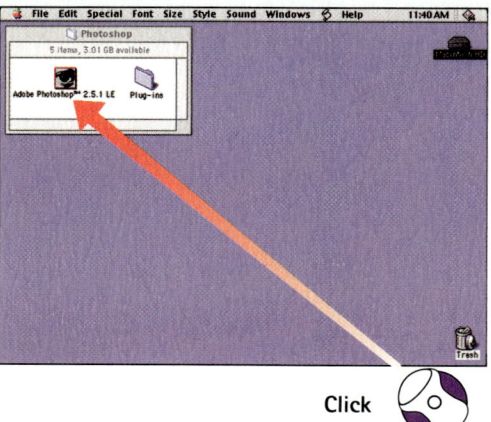

Click

### 2 Display the Get Info Window

Go to the **File** menu and select **Get Info** and then **Memory** from the submenu.

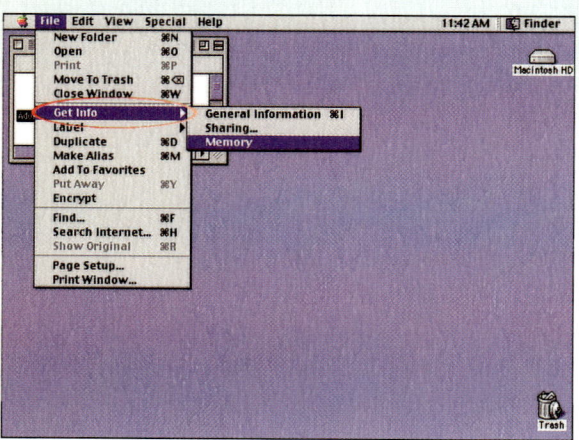

### 3 View the Memory Requirements

Look at the Info window. You'll see three sets of numbers. The top one can't be changed and is what the maker suggests for most users. (You might have problems if you use less memory than the suggested amount.) The second number is the minimum memory size the operating system will give the application. If less memory than this is available, the application will not be allowed to run. The third number is the preferred memory size. This is the amount of memory the application will be given if enough is available.

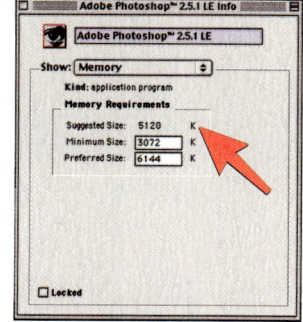

112  PART 8: INSTALLING AND REMOVING APPLICATIONS

## 4 Change the Memory Requirements

You can change the second and third sets of numbers. If an application tells you that it doesn't have enough memory, try increasing the **Preferred Size** in increments of 500 to 1000 until the problem disappears. If you want to always make sure the application always has enough memory, increase the **Minimum Size** also. In this case, I increased the **Preferred Size** to 8000K.

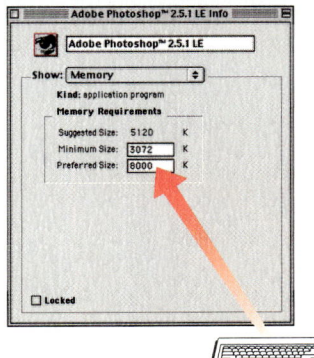

## 5 Confirm Your Changes

After you've changed a memory requirement, it's a good idea to launch the application with a document that requires quite a bit of memory and confirm that the problem is solved. If it isn't, try increasing the memory requirements again. (You can also decrease the **Preferred Size** if you're short of memory and need to run several applications at the same time.)

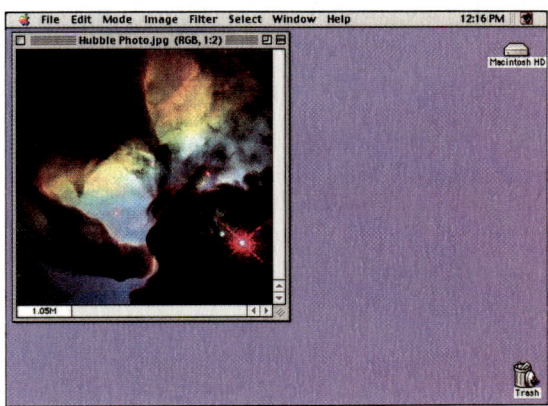

*End*

## How-To Hints

### Changing the Memory Setting
The memory setting can only be changed if the program isn't running. If you find you cannot make a change, check your Mac's Application menu and see if the program is running. If it is, quit the program and try again.

### Not Enough Memory
You cannot run a program if its memory requirement exceeds what's available on your Mac. If you try to launch a program after changing its memory allotment and you get a message that there's not enough memory, try quitting other opened programs (as listed on the Application menu). If that doesn't help, you may have to go back to the **Get Info** dialog box and **reduce** the **memory** allocated to the program (but don't go below the **Suggested Size** listed, as the program may not work properly).

### Other Ways to Change Memory Requirements
As always on a Mac, there are other ways to display the Info window. You can click on the application, press **Control+I**, and then select **Memory** from the pull-down menu. As an alternative, you can use contextual menus by holding down the **Control** key when you click on an application and then selecting **Get Info** and **Memory**. Note that selecting an alias does not enable you to change memory requirements. You must use an application's original icon.

How to Give an Application More Memory  113

TASK 5

# How to Remove Applications

Maybe you have stopped using an application. Or you want to prune your hard drive of files you don't need, in order to make room for those you want.

In either case, you'll want to remove the application and all the files connected with it.

## Begin

### 1 Launch the Installer

Some complicated programs give you an **uninstall** or "remove" option to remove all elements from your Mac's drive. To use this feature, place the program's **Installer CD** in your Mac's drive and double-click on the **Installer** icon.

### 2 Go to the Main Installer Screen

After you click a few **Continue** or **Next** buttons, you want to get to the main installer screen.

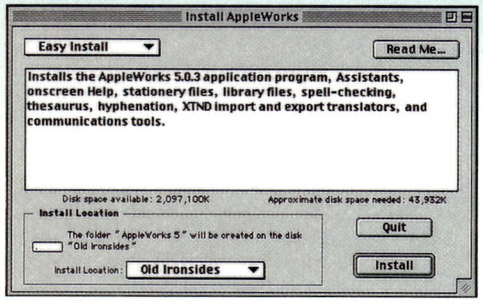

### 3 Look for the Remove Option

Click on the pop-up menu labeled **Easy Install** and look to see if there's a **Remove** or **Uninstall** option and select it. Then run the installer to remove the program. (Not all programs have this feature.)

114  PART 8: INSTALLING AND REMOVING APPLICATIONS

## 4 No Uninstall Option

If there's no **Uninstall** or **Remove** option, quit the **installer** and locate the **program's folder** on your Mac's drive.

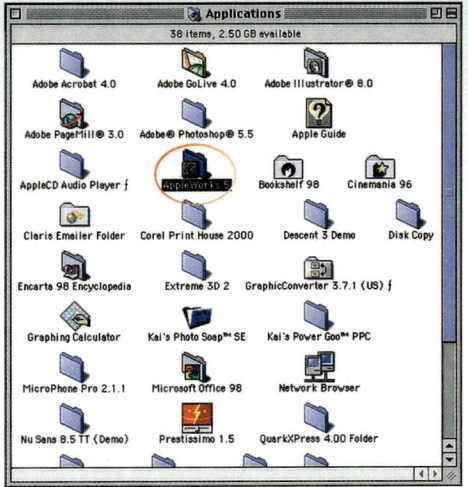

## 5 Drag the Folder to the Trash

Take the application folder, drag it to the **trash**, and then use the **Empty Trash** command to get rid of it.

## 6 Check the System Folder

Look at the Extensions, Contextual Menus, Control Panels, Control Strip Modules, and Preferences folders for files that bear the name of the application. (XTend Power Enabler is part of the AppleWorks installation.) Remove them and restart your Mac.

*End*

## How-To Hints

### If You Can't Delete

If a program has System Folder components loaded into your Mac's memory, you may get a message about files being in use. Just make sure you have quit the application before you try to remove them, and then restart. Then you should be able to use the **Empty Trash** command to get rid of its files. If you get a message about a file being locked, hold down the **Option** key to remove it.

### Check the Installation

If you're not sure what to remove, consult the **Installation Log**, which is often found in the Installer Logs folder, or the application's folder, or just on the top directory of your hard drive. If it's available (and not all programs make one), It'll be a text file you can open just by double-clicking. It'll show what was installed and where. Then you can just locate those files and be assured you've covered all bases and removed everything.

# Task

1. How to Change the Appearance Control Panel 118

2. How to Adjust Mouse Tracking Speed 120

3. How to Use the Date & Time Control Panel 122

4. How to Pick System Alert Sounds 126

5. How to Record System Alert Sounds 128

6. How to Use the Energy Saver 130

7. How to Adjust Your Display Settings 132

8. How to Customize for Multiple Users 134

# PART 9

# Customizing Your Mac's Look and Feel

When you bring your Mac home from the store, it has a neat desktop pattern, a menu bar clock, and it may look just great.

But as you get used to your Mac, you may find you'd like to change something. Wouldn't it be nice if you had another desktop pattern to select? Or perhaps you don't like the little beep you hear when the Mac has to put up an alert notice of some sort.

You notice, for example, that the time display shows the wrong time. Or perhaps you have family members or coworkers who want to use your Mac, but you don't want them messing with your files or accessing certain features.

Fortunately, there are easy answers to these questions, and they form the subjects discussed in the next few pages. In the pages that follow, we will discuss how to customize your Mac so it looks and behaves as you want.

## Task 1

# How to Change the Appearance Control Panel

The pattern you see on your desktop and the typefaces used for titles and directories are all set in one place—the Appearance Control Panel.

## Begin

### 1 Open the Appearance Control Panel

Go to the **Apple** menu, choose **Control Panels**, and select **Appearance** from the sub-menu.

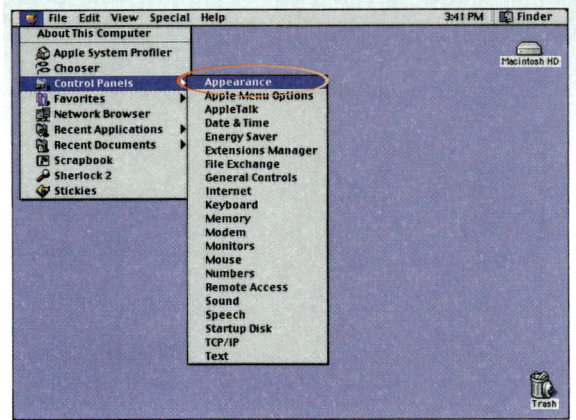

### 2 Pick a Theme

Click on the Themes folder tab. Themes are complete designs for desktops and display fonts. Push the scroll bar right or left to browse the available themes.

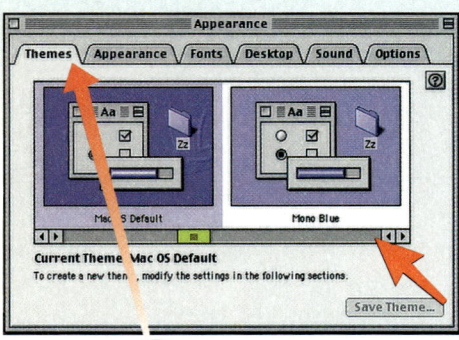

 Click

### 3 Save the Theme

When you find a theme design you like, double-click on the **Theme** to activate it. If you modify the theme, click the **Save Theme** button to save it.

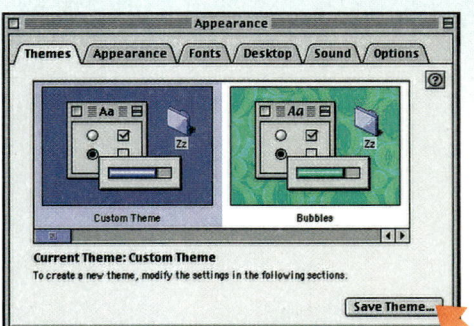

Click

118   PART 9: CUSTOMIZING YOUR MAC'S LOOK AND FEEL

## 4 Pick a New Desktop

Click on the **Desktop tab** and scroll through the list to find another pattern. You'll find a nice selection of desktop patterns to try.

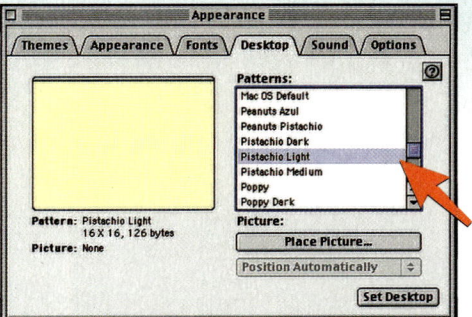

## 5 Set the Desktop

Once you find the desktop pattern you like, select it and click the **Set Desktop** button to make it appear.

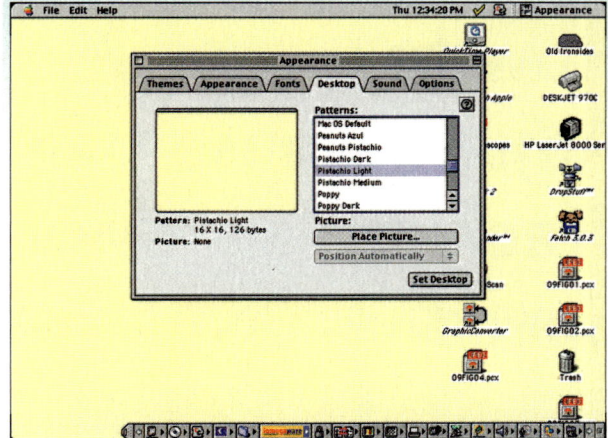

## 6 Change the Font

If you'd like to customize the display font used, click on the **Fonts** tab and make your selections from the pop-up menus.

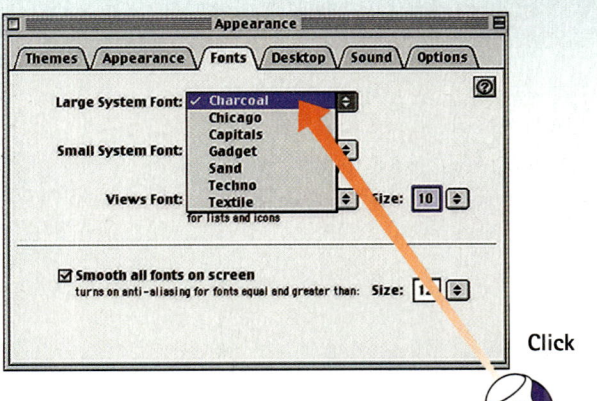

Click

*End*

# How-To Hints

### What About Those Options?

The **Options** tab gives you a **Smart Scrolling** option, which gives you variable sized scrollbars in some applications. Another option turns on the collapse feature, used to collapse a document, disk, or folder window to display just the title.

### Changing It Back

Absolutely. Feel free to experiment with desktop designs till you find the ones you want. You can also find more selections on your Mac OS CD. You can mix and match and develop a design that fits your needs and your personality.

HOW TO CHANGE THE APPEARANCE CONTROL PANEL    119

## Task 2

# How to Adjust Mouse Tracking Speed

When you turn on your Mac for the first time, you are likely to find that the Mouse moves a little too slowly. This is especially true if your Mac has a big-screen display. Fortunately, there's a way to change the setting.

## Begin

### 1 Open the Mouse Control Panel

Go to the **Apple** menu, choose **Control Panels,** and select **Mouse** from the sub-menu.

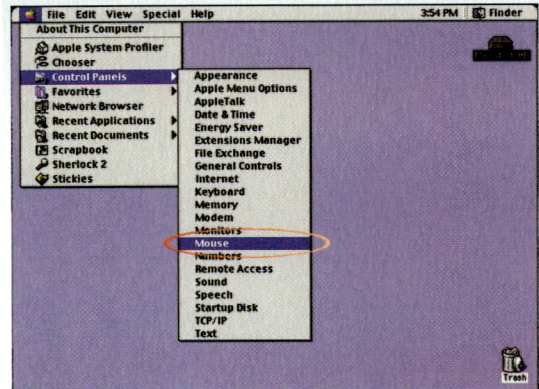

### 2 Change the Speed

Drag the slider back and forth to change how fast the mouse pointer moves on screen when you move the mouse.

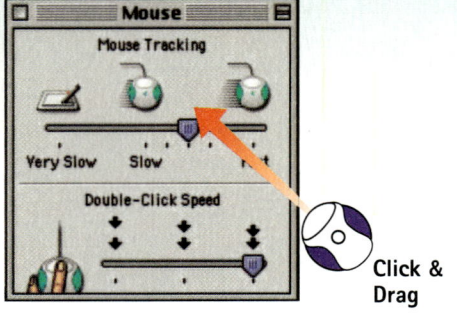

Click & Drag

### 3 Change Double-Click Speed

If you have difficulty making double-clicks, you may want to slow them down. Click and drag the slider at the bottom further left to give you more time to double-click.

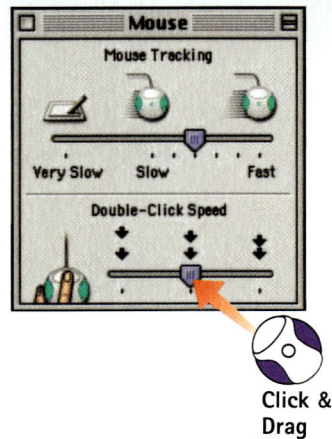

Click & Drag

## 4 Test the Setting

Results take effect immediately, so when you're finished with your settings, test the performance of your mouse and see if it's what you like.

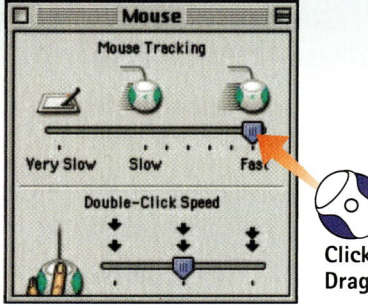

Click & Drag

## 5 Try it Again

If the setting doesn't suit you, feel free to go back to the **Mouse Control Panel** and fine-tune it.

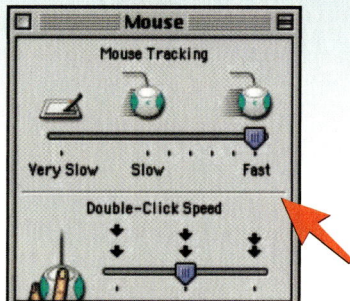

*End*

---

## How-To Hints

### Why Doesn't It Work with My iBook or PowerBook?

Tracking speed settings for an Apple laptop are done via the **Trackpad Control Panel**. You can also find it by going to the **Apple Menu** and choosing **Control Panels**. The settings also include the option to be able to double-click with your fingers on the trackpad. As with the Mouse Control Panel, the settings can be adjusted back and forth until you find the ones you like.

You aren't restricted to the mouse that comes with your Mac. You can buy a third-party mouse with more features: a trackball that works like an upside-down mouse, and drawing tablets that work like a pencil.

### Special Mouse Software

Special pointing devices, such as a mouse with extra buttons, will usually come with special software to activate those features. In that case, the Mouse Control Panel may not do anything at all. You'll have to use the Control Panel or application that came with the special mouse to adjust the settings.

## Task 3

# How to Use the Date & Time Control Panel

You're always conscious of the passage of time on your Mac because there's a clock right on the menu bar. But you might not know how to set or customize your clock, have it check the time over the Internet, or chime out the hours. That's what we'll be looking at in this chapter.

## Begin

### 1 Open the Date & Time Control Panel

Go to the **Apple** menu; choose **Control Panels** and then **Date & Time**. A **Date & Time** control panel should appear.

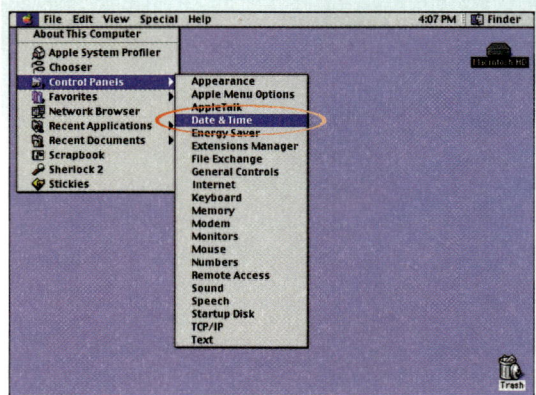

### 2 Set Your Time Zone

If you gave the Mac OS Setup Assistant a major city near where you live, you've already told your Mac what time zone you live in. But if you didn't choose a city, or if you've moved, you can specify your time zone by clicking on **Set Time Zone** in the **Date & Time** panel.

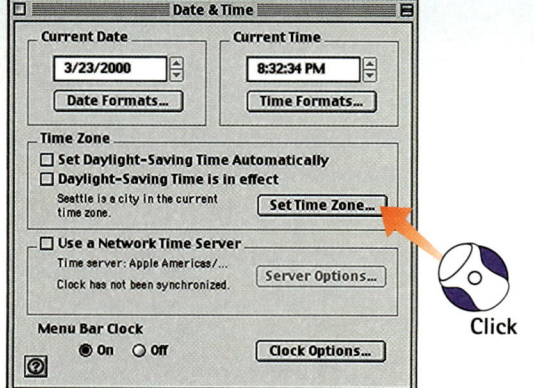

### 3 Specify Your City

A **Set Time Zone** window will appear, asking for a city that's close to you and in your time zone. You can locate a city by scrolling up or down the list or by typing the first few letters of its name. When you've found it, double-click on the name and you return to the **Date & Time** panel.

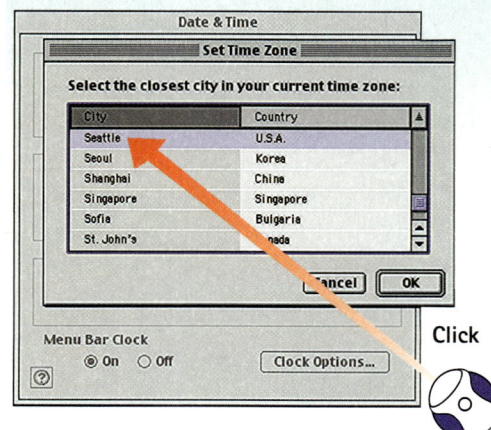

## 4 Set Date & Time Options

Now you'll want to set a few other options. Under **Time Zone**, specify whether **Daylight Savings Time** is in effect as well as whether your Mac should take care of that pesky twice yearly change for you. If you have an Internet connection, you might also want an Apple Computer server to keep your Mac's internal clock on time. If so, check the **Use a Network Time Server** box and click on Server Options.

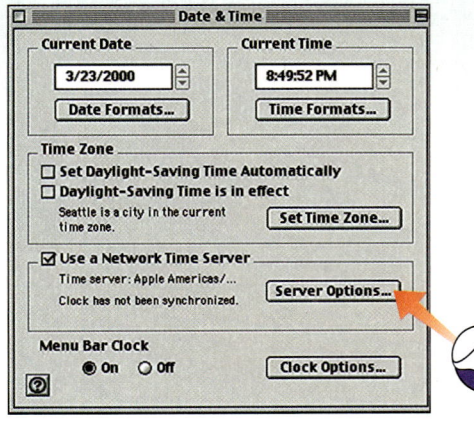

Click

## 5 Specify Server Options

A *server* is a distant computer that provides your computer with assistance; in this case, a server provides the correct time. In the pull-down menu, choose the location closest to you. You can also specify how often you synchronize. Unless the time is critically important to you, every two weeks should be often enough.

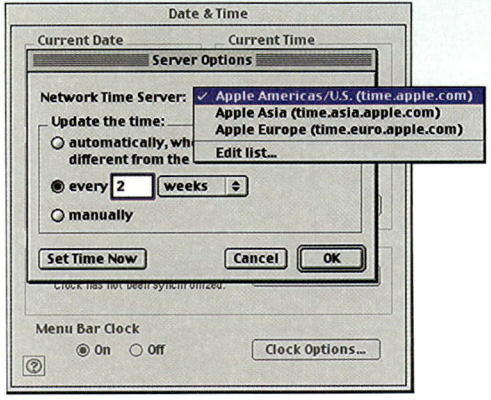

## 6 Setting the Date and Time

Next, you'll want to set the date and time if they are not already correct. Setting the date and time on a Mac is much easier than programming a VCR. Simply click on the digits you want to change and set them by typing the correct number or by using the arrows.

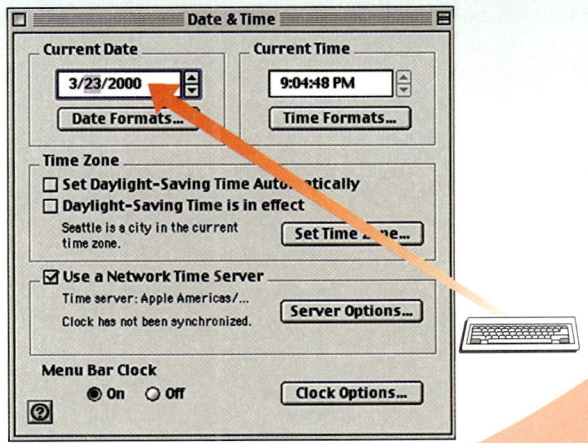

How to use the Date & Time Control Panel  123

## Date and Time Control Panel Continued

### 7 Set Display Formats

If you want to change how the date and time display, click on the **Date Formats** and **Time Formats** buttons. You can use the pull-down menus and accept the format used in your country or create your own unique format.

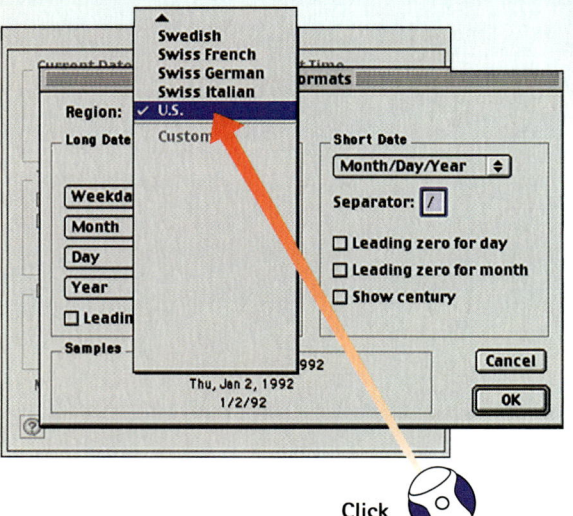

Click

### 8 Set Clock Options

Clicking on **Clock Options** in the **Date & Time** panel enables you to decide how the date and time are displayed in your menu bar. You can view the result of your changes in the **Sample** section at the bottom of the panel.

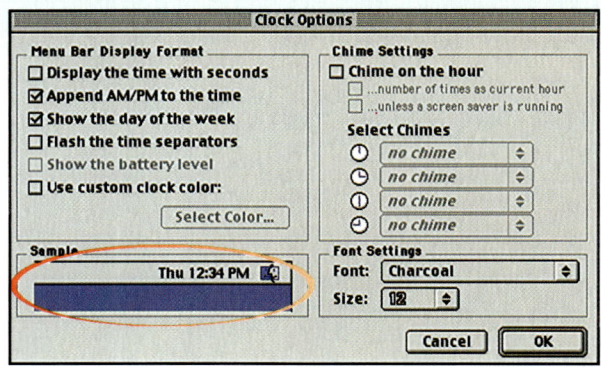

### 9 Chime the Time

Before you leave the **Clock Options** panel, you can also set your Mac to chime on the hour and quarter hour. If you don't like any of the sounds Apple provides, see Task 5 for details on recording your own sound.

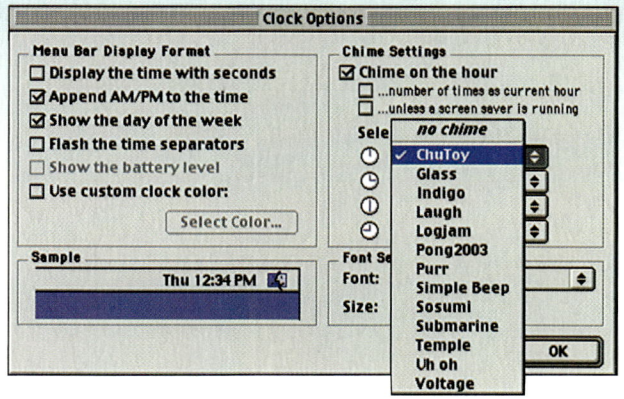

124  PART 9: CUSTOMIZING YOUR MAC'S LOOK AND FEEL

## 10 Use the Clock

Before you leave the **Date & Time** panel, make sure that the clock is turned on or off as you prefer. There's one more trick to learn about the clock. Normally the clock displays the time, but if you click on the time, for a few seconds the clock will display the current date.

*End*

## How-To Hints

### Can I Have an Hourly Chime, Please?

As you notice in Step 9, you can pick a sound that plays when the clock strikes the hour, the quarter hour, or the half hour. You'll learn about picking and adding system sounds later in this section.

### Why Do I Have Two Clocks?

Some programs, such as Power On Software's Now Up-to-Date, have Control Panels that put up their own menu bar clocks. First, you need to decide which clock you want to use. Then you can open the proper Control Panel and turn off the clock display you don't want.

## Task 4

# How to Pick System Alert Sounds

When you tire of hearing beeps, you'll be pleased to know you can easily select another sound or just turn the sounds off completely.

## Begin

### 1 Open the Sound Control Panel

Go to the **Apple** menu, choose **Control Panels**, and select **Sound** from the sub-menu.

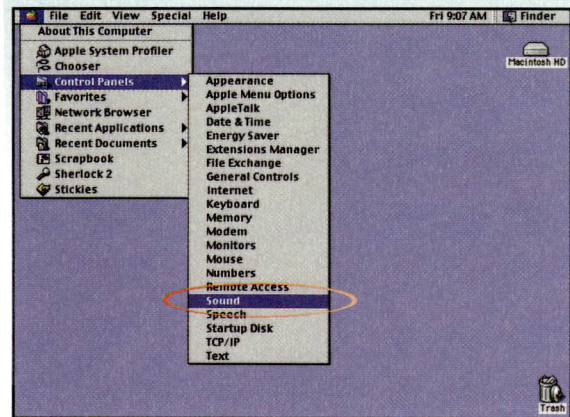

### 2 Choose Alert Sounds

Click **Alert Sounds** from the list of sound options.

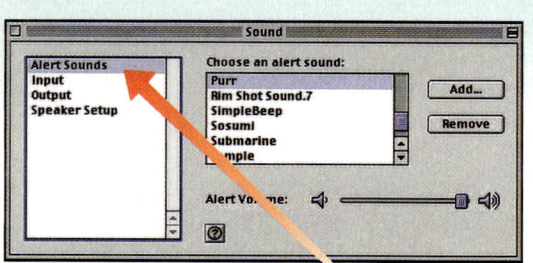

Click

### 3 Choose a Sound

Scroll through the list of alert sounds and select a sound by clicking on its name. You'll hear a playback of the sound in your Mac's speaker.

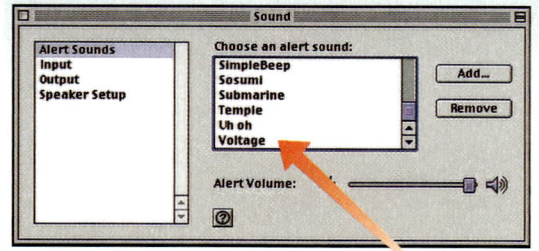

Click

126  PART 9: CUSTOMIZING YOUR MAC'S LOOK AND FEEL

## 4 Change the Volume

If the volume level isn't want you want, click and drag the **Alert Volume** slider to the level you want.

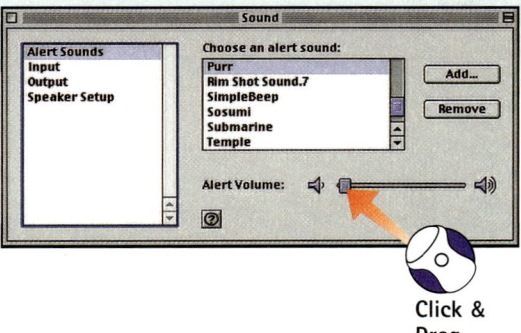

Click & Drag

## 5 Silence It

If you move the volume slider all the way to the left, the sound will be turned off, and your Mac's menu bar will flicker when an alert is announced.

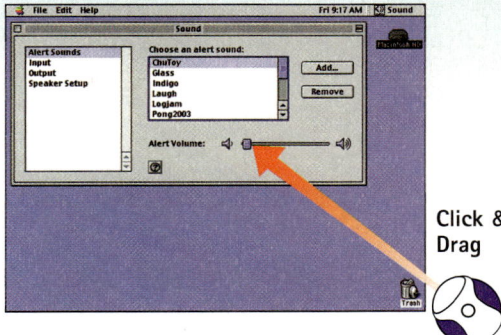

Click & Drag

## 6 Remove It

Don't want a sound available? Just click on the sound's name and then click the **Remove** button (you'll be asked to confirm your decision). The sound will quickly disappear from the list.

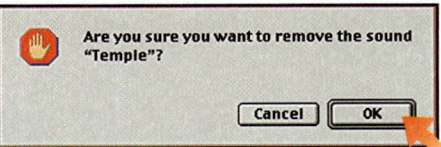

Click

*End*

# How-To Hints

### Can't Hear a Thing?

If you've turned the volume slider all the way up and it still doesn't produce audio, click the **Output** button on the **Sound Control Panel** and move the slider to the right. If you have extra speakers connected to your Mac, and higher volume settings have no effect, make sure that the speakers are properly hooked up, and the volume level is turned up enough for you to hear it.

### Adding Sounds Is Easy

Your **Mac OS CD** may have some extra sound files. Or you may find Mac sound files on the Internet. To add them, just drag them to the closed **System Folder** icon. The clever Mac OS Finder will put them in the right place (right inside the System file). Then they'll show up among the list of available alert sounds.

### No Sound Control Panel?

Before Mac OS 9, Apple put the settings of the **Sound Control Panel** in the **Monitors & Sound Control Panel**. Most of the settings described here, though, are the same. You just have to click the **Sound** icon to get to them.

TASK 5

# How to Record System Alert Sounds

Perhaps you're tired of the selection of system sounds you have, or you just want to make one of your own. You can easily add a system sound with your own voice or from a recorded piece. I'll tell you how to do this next.

## Begin

### 1 Open the Sound Control Panel

Go to the **Apple** menu, choose **Control Panels**, and select **Sound** from the sub-menu.

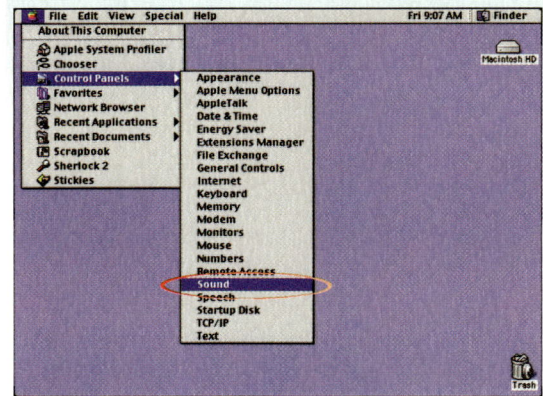

### 2 Check Your Sound Input Setting

Click **Input** and make certain that the input source for your sound is chosen, whether it's a mike or CD.

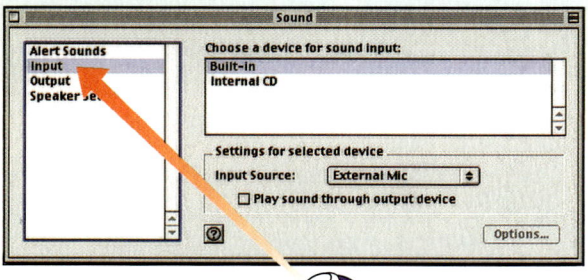

Click

### 3 Choose Alert Sounds

Click on the **Alert Sounds** button to bring up the screen where you can add custom sounds.

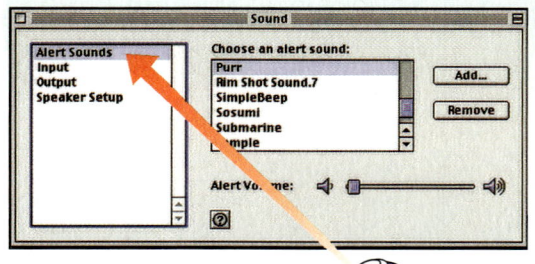

Click

128   PART 9: CUSTOMIZING YOUR MAC'S LOOK AND FEEL

## 4 Add It

Click the **Add** button to bring up an interactive tape recorder display.

Click

## 5 Record It

When you're ready to record your production, click the **Record** button. Click **Stop** when you're done. It's that simple.

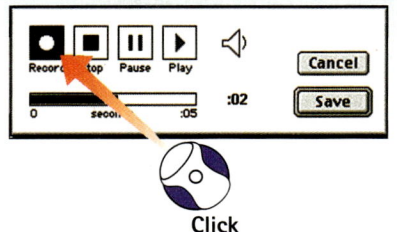
Click

## 6 Play It Back

After you're done, click the **Play** button to hear what you did. If you don't like the result, feel free to record over and over again until you're satisfied.

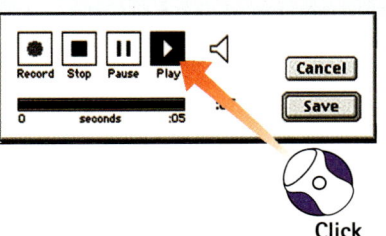
Click

## 7 Save It

Click the **Save** button and give your sound a descriptive name in the box that appears. Then click on the **OK** button and it will end up among the list of alert sounds. You can now select it as a regular Mac sound.

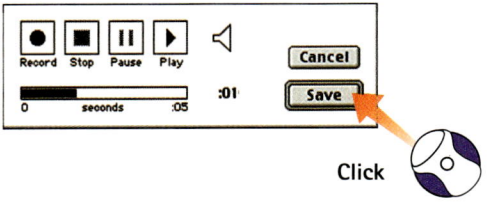
Click

*End*

---

## How-To Hints

### If You Have No Mike

Not all Macs come with mikes. And the Apple iBook doesn't even have a jack for one (or at least the one shipping when this book came out didn't). Fortunately, there's relief for either condition. You can buy a mike for your Mac at your dealer (make sure it's the special Macintosh compatible version). And there are also USB mikes for the iBook available.

### If the Sound Is Too Low

You don't really have special level settings when you record an alert sound. If you're using a mike, get closer to it, and try recording again. Don't shout because that will simply distort the sound. You can record your little production over and over again, and experiment with different levels until you're happy with what you've done. Then you'll be ready to save it as a sound file.

HOW TO RECORD SYSTEM ALERT SOUNDS   129

TASK 6

# How to Use the Energy Saver

Your Mac can be set to go into a sleep or idle mode if you haven't used it for a while. This can result in a slight savings on your electric bill and may cause less wear and tear on your Mac's hard drive. The settings for this feature are all made in the Energy Saver Control Panel.

## Begin

### 1 Open the Energy Saver

Go to the **Apple** menu, choose **Control Panels**, and select **Energy Saver** from the sub-menu.

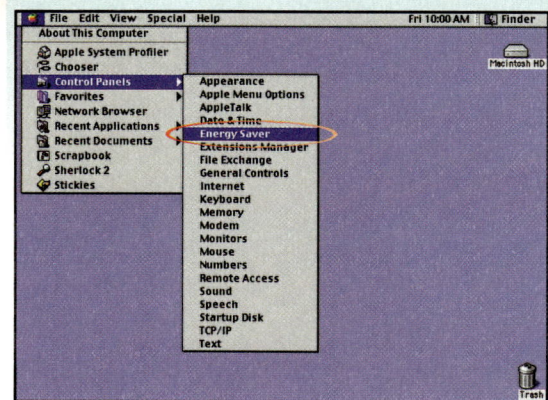

### 2 Pick a Sleep Mode

Drag the slider back and forth to select the amount of idle time before your Mac and its display go into sleep mode.

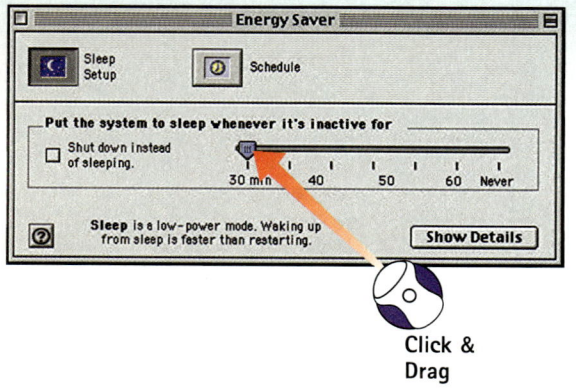

Click & Drag

### 3 Shut Down Instead

If you'd rather have your Mac automatically turn itself off after a predetermined amount of time, click the **Shut down instead of sleeping** checkbox. This will not affect a separate Mac display, nor any external devices plugged into the Mac, such as a scanner or removable disk drive.

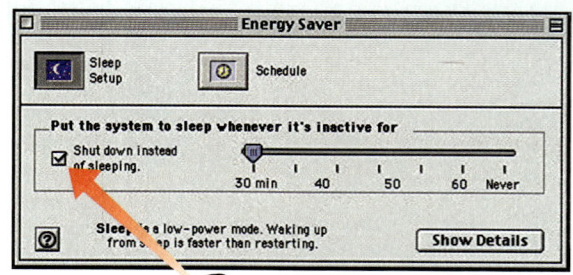

Click

130   PART 9: CUSTOMIZING YOUR MAC'S LOOK AND FEEL

## 4 Choose Additional Settings

To display more customized settings, click the **Show Details** button. The panel will enlarge and let you separate delays for display and hard disk sleep.

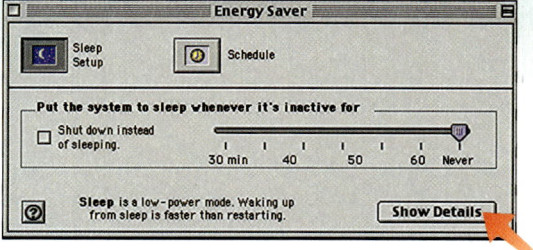

Click

## 5 Set a Schedule

Click the **Schedule** button to set your Mac to automatically turn itself on and off at a preset time. Of course, you have to have it plugged in to a regular power source. And the setting won't affect any devices not powered by the Mac itself.

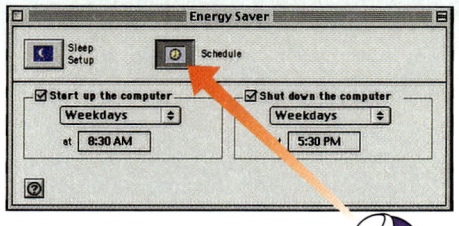

Click

## 6 Schedule Your Computer

If you have regular work hours, you can set your Mac to be ready to go when you arrive at work and shut itself down after you leave. Just set the times in the Schedule panel.

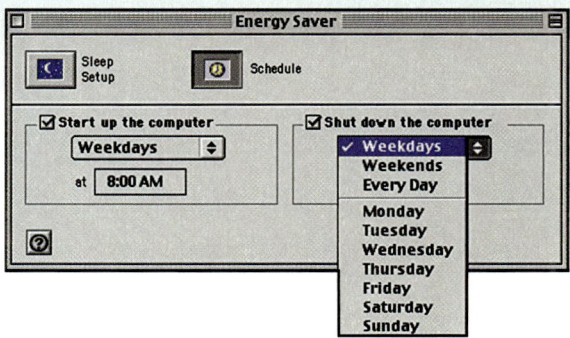

*End*

# How-To Hints

## Laptops Have More Options!

There are separate settings for AC Power and Battery if you are using an iBook or PowerBook. This way you can conserve power to get the longest possible battery life, and you can choose the best performance when you are hooked up to an AC outlet. The Energy Saver will automatically configure itself, depending on your power source.

## Display Doesn't Sleep

Your Mac's display has to be "energy-star compliant" for it to go into sleep mode at the time set via Energy Saver. Many older displays don't support this feature. Check your product manual or check with the manufacturer for details.

TASK **7**

# How to Adjust Your Display Settings

What if you look at your desktop display, and your icon titles are too large or too small? Or you want to display more colors to get a better color display? Such changes are made with the Monitors Control Panel.

## *Begin*

### **1** Open the Monitors Control Panel

Go to the **Apple** menu, choose **Control Panels**, and select **Monitors** from the sub-menu.

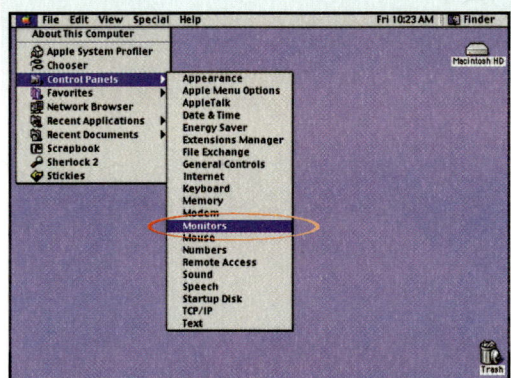

### **2** Change the Resolution

The resolution setting determines how big or how small desktop items will appear. Depending on your monitor, you will have one or several choices. Click on a **setting**, and it'll take effect in a few seconds.

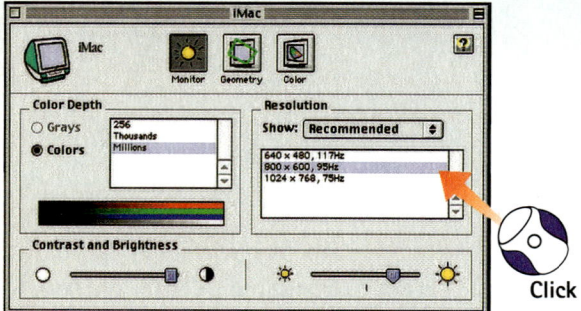

### **3** Change the Color Depth

Depending your resolution setting and the graphic capability you have, there may be one or more options for color depth. Click on a **setting** to change it.

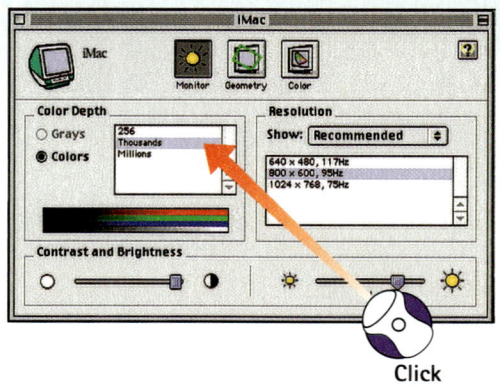

## 4 Change Contrast and Brightness

The iMac and some other Macs have built-in slider settings for contrast (relationship between dark and light) and brightness settings. Contrast is normally turned all the way up. Brightness usually goes half to three quarters of the way.

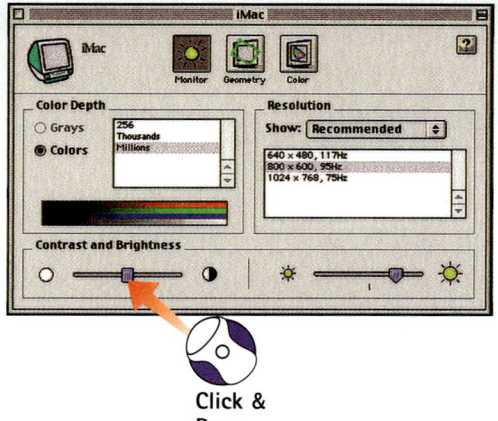

Click & Drag

## 5 Calibrate Color

You can calibrate the color of your display to make it more accurate. Click on the **Color** button and then follow the prompts to calibrate color.

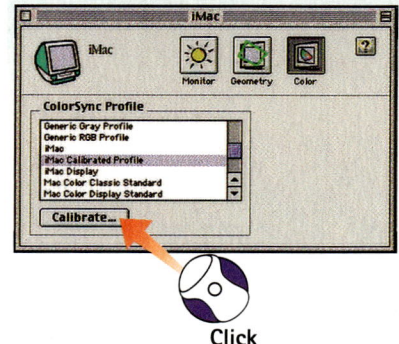

Click

## 7 Set for Gray Images

If you'll be working with black and white images, you may want to set your monitor to grays rather than colors. Just click on the **Grays** button.

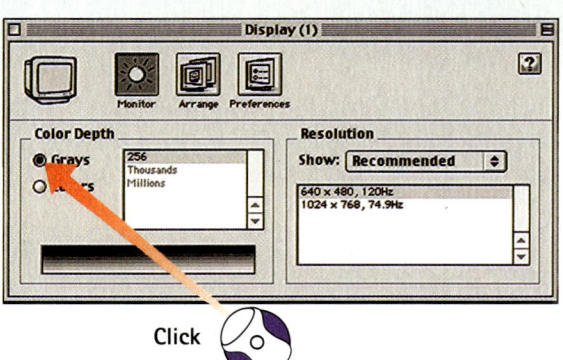

Click

*End*

## How-To Hints

### Why Don't I Have Thousands or Millions of Colors?

The ability to display those color settings depends on your resolution setting (higher uses more memory) and the amount of video memory you have on your Mac. You can try a lower resolution and see if it delivers more colors.

### No Brightness and Contrast Display

Unless you have an iMac or certain Apple displays, the setting for brightness and contrast is done on the display's front panel. Sometimes, there's a control knob. Other times you click a few buttons to bring up a settings menu. Your display's manual will explain how to make the necessary adjustments.

Task 8

# How to Customize for Multiple Users

Normally, your Mac is designed to be customized for just one user. But if you have several people who use your Mac, either at home or at the office, you may want to look into Mac OS 9's Multiple Users feature.

Multiple Users lets you create a custom set of user experiences for each person who will use the Mac. You can deliver a simplified interface (called Panels) for those who don't have much experience on a computer. Or you can restrict files and disks from prying eyes.

## Begin

### 1 Open the Multiple Users Control Panel

Go to the **Apple** menu, choose **Control Panels**, and select **Multiple Users** from the sub-menu.

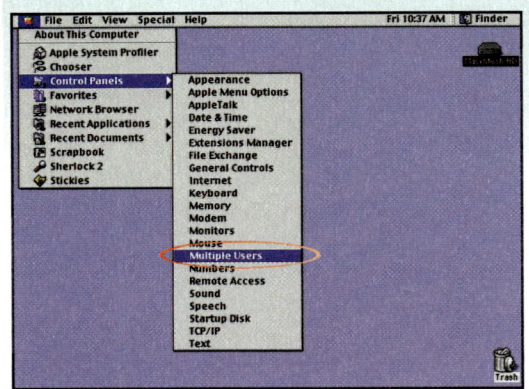

### 2 Turn It On

The name that was set in the **Mac OS Setup Assistant** is listed as the owner. When you bring up **Multiple Users**, first turn it on by checking the **On** button.

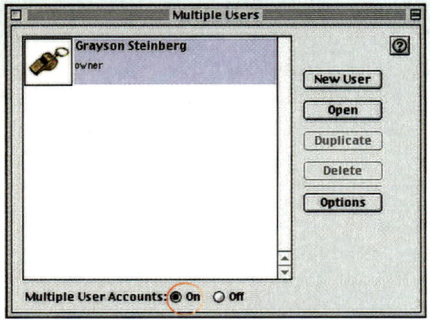

### 3 Add a User

Click on the **New User** button to bring up a settings screen where you can customize the settings for another person. Then enter the new user's name and password.

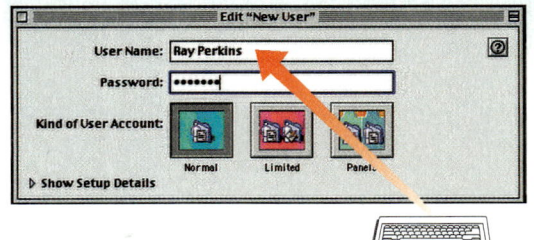

134  PART 9: CUSTOMIZING YOUR MAC'S LOOK AND FEEL

## 4 Choose the User Account

The **Normal** account lets a user access the same basic features as you do (minus what you restrict). **Limited** and **Panels** put in more restrictions, which allows the owner of the Mac to set severe limits on which files, programs, and even disks those users can access.

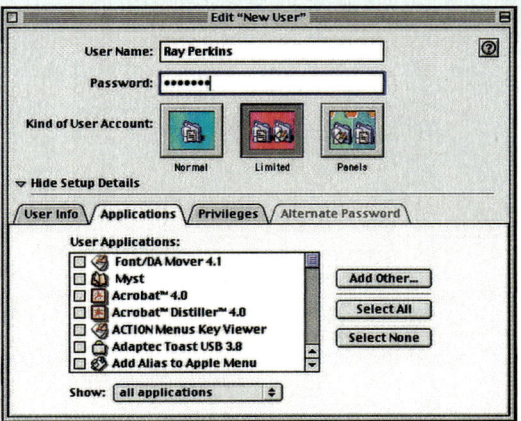

## 5 Click the Tabs

To customize each area of a user's access on your Mac, click a **tab** and enter the **settings**. Click the **close** box on the setup screens to store the settings.

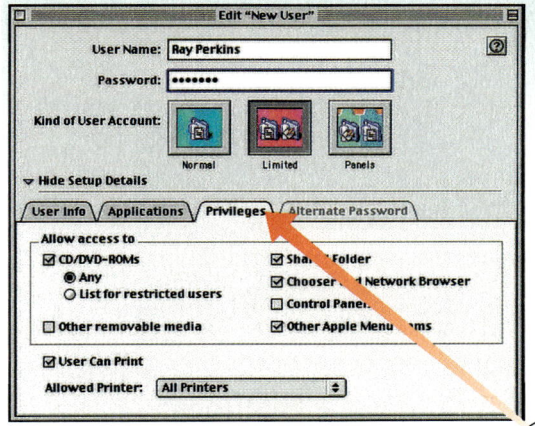

Click

## 6 Log In and Out

When you're finished using your Mac, choose **Log Out** from the **Special** menu or **restart**. Then when other people want to use your Mac, they will need to choose their user icon and enter the correct password to get access.

*End*

# How-To Hints

## Can I Use My Voice as a Password?

Yes, one of the great features of Mac OS 9's Multiple Users setup is the ability to log in by using your speaking voice. The capability to store the voice is done when you click the **Options** button. You just repeat a word or phrase four times, and it's recorded. Next time you log in, just speak your word or phrase and you'll get access. If you get a sore throat, don't worry. You can still type in a password instead.

## Is Multiple Users Foolproof?

No, but it's good for normal purposes. If you need a more secure setup, consider buying special security software for your Mac. Your dealer will tell you about such programs as ASD Software's DiskGuard and FileGuard and Power On Software's DiskLock and OnGuard. These programs are designed to offer additional security levels on your Mac.

# Task

1. How to Set Up a Printer  138

2. How to Use the Page Setup Dialog  140

3. How to Use the Print Dialog  142

4. How to Stop and Resume a Print Job  144

5. How to Use Desktop Printing  146

6. How to Use PrintMonitor  148

7. How to Cope with Printer Problems  150

# PART 10

# Printing from Your Mac

For years, some have claimed that personal computers will usher in a paperless society. That hasn't happened yet and might not happen anytime soon, ut computers have dramatically changed when and how we use paper. If you use a computer, you'll need to know how to use the printer that's attached.

In the pages that follow, we'll explore virtually everything you need to know about printing with your Mac. I'll show you how to install a printer and how to tell it to handle paper. If you need more than one copy, I'll even show you how to print as many copies as you like, all in the order you desire.

We all make mistakes, but there's no reason to print them out for the world to see. Just because you sent a document to the printer doesn't mean that you can do nothing to keep it from being printed. You can save that paper for a corrected version. I'll show you how.

Last but not least, printers wouldn't be printers if they didn't jam on a piece of paper from time to time. I'll show you how to handle that problem with finesse and skill. ●

## Task 1

# How to Set Up a Printer

Seeing everything on your Mac's display is just half the battle. The next part is seeing it in print.

You have a wide selection of printers available for your Mac. They range from inkjet printers, which spray minute particles of ink on a page, to laser printers, which function similarly to regular copy machines.

Most inkjet printers print both color and black and white. Most laser printers are black and white, and only expensive ones reproduce color.

Whether you use a low-cost printer or a huge office printer, the basic setup is similar.

## Begin

### 1 How to Set Up a Printer

Just about every printer is protected with tape, cardboard, or other packing materials during shipment. The first thing you'll want to do is consult the setup instructions and remove all the little fittings.

### 2 Install the Software

Most laser printers work fine with the LaserWriter software you already have installed on your Mac, but they may include added files. Inkjet printers all require special software (called drivers) to run.

### 3 Restart Your Mac

In order for the printing software to work, you need to restart your Mac. Normally, the printing software installer will produce a **Restart** prompt. Otherwise, you can choose restart from the Special menu.

Click

138  PART 10: PRINTING FROM YOUR MAC

## 4 Connect the Printer

Attach the cables from the printer to the proper connection port on your Mac (printer port, Ethernet port, or USB port).

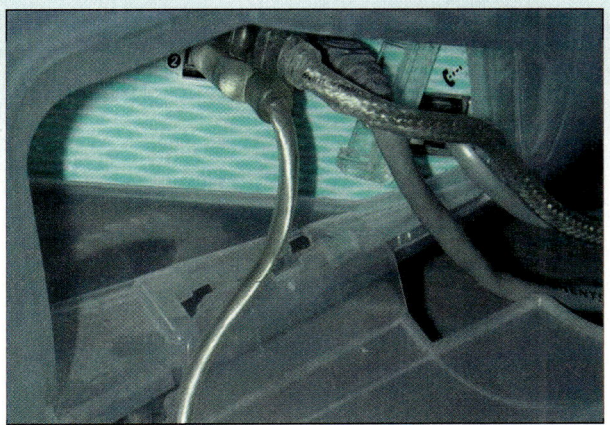

## 5 Turn on the Printer

Switch on your printer. Give it a few moments to finish its startup sequence. How long that takes depends on the printer, so be patient.

## 6 Select the Printer

Go to the **Chooser** in the Apple menu look for the **name** of the printer or printer driver, and select it. Click **Setup** or **Create** to finish the process.

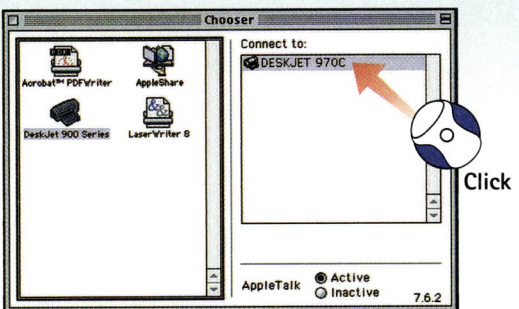

Click

*End*

# How-To Hints

### Printer Cable

Most printers don't come with connection cables. That's because they normally have two or three different ports for Macs and Windows-based PCs, and you'd be paying for cables you don't need. When you buy a printer, ask the dealer which cable you need.

### If Your Printer Is Not in the Chooser

If the printer software is not shown in the Chooser, make sure that you have the right network connection. For example, if a printer is hooked up via Ethernet, you have to go to the **Apple Menu**, pick **Control Panels**, and then pick **AppleTalk** to switch on your network.

HOW TO SET UP A PRINTER   **139**

## TASK 2

# How to Use the Page Setup Dialog

Before you print a document, you need to make sure that your printer is properly set up to work with the sort of paper you're using. In addition, there are other settings you may want to make, depending on the kind of printer you have.

These settings are all made via the Page Setup box.

## *Begin*

### *1* Open Page Setup

First, open a document you want to print. Then go to the **File** menu and select **Page Setup**.

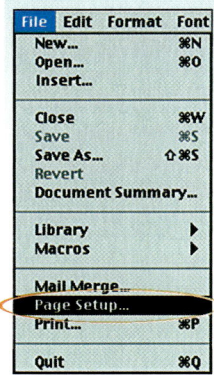

### *2* Check the Layout

Make sure that the proper paper size and orientation is selected.

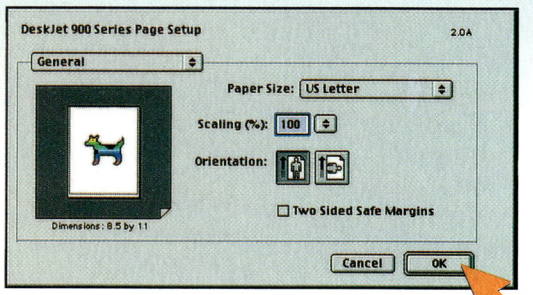

### *3* Change Paper Orientation

The straight-up layout is the standard one, called **portrait**. If you have a sideways image, click on the second option, called **landscape**.

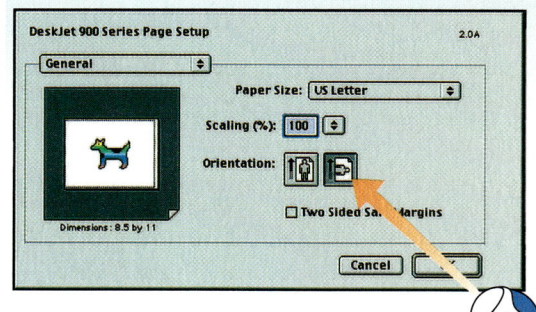

Click

140 PART 10: PRINTING FROM YOUR MAC

## 4 Change the Image Size

If the page size of your document is too large for your printer, click the **Scaling** menu and change it. For some printers you'll actually have to type in the figures.

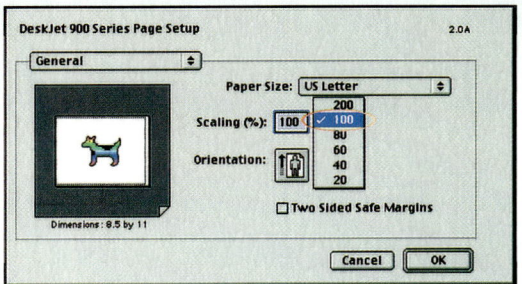

## 5 Change the Paper Size

Normally, a printer is set to use regular letter-sized paper. Click the **Paper Size** pop-up menu to change the setting. A4 is the standard paper size in Europe.

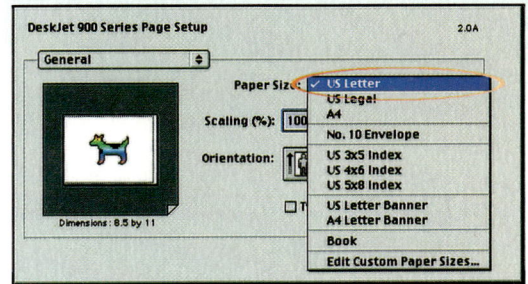

## 6 Check Paper Dimensions

Normally, a printer requires a small margin at the edges of a page. Click the paper icon at the left of a **Page Setup** box to see what those dimensions are. A few printers are capable of "full bleed," which means they can print a document from edge to edge.

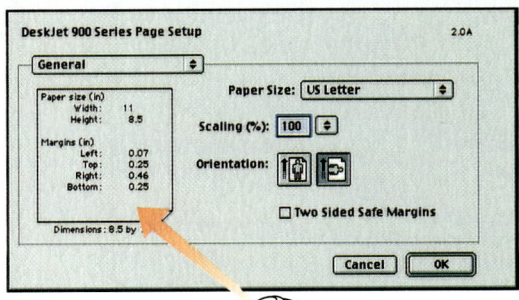

Click

*End*

## How-To Hints

### Dialog Box Different

Every printer manufacturer has a different layout for the Page Setup dialog box. The example shown here is for an HP DeskJet 900 Series printer. Epson printers, have a completely different design, but many of the page setup procedures will be exactly the same. In addition, different programs will add their own special features to a Page Setup box.

### Page Setup Missing?

If you can't bring up the Page Setup box, go back to the **Chooser** and make sure that you've selected the proper make and model **printer**.

TASK 3

# How to Use the Print Dialog

After you've checked and adjusted your Page Setup box, you're ready to print your document.

## Begin

### 1 Open the Print Dialog Box

Go to the **File** menu and choose **Print**. You can also type ⌘+P.

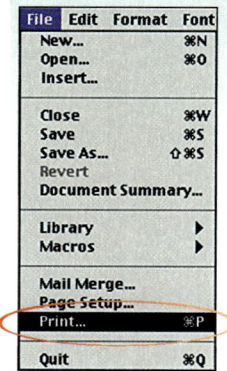

### 2 Check the Print Dialog Box

By default, pressing the **Print** button will print one copy of each page in your document.

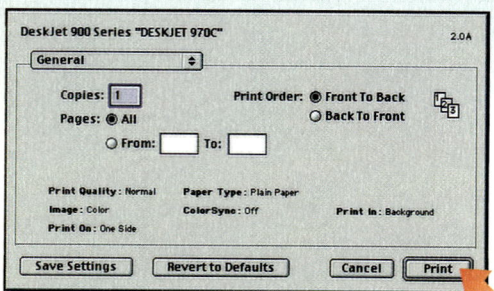

Click

### 3 Change the Number of Pages

If you want to print more than one copy of a document, click on the **Copies** box and enter the number in the copies box. If you want to print only selected pages, click the **From** radio button and enter the **specific page numbers** that you want to print, in the two boxes.

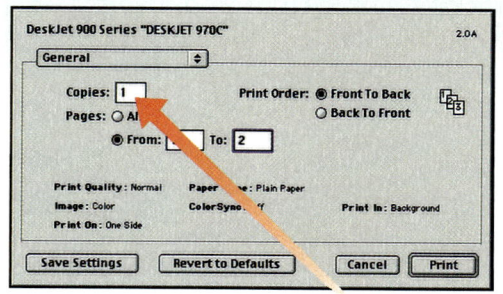

Click

142   PART 10: PRINTING FROM YOUR MAC

## 4 Change Print Order

Normally, the **Print** function will print pages in front to back sequence. If you want to change the print order, click the **Back to Front** radio button.

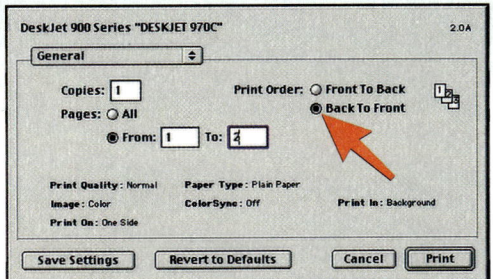

## 5 Change Print Quality

Some printers also give you the chance to change the setting for print quality and the type of paper used. Click the pop-up menu named **General** to locate the **Paper Type/Quality** option and other selections.

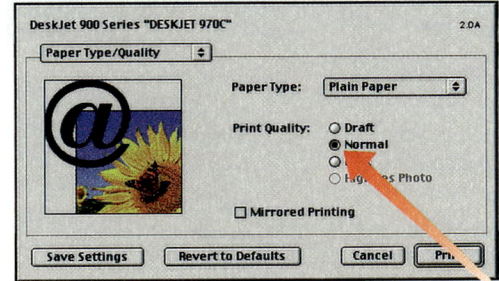

Click

## 6 Save the Settings

If you want to save new Print settings so they'll be available whenever you bring up a Print dialog in an application, click the **Save Settings** button. Check your settings and then click **OK** to store them.

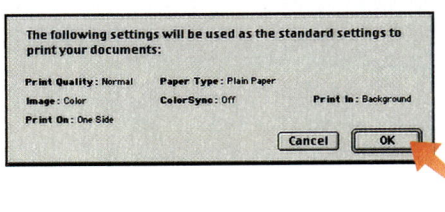

Click

*End*

### How-To Hints

#### Doesn't Look the Same

As with a Page Setup box, Print dialog boxes vary from printer to printer and from program to program. But basic settings, such as the number of copies, specific pages to print, and the order of printing, will essentially be the same.

How to Use the Print Dialog    **143**

## Task 4

# How to Stop and Resume a Print Job

You just clicked Print. The job is being processed, but wait, something's wrong. You made a mistake, and you need to correct the document first. Or you just made the wrong settings in the Print dialog box. Is there a way to stop the job? If you catch it in time, usually the answer is yes.

## *Begin*

### *1* Check the Desktop Printing Icon

If the Desktop Printing icon still shows a document on top of the printer icon, you can still stop the print job.

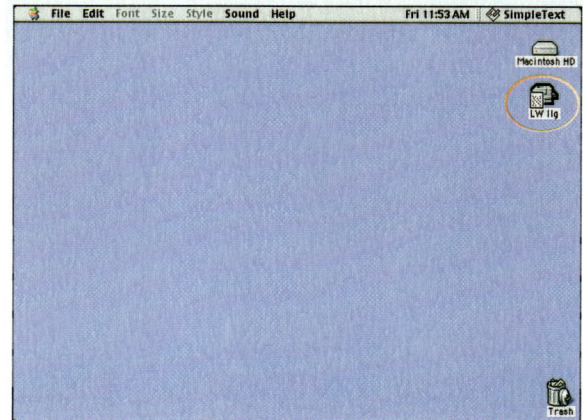

### *2* Open the Desktop Printer

Double-click on the **desktop printer icon** to open it.

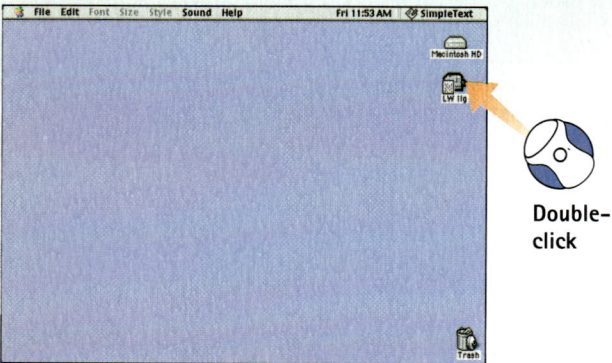

Double-click

### *3* Select the Job

Click on the **job's name** in the top portion of the window to select it.

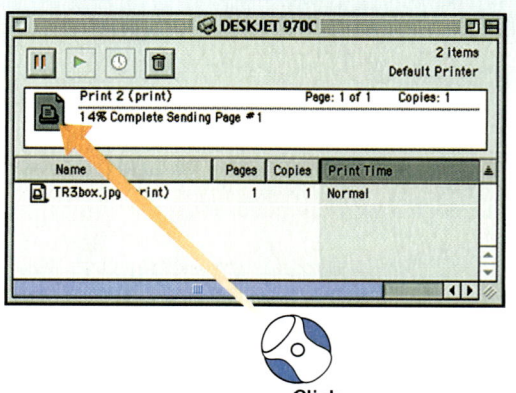

Click

144   PART 10: PRINTING FROM YOUR MAC

## 4 Click the Trash Icon

When you click the **Trash** icon, the job is stopped, and the printer file is deleted.

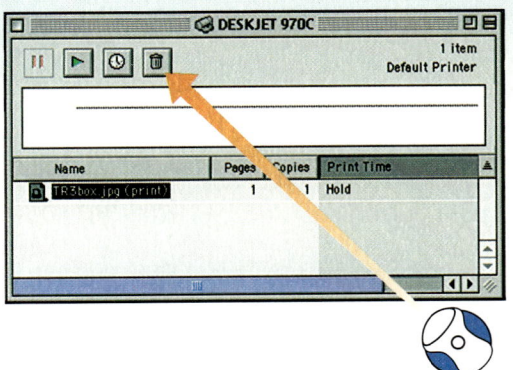

Click

## 5 Hold the Job

If you just want to stop the job temporarily, click the **Stop** button instead, and the job will be moved to the bottom of the desktop printer window.

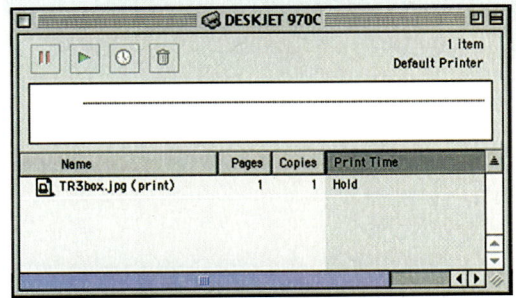

## 6 Resume the Job

If you want to start printing again, click on the **job** that's being held and then click the **Start** button (the one with the right arrow) to resume the printing process.

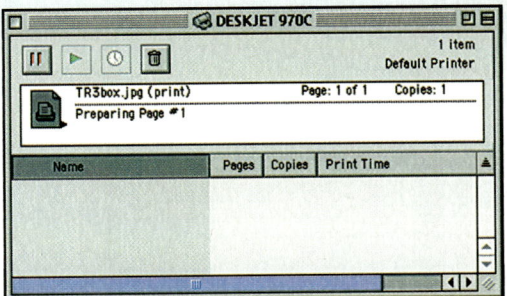

*End*

### How-To Hints

*Locating Your Desktop Printer*

Canon and Epson printers and some other models do not use Apple's desktop printing feature. For these models, you'll have a PrintMonitor application that you can use to control the print queue. This will be explained in more detail in Task 6.

## Task 5

# How to Use Desktop Printing

Many printers use Apple's desktop printing feature to let you manage jobs. Not only does it let you stop and resume a job, but you can also have printing automatically begin at a preset time.

## Begin

### 1 Open the Desktop Printer

Look on the right side of your screen for the **desktop printer** icon and double-click on it. (If you have more than one printer, you might have more than one printer icon.)

Double-click

### 2 Reschedule a Job

First, start a typical print job by opening one of your documents and starting it printing. Then, as that job begins to print, select it by clicking on its title in the desktop printer list.

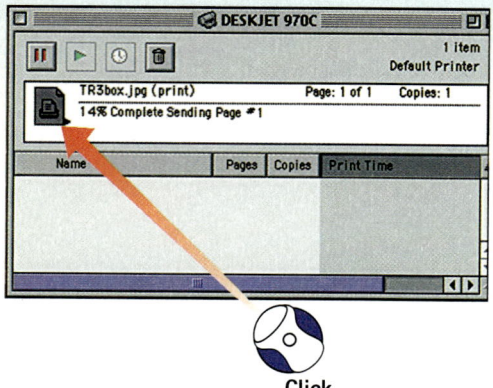
Click

### 3 Stop the Printing

Before the job has time to print, stop the printing by clicking on the **Stop** button (the one with two vertical lines).

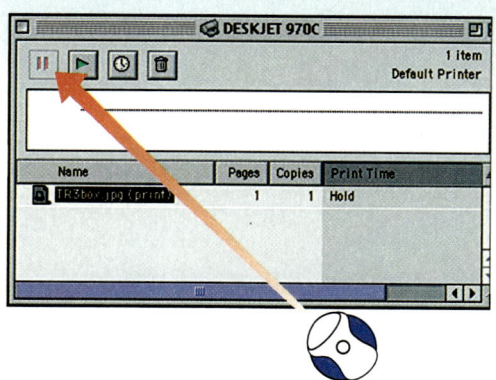
Click

## 4 Schedule Later Printing

You might want to schedule something to print later. If so, click on the **Schedule** button. (The **Schedule** button looks like a clock.)

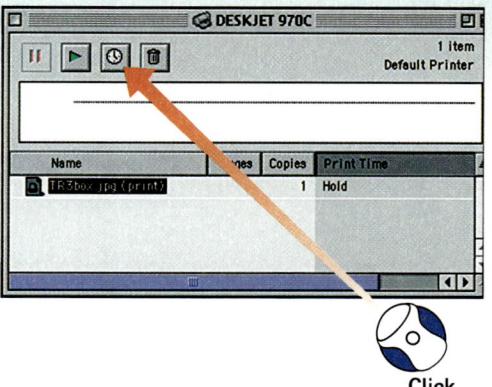
Click

## 5 Set the Print Time

Click **Urgent** to have a document print next or click **Normal** to have it take its place in the line of documents to be printed. To schedule a later print time, click on the **At Time** button and set the date and time in the two boxes. When everything is set, click the **OK** button.

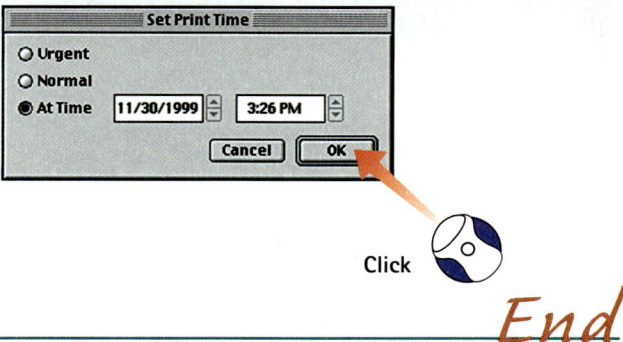
Click

*End*

---

## How-To Hints

### Drag-and-Drop Printing!
You do not have to launch a program first before you print a document. Just drag the document's icon to the desktop printer icon. The application will automatically open, and you'll see a **Print** dialog box. When you click **Print**, the document (or all documents dragged to the desktop printer icon) will print. Then the application closes.

### Wrong Default Printer
You can easily switch from one desktop printer to another without a trip to the **Chooser**. Just open a desktop printer window and choose **Set Default Printer** from the **Printer** menu.

## Task 6

# How to Use PrintMonitor

Some printers don't use the desktop printing feature. And if you have an older Mac with an older version of the Mac OS, you may not be able to use desktop printing at all.

Instead, you'll be working with an application known as PrintMonitor, which appears in your application menu only when a print job is in progress.

## Begin

### 1 Start the Job

In order to launch **PrintMonitor**, first open a document and then click the **Print** command.

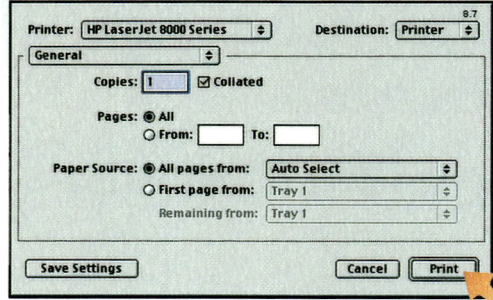

Click

### 2 Open PrintMonitor

Go to the **Finder's** application menu on the far right of the menu bar and choose **PrintMonitor**. This window will appear.

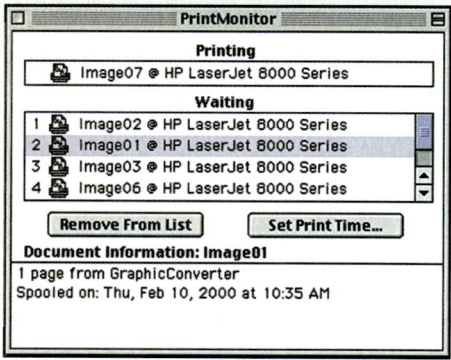

### 3 Stop the Job

If you want to stop a print job, click the job's name to select it; then click the **Cancel Printing** button.

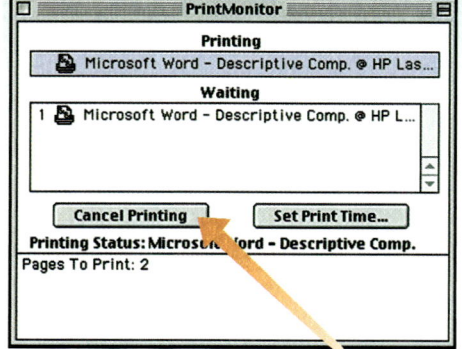

Click

148   PART 10: PRINTING FROM YOUR MAC

## 4 Change the Schedule

To print a job at a later time, simply click the **Set Print Time** button; then specify the time the job is to be printed on the **Set Print Time** window.

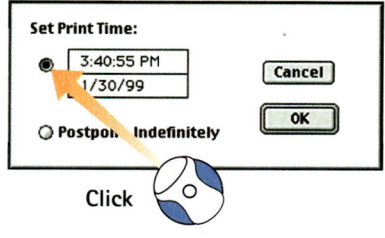

Click

## 5 Change the Print Order

If several jobs are being printed, you can click on one of the waiting jobs and drag it into a new position. You cannot put it ahead of a job currently being processed, of course.

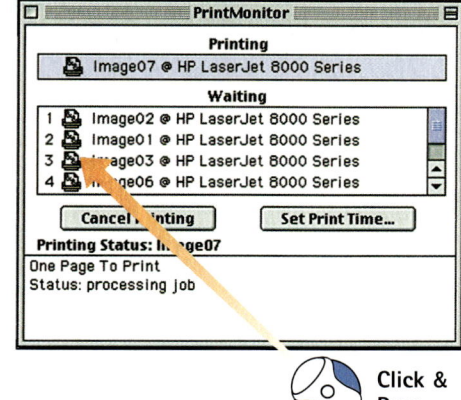

Click & Drag

*End*

---

## How-To Hints

### PrintMonitor Disappears
After a job is finished, PrintMonitor quits automatically. It's only designed to be present when documents are actually being processed for printing.

### Not Enough Memory
If PrintMonitor doesn't have enough memory to process a job, it'll put up a warning notice, asking if you want to give it more memory. When you **OK** the message, PrintMonitor will use more of your Mac's RAM to complete the job.

TASK 7

# How to Cope with Printer Problems

Printing on a Mac is usually trouble free. You click Print and in a few moments your job appears. But sometimes a job is too complex for the printer, or you made the wrong printer setting. And, as with regular copying machines, paper can get jammed.

In this section, I'll give you a few techniques to help handle these problems.

*Begin*

### 1 Stop the Job

If the job seems to be taking a very long time to print and nothing is happening, go to the desktop printer icon (or PrintMonitor) and stop the job. Then try printing it again.

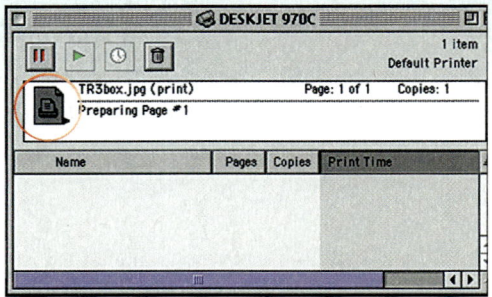

### 2 Restart the Printer

If you're using a regular laser printer, sometimes the printer's memory gets overwhelmed, and it cannot handle the document. You should just **stop** the job. Then turn the printer **off** and **on** again.

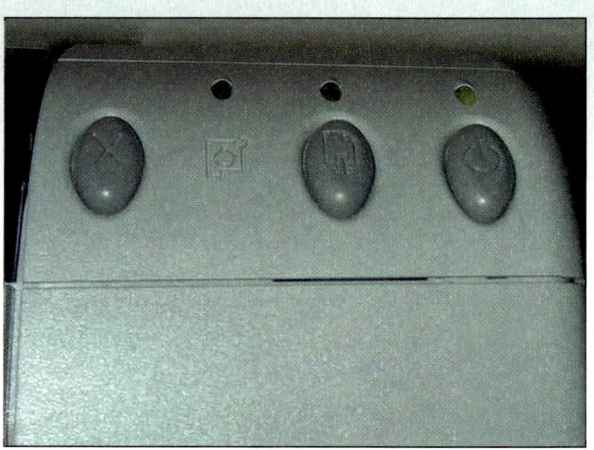

### 3 Restart the Job

After the printer has started functioning again, go back to your desktop printing window or **PrintMonitor** and **restart** the print job.

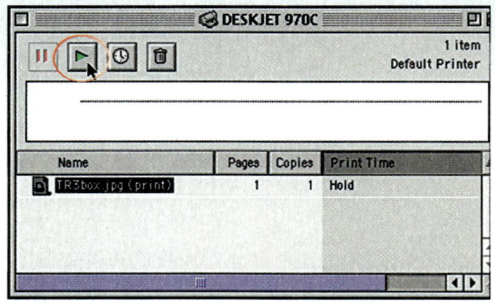

150   PART 10: PRINTING FROM YOUR MAC

## 4 Restart Your Mac

If restarting a printer doesn't help, stop the job, go to the **Special** menu, and choose **Restart**. After your Mac has restarted, resume the job.

## 5 Simplify the Document

Go back to your document and make it less complex. Remove fonts or extra illustrations and try printing again. Some lower-priced laser printers are not able to handle complex jobs unless you install extra RAM in those printers.

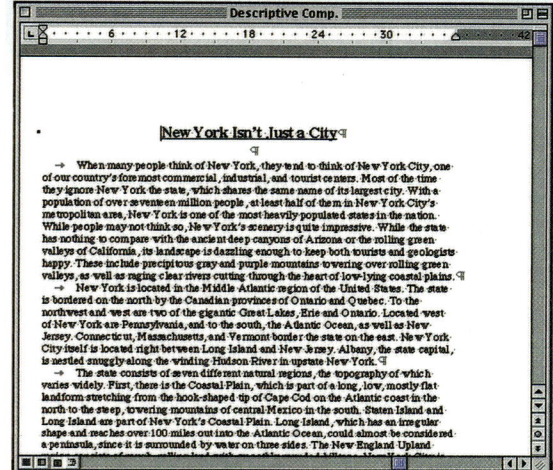

## 6 Clear a Paper Jam

If the paper has jammed in the printer, open the paper tray and covers and remove the paper. Check the printer's manual for the safest way to clear a jam.

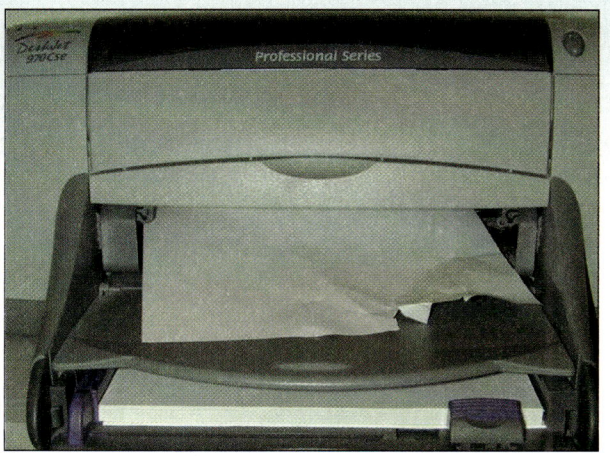

*End*

## How-To Hints

### If Your Mac Crashes While Printing

A software conflict may cause your Mac to freeze when you try to print a document. Should this happen to you, you'll want to read "Part 15, Solving Problems," for additional assistance.

### Low Toner or Ink

If your printer is low on ink or toner, it'll usually put up a warning notice or light. Some printers will just begin to print light documents. Each way, check your printer's documentation on how to check and replace these consumables.

HOW TO COPE WITH PRINTER PROBLEMS   151

## Task

1. How to Hook Up a New Drive  154
2. How to Format a New Drive  156
3. How to Start from Another Drive  158
4. How to Check for Hard Drive Damage  160
5. How to Optimize a Hard Drive  162
6. How to Back Up a Drive  164

# PART 11

# Hard Drive Setup and Maintenance

Every Mac made today comes with a hard drive. A hard drive is a box that contains several spinning platters, coated with magnetic material. All of the files you have on your Mac are stored in these delicate devices. And almost every time you use your Mac, the hard drive is busy.

If you find that your hard drive is just getting filled up too rapidly and you need more space, you can easily add another storage device to your Mac. I'll show you how in this section.

With Apple issuing a new version of its operating system at least once a year, you may find yourself wanting to start your Mac under two different versions. Sometimes you'll want to use the latest version for its hot new features. At other times, you may want to turn to an old and trusted version to make sure an aging application doesn't give you trouble. With the Mac you can do both; you can decide before you restart which drive (an operating system) you'll be using.

Hard drives aren't perfect. Due to a system crash or just due to wear and tear, the drive's table of contents, which tells your Mac where your files are located, can get damaged. So you also need to develop a regular routine to make sure the drive is healthy and ready to store your files reliably.

You'll learn how to do that here.

In addition, you'll discover ways to protect your valuable files, by making extra copies on other drives, or backups, so you'll have a copy you can use if anything happens to the original.

## Task 1

# How to Hook Up a New Drive

As you use your Mac, you may find a need for an extra storage device. Maybe you've run out of room on your regular drive, or you want to have a place to store backups. If so you can hook up an external drive to your Mac in minutes.

You can install an extra internal drive on some desktop Macs (but not the iMac), and save money, but you'll want to check the instructions before you buy. It involves a more difficult setup process, since you have to open up the computer's case, and deal with small screws and flimsy connection cables.

## Begin

### 1 Open the Box

Check your new drive and the installation instructions it came with. The product I'm showing here is a VST Technologies FireWire Hard Drive, which can be attached to any Mac with a FireWire connection port (such as many newer desktop Macs and iMac DV series).

### 2 Shut Down Your Mac

If the drive isn't a FireWire or USB drive (the newest technologies on an Apple computer), you must shut down your Mac before installing. Choose **Shut Down** from the Finder's **Special** menu.

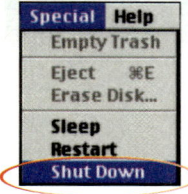

### 3 Connect the Cables

Take the **cable** and connect it from the drive to your Mac; then attach the **AC power plug**. If you have several drives already hooked up, you'll want to attach it to the drive that will be put in front of it.

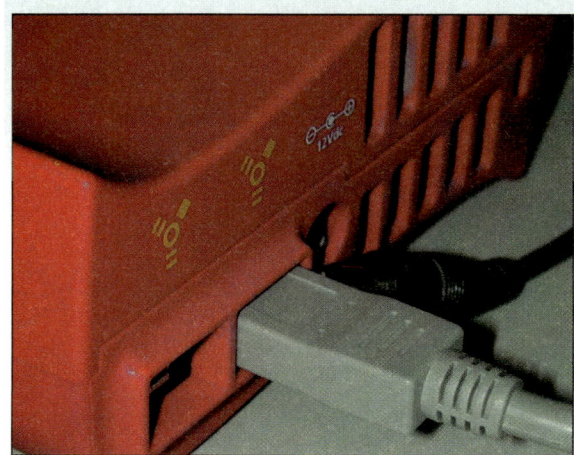

## 4 Turn Everything On

Turn on the **drive**; then turn on your **Macintosh**. Double-click on the drive icon to check it out.

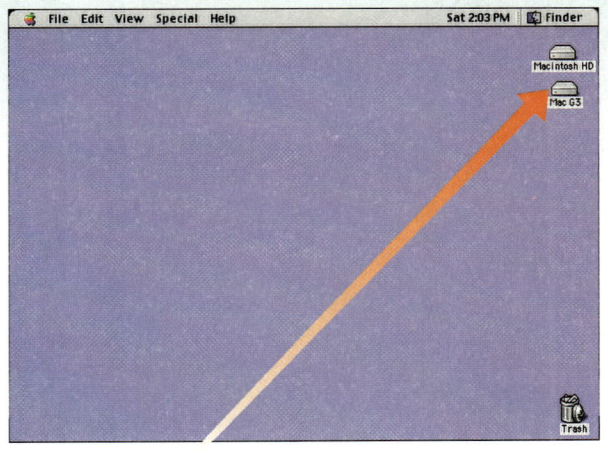

 Double-click

## 5 Need to Install Software

Some drives, such as Zip drives or other drives with removable media, may require that you install software in order to use them. So, insert the **CD** in the Mac's drive and run the **installer** from it. I'm showing the installer for Iomega's software for their Jaz and Zip drives here.

Click

*End*

---

## How-To Hints

### Drive's Icon Isn't There

When a new drive is on (or a removable drive has media in it), the icon should appear on your Mac's desktop. If it's not there, power down and recheck your connections. If that doesn't solve your problem, check the directions and see if you need to install special software. For a hard drive, you may have to format first (see the next section).

### Can You Connect a Drive Without Shutting Down?

Yes, you can do it if your Mac uses FireWire or USB ports for extra devices. You can easily plug in new devices with these two technologies without shutting down. But, if you attach a SCSI drive, you should not try to hook up the drives with the power on, or you'll risk damaging both components.

### What About SCSI?

If you are attaching a SCSI hard drive to your Mac's SCSI port, please check the manufacturer's instructions about setting SCSI ID numbers and termination for the product. These settings must be correct for the drive to work properly on your Mac.

TASK 2

# How to Format a New Drive

Most drives you buy will come ready to run. But if they aren't, you'll have to format them. Formatting is a process of clearing out the contents of a drive and getting it ready for you to use. After you've installed a drive following the instructions above, follow these steps to format it.

**And just remember:** *When you format a drive, you wipe out all the files on it, if any. So don't attempt this operation unless you have a backup for the files, don't need them, or you're setting up a brand new drive.*

*Begin*

### *1* Locate the Format Program

If Apple doesn't provide your hard drive, the company who sold it to you should have a disk with formatting software. Otherwise, go to the **Utilities** folder on your Mac and look for the **Drive Setup** folder and open it.

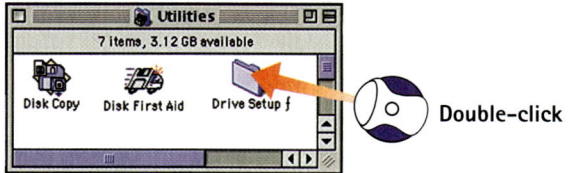

### *2* Launch the Program

Double-click on the **formatting software** to launch it. This will bring up the program's main work area.

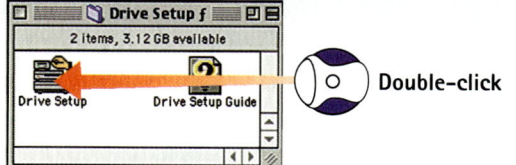

### *3* Select the Drive

You should see the **name** of the **drive** in the program's window. Sometimes, it will be identified by the type of drive, rather than the name you gave it.

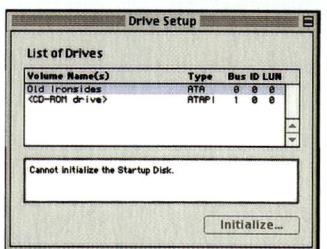

PART 11: HARD DRIVE SETUP AND MAINTENANCE

## 4 Initialize the Drive

After **selecting** the **drive's name**, click the **Initialize** command (it may be called **Format** in some programs). Be prepared to wait a few minutes or even an hour or two for the operation to be complete.

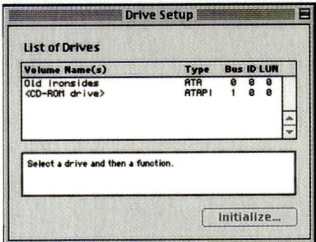

## 5 Finished

When the formatting operation is done, check your Mac's desktop for the new icon for your drive.

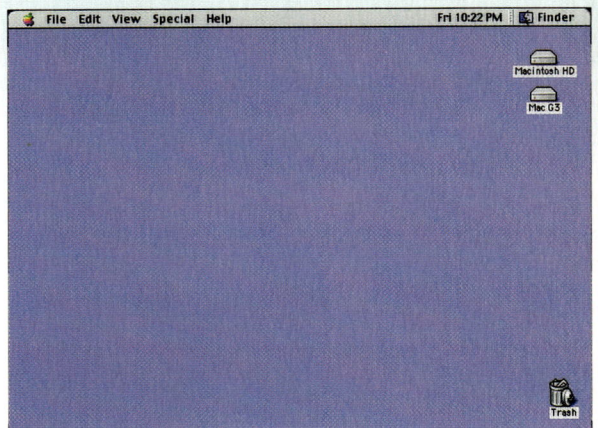

*End*

## How-To Hints

### Format/Initialize Command Grayed Out

Apple's Drive Setup is set up to work with hard drives that come with your Apple pro-duct. Some drives, though, don't work with this software. If you cannot get Drive Setup to work, ask your dealer for a program that will run. Normally, you'll find the program on the drive itself (if it has been formatted already). Otherwise, it will be on a separate floppy disk or CD.

### Format and Initialize—What's the Difference?

Formatting a drive wipes the files clean and then creates a new directory or table of contents. Initializing is faster. It just wipes out the table of contents, and tells the Mac operating system that new files can be written on the drive (even if there are files there, because they won't be cataloged anymore).

HOW TO FORMAT A NEW DRIVE  **157**

TASK

# How to Start from Another Drive

Your Mac can start from another hard drive if it has a regular System Folder. The extra drive can be located inside your Mac or connected to it via cable.

*Begin*

## 1 Go to the Apple Menu

Move on to the Apple menu **Control Panels** and then **Select Startup Disk** from the sub-menu.

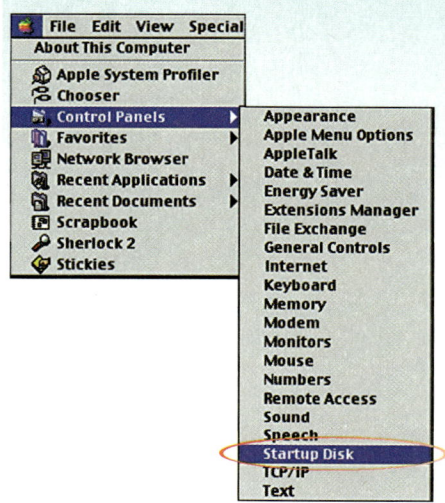

## 2 Select the Disk

In the **Startup Disk** window, click on the **name** of the **disk** you want to start from. Click the close box to save your changes.

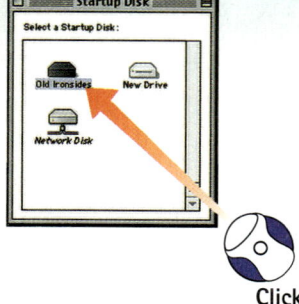

## 3 Restart Your Mac

Click on the desktop; then go to the **Special** menu and choose **Restart**.

158   PART 11: HARD DRIVE SETUP AND MAINTENANCE

## 4 Make Sure It's the Right Disk

If you have started from the correct disk, its icon will be displayed right at the top right on your Mac's desktop.

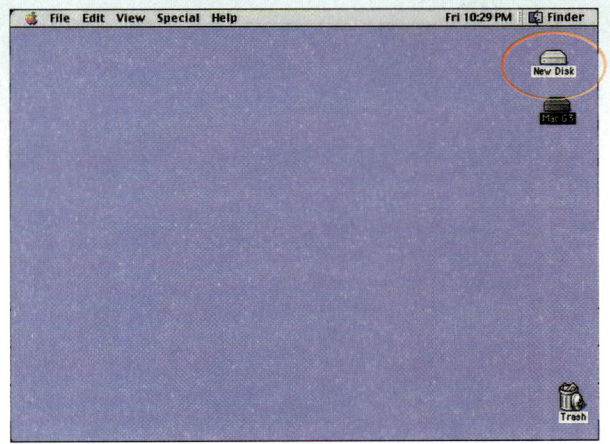

## 5 Change it Back

When you're ready to start from the original disk again, you can revisit the **Startup Disk Control Panel**, change it back, and **restart**.

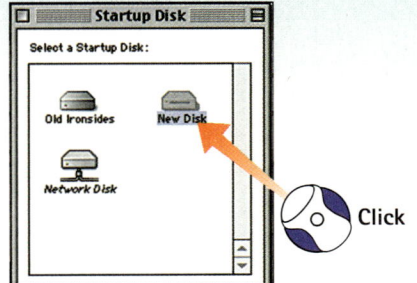

Click

*End*

---

## How-To Hints

### Doesn't Start from the New Drive
Even if the drive's icon is listed in the Startup Disk Control Panel, your Mac won't boot from it unless it has a real System Folder on it. Should your Mac start from the original drive, check the other drive and see.

### Question Mark Icon
When a drive selected in the Startup Disk Control Panel doesn't have a working System Folder, you'll see this icon, but usually your Mac will just revert to your original drive with a System Folder and start from it after a short time.

### Can't Boot from FireWire or USB Drives
At the time this book was written, you could not start your Mac from either a FireWire drive or a USB drive connected with the original generation iMac, iBook, PowerBook G3, or Blue & White Power Macintosh G3. The newest iMacs and Power Mac G4 can boot from a USB drive. Support for booting from FireWire drives may come at a later date (perhaps when this book is out).

How to Start from Another Drive  159

Task 4

# How to Check for Hard Drive Damage

As I said at the beginning of this section, over time your Mac's hard drive may become corrupted, perhaps due to a system crash or wear and tear on the drive. Fortunately, there are ways to check your drive and repair many problems, and the tool to do so comes right from Apple.

*Begin*

## 1 Locate Disk First Aid

When your Mac is set up from the factory or you reinstall system software, you'll find a copy of **Disk First Aid** in your **Utilities** folder.

Click

## 2 Launch the Program

Double-click the **Disk First Aid** icon, which brings the program's window to your Mac's display.

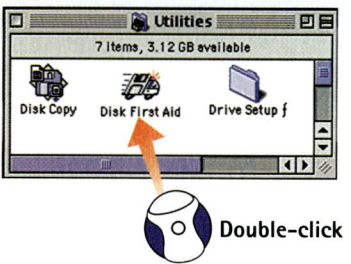
Double-click

## 3 Select the Drive

At the top of the window you will see a list of available drives. Click on the first drive you would like check and **Shift+Click** on any others.

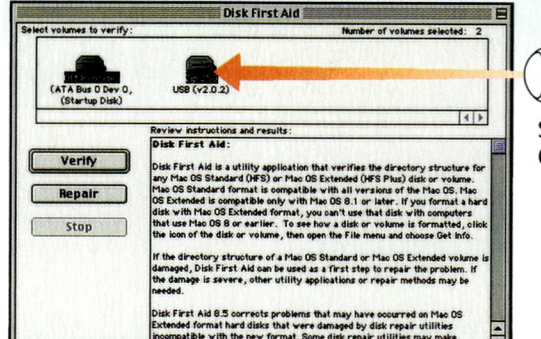

Shift+ Click

160  Part 11: Hard Drive Setup and Maintenance

## 4 Click Repair

Click the **Repair** button to scan your drive and then make any needed directory repairs. You'll see the progress of the scan listed in the program's window.

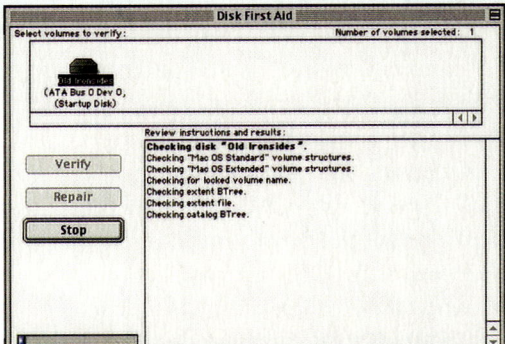

## 5 Did It Fix Any Problems?

If **Disk First Aid** finds a problem and fixes it, it's always a good idea to run it again. That's because one problem may obscure another one. So click **Repair** again for a second scan (which is shown in progress).

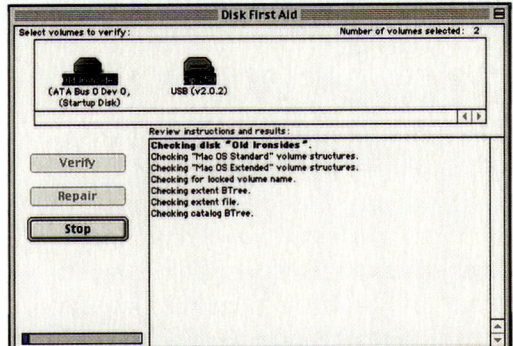

*End*

---

## How-To Hints

### Damage Not Fixed
While Disk First Aid can handle most problems you'll encounter with a hard drive, it isn't perfect. If you see a report that some problems were not fixed, try running Disk First Aid again. If that doesn't work, consider getting a copy of a commercial disk repair program. These include Alsoft's DiskWarrior, MicroMat's TechTool Pro, and Symantec's Norton Utilities for the Macintosh.

### Don't Leave It Unfixed!
When directory damage cannot be fixed on your hard drive, you shouldn't leave it as is. Disk directory damage can get worse and worse over time, and eventually files may end up being damaged. If all your efforts cannot fix the problem, you should seriously consider backing up your files and reformatting your hard drive.

## Task 5

# How to Optimize a Hard Drive

The files stored on your hard drive are written in short semi-circular segments on a series of concentric circles. Over time, the segments that make up each file can get scattered all over a drive. Mac's operating system has no problem keeping track of all these pieces, but gathering them can slow down operations, especially when you open or save a file.

Optimization keeps this problem under control. It gives your drive a "spring cleaning" "—rearranging files and putting each file's segments in their proper order. Apple doesn't supply anything that does this, but you can optimize with software such as Alsoft's PlusOptimizer, MicroMat's TechTool Pro, and Symantec's Norton Utilities.

## Begin

### 1 Restart from the CD

A non-startup drive can be optimized as is, but to optimize your start-up drive, you must start from another drive or from the CD-ROM that came with the optimizing application. To do the latter, insert the CD-ROM in your CD drive and choose **Restart** from the **Special** menu. Then, as the Mac restarts, hold down the **C** key on your keyboard, releasing it when you see the Happy Mac icon. (For the new procedure for the latest Macs, see the "How-To Hints" that follow.)

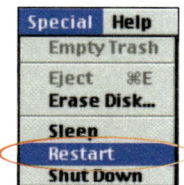

### 2 Speed Disk

Double-click on the **Norton Utilities** icon and then click on the **Speed Disk** button in the menu that appears.

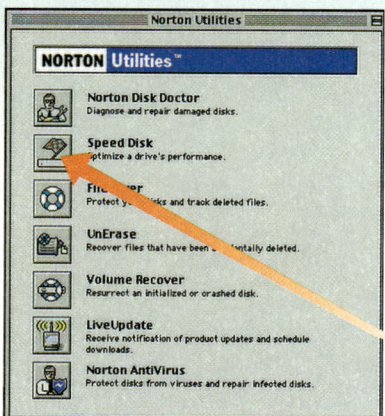

Click

### 3 Select a Drive

**Speed Disk** will display a list of your optimizable drives on the right. Click the drive you want to optimize. (Use Shift+click to optimize more than one drive.)

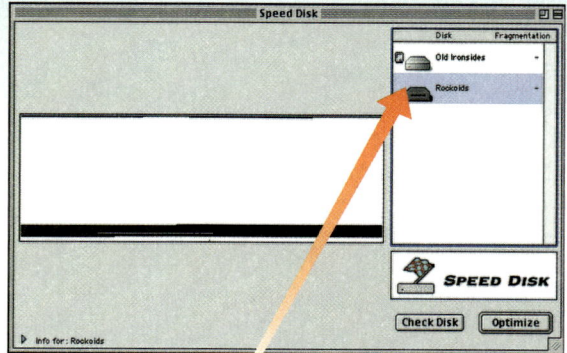

Click

162 PART 11: HARD DRIVE SETUP AND MAINTENANCE

## 4 Start Optimization

Click the **Optimize** button in the lower-right corner to begin. You can click on **Check Disk** if you want to see if whether the disk is in need of optimization before getting involved in a time-consuming optimization.

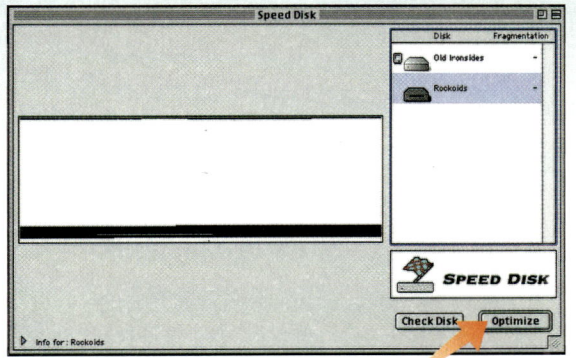

Click

## 5 Optimization in Progress

You could watch Speed Disk do its work, but the process can take a half-hour or more, so you might prefer to do something else. If you need to stop the process, click on the **Stop** button. No harm will come to your hard drive.

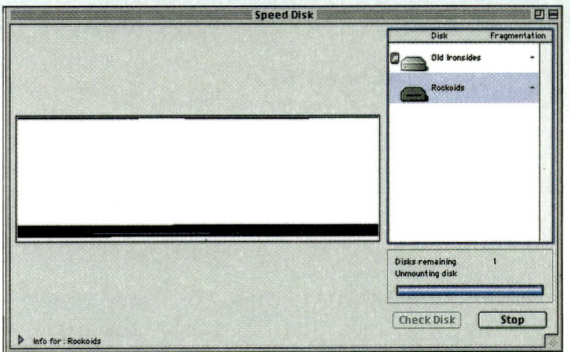

*End*

## How-To Hints

### Use the Latest Version

From time to time, updates to the operating system will change how your Mac stores files on a hard disk. When these changes occur, there is a possibility that an optimization program will damage files as it moves them around. So, to be safe, when you optimize, always use software that you know is safe with your version of the Mac OS. (The manufacturer can tell you this.) When you upgrade your OS, it might also be a good time to upgrade your disk repair and optimization software.

### New CD Startup Scheme

If you have an iBook, second generation iMac, Power Mac G4, or any later model, you start from a CD this way: **Restart** and hold down the **Option** key. You'll see a list of available startup drives. Click on the **CD** icon and then the **right arrow** to continue the startup process direct from the CD.

### Can't Optimize?

Before any of these optimizing programs will run, they'll check the drive to make sure there's no directory damage. If they find any, you'll see a warning notice to run a diagnostic program first. Since lots of files are being recopied, you need to make sure that the drive's directory is in good shape.

### Can't Optimize the Startup Drive?

Except for MicroMat's TechTool Pro, you need to start from another disk or CD to optimize the startup drive. And even TechTool Pro doesn't support the feature for Mac OS 9, because of changes made in the way the system is setup.

HOW TO OPTIMIZE A HARD DRIVE   163

## Task 6

# How to Back Up a Drive

There's an old commercial about a certain type of junk food, saying nobody can eat just one. When it comes to your Mac and your files, nobody should keep just one copy of anything important.

There's always the danger of hard drive damage. In addition, you may find other possibilities for loss, such as a natural disaster or theft.

Even if the possibilities are small, it is important that you have a backup of your most critical documents. You could even back up all the material on your Mac's drive.

This section will tell you about a basic backup program.

## *Begin*

### *1* Install an Extra Drive

At the start of this section, I discussed adding an extra drive. Once it's set up, make sure that it's up and running. For backup storage, a removable drive, such as a **Jaz** or **Zip** is ideal.

### *2* Select the Files to Backup

Click to select the **folder** or **disk** you want to backup. Shift+click for more than one file or folder.

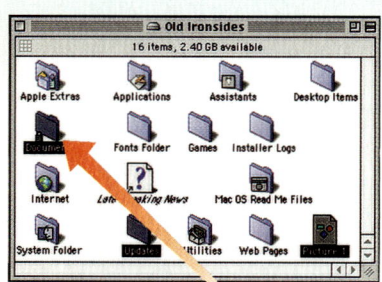

Shift+Click

### *3* Drag the Files to the Other Drive

Drag the files to the icon of the disk to which you want to copy those files.

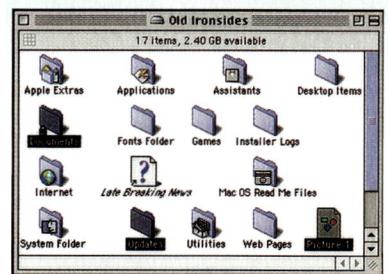

## 4 Watch the Progress

You'll see a progress display as files are copied over.

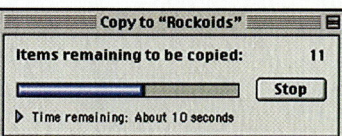

## 5 Select More Files if Necessary

If your removable driver runs out of space, so that you need to insert more media or you need to add additional files, follow steps 2 through 4 with the additional material.

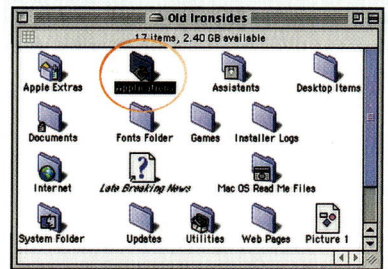

## 6 Store Removable Media

After you have copied the files you want, click and drag the **icon** of the removable drive media to the trash, which ejects it. Then put it in a place for safekeeping. It is a good idea to make an extra backup and store it in another location (perhaps a bank vault).

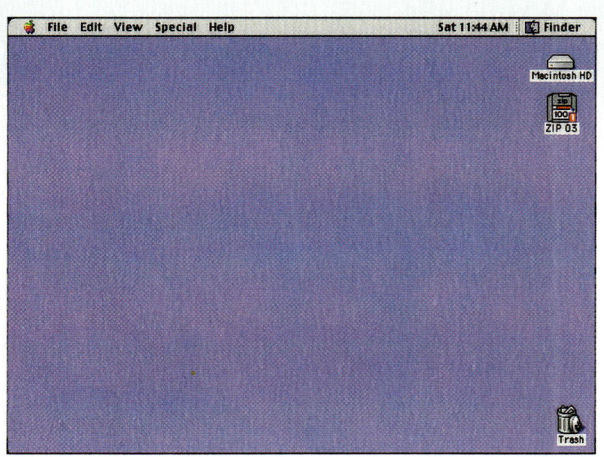

*End*

---

## How-To Hints

### There Is a Simpler Way

There are dedicated backup programs that can actually automate the process of backing up your files. Once you set them up as to what files to copy and where, they can do their stuff at the times you want, so you don't have to baby-sit the Mac. Such programs include Retrospect and Retrospect Express from Dantz Development, and Personal Backup from ASD Software.

### Consider a CD for Permanence

If you want to archive files for a number of years, consider getting a drive that writes CDs. CD media can last indefinitely, and the CD blank media is cheap enough (from one to two dollars each in reasonable quantities) so that you can toss it away without regret when you don't need it anymore.

How to Back Up a Drive  **165**

# Task

1. How to Install a Scanner  168

2. How to Install a Keyboard or Pointing Device  170

3. How to Install a Desktop or Digital Camera  172

4. How to Install a New Modem  174

5. How to Add Speakers  176

6. How to Add a Hub  178

PART *12*

# Adding Accessories to Your Mac

**Y**our Mac doesn't work in a vacuum.

Even if you have an all-in-one model, such as the iMac or an Apple iBook or PowerBook, you will soon want to explore the tremendous number of products you can add to your Mac that provide a huge number of extra features.

For example, you may want to take family photos and send them on to the rest of the family. So you get a scanner, which is a device that will digitize artwork so you can see it on your Mac.

Perhaps you'd like to join the new world of digital cameras, which take great quality pictures without needing film or processing.

Or you aren't pleased with the sounds your Mac's little speaker produces, and you want to enjoy a computer game or a DVD (if you have a Mac with a DVD drive) in all its glory.

You'll find that there are hundreds and hundreds of accessories you can add to your Mac. We'll cover some of those choices and how to install them here. Whether your interest is a scanner, a new keyboard, or whatever, you'll find help here. ●

## Task 1

# How to Install a Scanner

A scanner is one of the best accessories you can buy for your Mac. You can use it to copy photos and artwork. Also, with special software, you can use it to make copies of printed material that you can edit with word processing software.

## Begin

### 1 Unpack the Scanner

Remove the scanner and pry apart the packing materials.

### 2 Unlock It

This is critical because scanners have delicate optical assemblies. Manufacturers use a locking switch to protect the scanner during shipment. Check the directions on how to **unlock** it. You may find the switch in the back, under the cover, or on the bottom of your scanner.

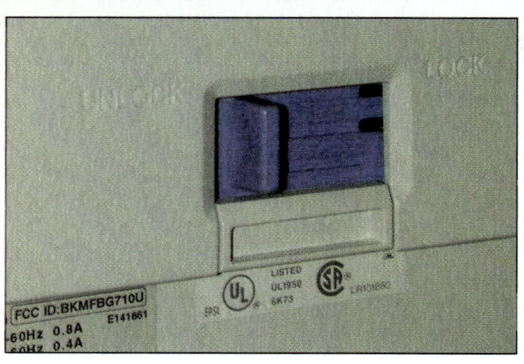

### 3 Install the Software

A scanner will just sit there if you don't install its software. Place the **scanner's CD** in your Mac's drive, locate the **installer**, and double-click on the icon (I'm showing software for an Epson scanner here). Then click on the **Install** button.

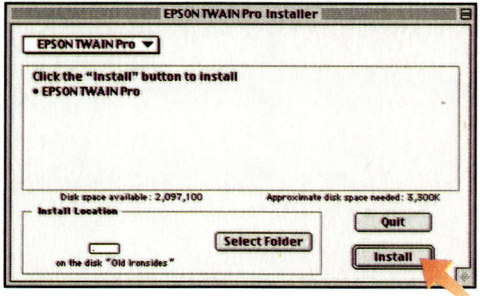

Click

168  Part 12: Adding Accessories to Your Mac

## 4 Shut Down the Mac

After the software is installed, you will probably have to **restart** your Mac. After that's done, choose **Shut Down** from the **Special** menu to turn it off.

## 5 Connect It

Take the connection cable and attach it to the scanner and the proper connection port on your Mac (USB, FireWire, or SCSI). Turn on the scanner and then the Mac.

## 6 Test It

After your Mac is running, locate your scanning software, put some artwork in the scanner, and try it out to make sure it works properly.

*End*

# How-To Hints

### Can You Use an Old Scanner on a New Mac?

Old scanners used a standard called SCSI to connect to Macs. But most new Macs don't have SCSI capability. If you have a Mac to which you can add a SCSI card, you can use that old scanner. Otherwise, you may want to retire the unit and consider one of the new models available for Macs with USB or FireWire ports.

### Scanner Isn't Recognized

Make sure that you installed the software. It may require a restart for the scanner to be recognized by the Mac. If it still doesn't work, verify that the scanner is on and that cables are properly connected. Also, make sure that you did unlock the scanner before you attached it to your Mac. Unless you have a USB or FireWire scanner, don't try unplugging anything until the Mac and the scanner are turned off.

## Task 2

# How to Install a Keyboard or Pointing Device

New iMacs and professional Macs come with a small keyboard and round mouse. Many people like them just fine. But some don't. Fortunately, there are plenty of replacement keyboards and pointing devices to pick from. You can choose keyboards that match the old Apple extended keyboard style (similar to a PC keyboard) or keyboards that are ergonomic, meaning they are designed to help reduce hand and wrist injuries. Pointing devices range from mice to trackballs (upside down mice) and joysticks. Artists use graphics tablets, which have special pen-like devices that you use to draw on them (similar to drawing on a sheet of paper).

## Begin

### 1 Connect the Keyboard

After unpacking the keyboard, take the cables and attach them to your Mac. If you have an older Mac with an ADB port, you'll need to shut down the Mac before you hook up the keyboard. If you have a newer Mac with a USB port, you don't have to shut down.

### 2 Attach Mouse to Keyboard

After the keyboard is connected, attach the mouse to it and test it to be sure it works properly.

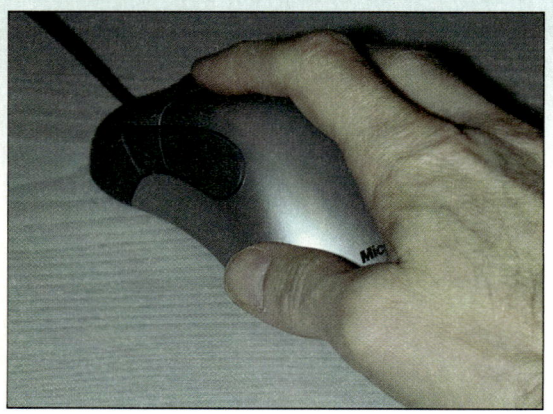

### 3 Connect New Pointing Device

If you have a new pointing device for your Mac, be it a mouse, trackball, joystick, or graphics tablet, you can plug it in along side or instead of your old mouse.

## 4 Install Software if Necessary

A pointing device with extra buttons may require special software to activate its extra features. If you have such software, **install** it next and then **restart** the Mac so it recognizes the software.

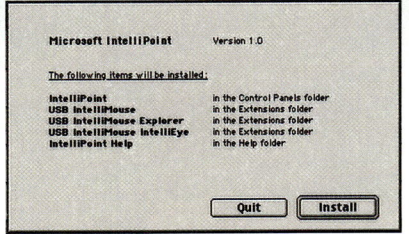

## 5 Configure the Software

The software for your new pointing device may need to be adjusted to access special features. These features may include adding custom functions to those extra buttons (such as bringing up contextual menus). The software here is for a Microsoft IntelliMouse Explorer.

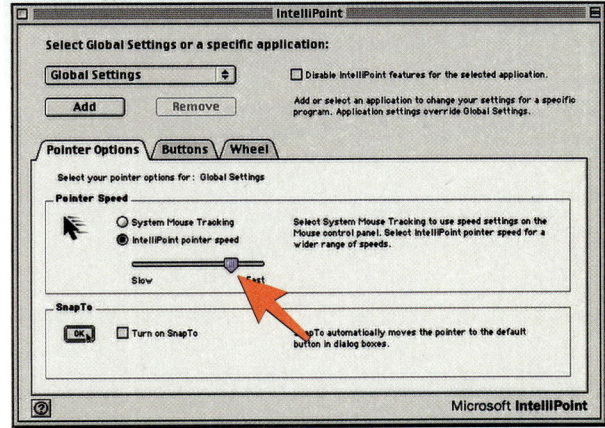

*End*

## How-To Hints

### Input Device Is Too Slow

Apple's Mouse Control Panel may not work with a pointing device that requires special software. Check the directions for the device to see whether additional software is needed or not. Some products actually require a visit to a company's Web site to get needed software.

### More Than One

The Mac's USB port lets you hook up to 127 daisy-chained devices. So you can definitely have a mouse, a trackball, a joystick, and a graphics tablet all work together. Just move the one you want to use into position. You'll probably have to install special software, of course, for some of these extra pointing devices. You can also have two keyboards at hand. Perhaps a family member likes the regular one, while you prefer the "ergonomic" type instead.

## Task 3

# How to Install a Desktop or Digital Camera

The Mac is presented as a multimedia machine. And multimedia means video. There are a number of cameras you can connect to your Mac. They range from a little desktop camera you can use as an interactive video camera, to a digital camera that takes real pictures (like one that uses film).

## Begin

### 1 Install the Software

Cameras require special software to work with your Mac. After **installing** the software, **restart** your Mac, so it will recognize the camera when it's connected.

### 2 Connect the Camera

Take the cables and attach them from camera to Mac.

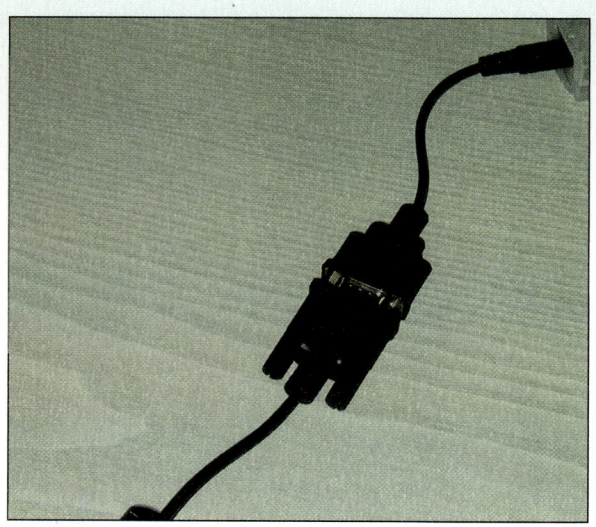

### 3 Check the Desktop Camera

Have a look at the image the camera captures to make sure it looks all right.

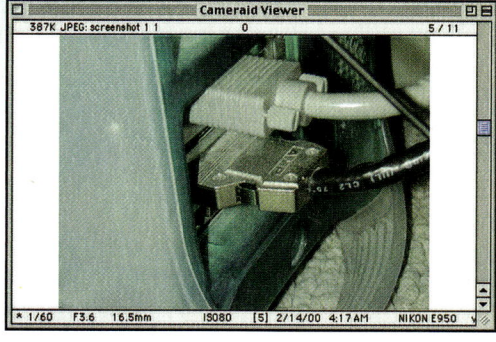

## 4 Adjust the Software

If the image doesn't look clear, check the software for ways to improve the quality of the image. Also, see if there is a focusing wheel on the camera.

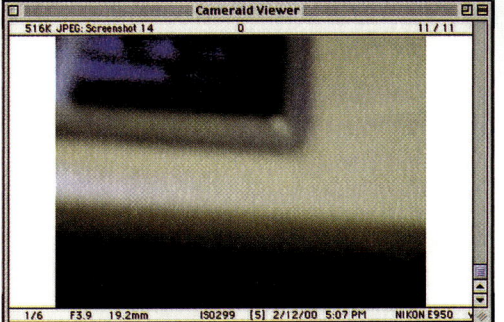

## 5 Test Digital Camera

Take pictures with your digital camera, just as you would with a roll of film. Make sure that you can bring the pictures into your Mac without any problems. Normally, the process requires that you attach the camera to your Mac through a cable and use their software to deliver the pictures to your computer. Once you do that, you'll want to look at the quality of the pictures to make sure they are satisfactory.

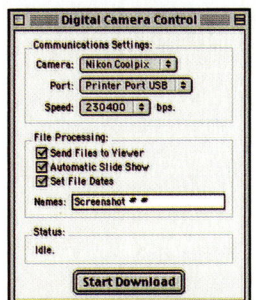

*End*

---

## How-To Hints

### What If Your Mac Can't Recognize the Camera?

Even if your camera had the right connection cables, don't forget the software. If it still doesn't work, visit the manufacturer's Web sites for updates. Also, try turning the camera off and on, to see if that makes it work properly.

### What Do You Do with Digital Camera Pictures?

A digital camera may create pictures in a special format, but if the software gives you an option of file format, choose JPEG. A JPEG file can be read by computer users with Macs and Windows-based PCs. If you send them to a Windows user, make sure that the name of the file has a .jpg suffix (this tells Windows what sort of file it is).

# Task 4

## How to Install a New Modem

If you have an older Mac, you may find that your connections to the Internet just seem too slow. Fortunately, 56,000 bps (56K) modems are in plentiful supply and cost less than many slower speed models did just a few years ago. Here's how to set one up.

## Begin

### 1 Install the Software

If your modem will do double-duty as a fax machine, you'll need to install the special software that comes with the unit. After installing the software, **restart** your Mac so it recognizes the software.

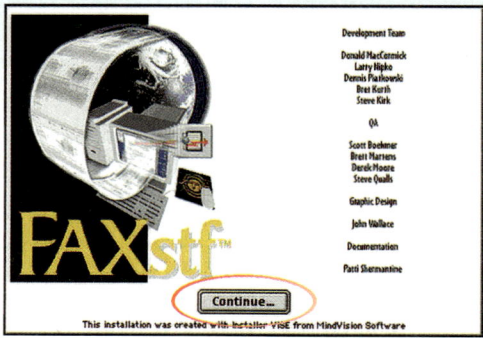

### 2 Connect the Modem

Connect the **cable** from modem to Mac. If you're using a Mac with the regular modem (serial) port, it's a good idea to **shut down** the Mac first. Then **turn on** the modem and the Mac.

### 3 Configure for a Modem

Open the **Modem Control Panel** and choose a **modem profile** that matches (or closely matches) the make and model of your modem.

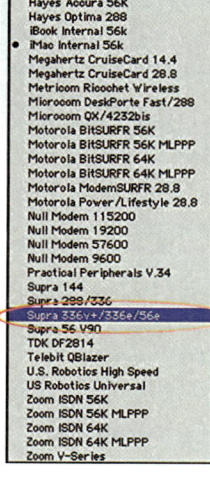

**174** PART 12: ADDING ACCESSORIES TO YOUR MAC

## 4 Test the Modem

Connect to your **ISP** to make sure the modem works properly.

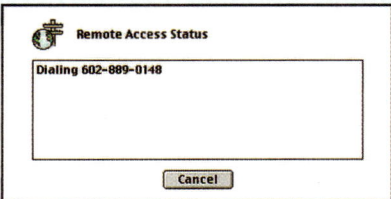

## 5 Test a Fax

If your modem will be used for sending and receiving faxes, send a test fax to someone you know to make sure that it runs properly.

*End*

## How-To Hints

### Modem Not Recognized

First, check your connection cables and make sure the modem is on. Also make sure that the needed software is installed. An external modem has little lights that show it's connecting and transferring data. If nothing is working, contact the manufacturer for assistance. Modems usually have long warranties.

### For AOL and CompuServe Users

You have to use AOL and CompuServe's own software to configure your new modem. Each program has a settings panel that can be used to select the proper modem driver (or script).

### 56K Modems Don't Connect at 56K

Due to FCC limits, the maximum possible speed for a 56K modem is 53K. However, that's not the only limiting factor. Your local phone lines will seldom handle connections faster than 40,000 to 44,000 bps, so don't be concerned if you get connections in that range or a bit lower. If you do better, consider yourself lucky.

HOW TO INSTALL A NEW MODEM

TASK 5

# How to Add Speakers

I won't mince words. The speakers you get on most Macs are not very high quality. Even a normal table radio may be better. If you have a new "slot-loading" iMac, of course, you do have better quality speakers.

For the rest of the Mac, iMac, iBook, and PowerBook line, you'll find a wide variety of speaker systems to pick from. Some of the best come from the same companies that make home audio and car audio systems. You'll want to look at products from such firms as Advent, Bose, Boston Acoustics, Cambridge SoundWorks, JBL, and Monsoon, to name just a few.

Speakers come either as two pieces (satellites) that are placed at each end of your Mac's display or as three pieces, offering a woofer module you place on the floor for enhanced bass quality.

## Begin

### 1 Audition the Speakers

You don't buy a home audio system without listening first, and the same is true for speakers. Listen to several in your price range before you buy.

### 2 Connect Them

Attach the **speaker cables** from speakers to Mac. Connect the **power cable** to the AC outlet.

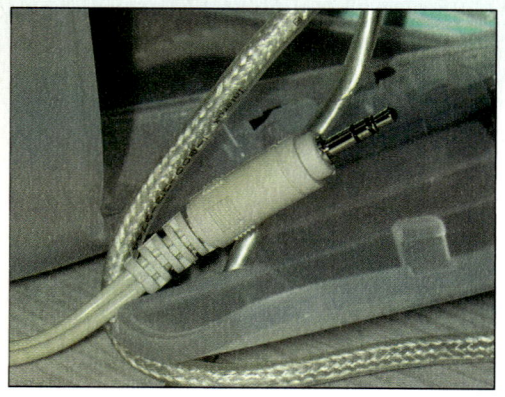

### 3 Turn the Unit On

Turn on the speakers and set the volume levels.

PART 12: ADDING ACCESSORIES TO YOUR MAC

## 4 Set Levels

After you set the sound levels, there are other adjustments that you may want to make. Some speakers, for example, have a balance control, which shifts the signal from left to right. Apple's Sound Control Panel can also be used to make this adjustment.

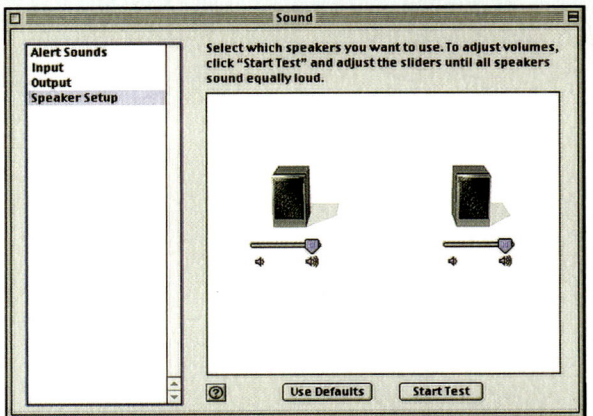

## 5 Check the Sound Control Panel

You can also adjust the speaker balance and overall levels with the **Sound Control Panel**.

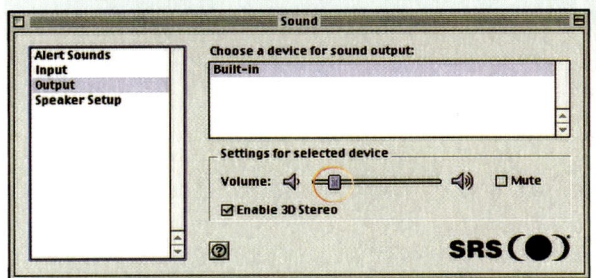

*End*

## How-To Hints

### No Sound

Look at cables and make sure that the speakers are on. Also double-check the **Sound Control Panel** (or Monitors & Sound on older Macs). Make sure that the **"mute"** checkbox hasn't been checked by mistake under **Output**. Some speakers also have a separate mute switch, and you'll want to push the switch to see if the sound doesn't return.

### Picture Distorts

Computer speakers must be magnetically shielded so that their magnets don't affect color purity and image quality at the edges of your Mac's display (obviously, a laptop isn't affected). If you see a problem with the display, move the speakers apart a bit. If the problem persists, look at the instructions or check with your dealer to make sure that the speakers are designed to work with computers. As to the distorted picture, just turn the Mac's display off and on (you need to just restart an iMac) to "clear" or degauss the display.

HOW TO ADD SPEAKERS 177

TASK 6

# How to Add a Hub

When you network your Mac via Ethernet, you can use a single cable, called a crossover cable, for one connection. But if you need to connect to more than one device, you will have to buy a hub. A hub is a central connection device that manages such hookups.

You also need a hub if you want to expand the number of USB and FireWire ports on your Mac.

## Begin

### 1 Install the Hub

Take the hub and attach it to the **AC** outlet (USB hubs don't need an AC connection unless you connect several devices, or ones that take extra current).

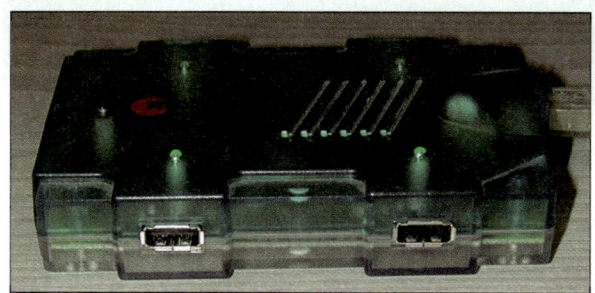

### 2 Connect the Cables

You don't have to turn the Mac off, but be sure that cables are run from the Mac's connection port (Ethernet or USB) to the hub. And then they should be run from the hub to the other devices.

### 3 Check the Network

If you have an Ethernet hub, you'll need to make sure you have the right network connection. Go to the **Apple** menu, choose **Control Panels**, and select **AppleTalk** from the sub-menu.

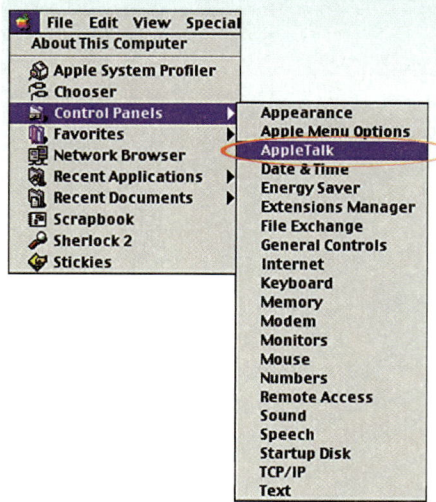

## 4 Pick Your Network

Click on the **Connect via** pop-up menu to change the network, if the wrong one is chosen. Then click the **close** box.

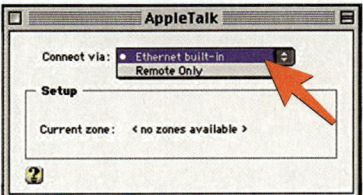

## 5 Save the Changes

When you change settings in the **AppleTalk Control Panel**, you get a dialog box asking to save the changes. Click **Save**.

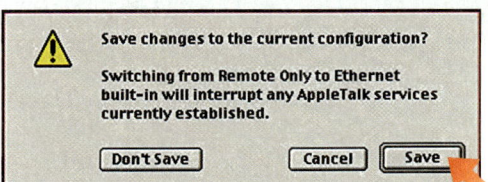

*End*

---

# How-To Hints

### Ethernet Network Not Recognized
On older Macs, you may have to reinstall system software to include the proper Ethernet software. If your Mac has an Ethernet card made by a company other than Apple, it will also come with a floppy or CD that contains the software you need.

### USB Device Not Recognized
If you cannot get your Mac to recognize a USB device, you should make sure that its software is also installed. All the hub does is provide a place to connect; it doesn't replace the software. After the software is installed, the device should be recognized and should work.

# Task

1. How to Connect to a Network  182

2. How to Set Up File Sharing  184

3. How to Set Permission Levels  186

4. How to Turn Off File Sharing  188

5. How to Diagnose Network Problems  190

# CHAPTER 13

# Networking Your Mac

Your Mac need not live in isolation.

Every Mac comes with built-in networking capability. This allows you to connect it to other Macs or networked printers, so you can all share files with each other and send your print jobs to the same printer. All but the oldest Macs come with standard support for Ethernet, a high-speed networking standard that works just as well on the smallest networks as the largest ones that consist of hundreds of computers. You can set up an Ethernet network with as few as two Macs or one Mac and a printer, or as many as hundreds of computers, printers, and other network resources.

In this section, you'll learn how to attach your Mac to a network, be it another Mac or a central network connection point (a hub). You'll also learn how to share files with other Macs and how to protect access so unauthorized people cannot access your files. And if problems should arise, you'll learn what to check to fix those problems.

## Task 1

# How to Connect to a Network

Get your cables ready; you'll find hooking up to a network is easy. If you're going to connect to the Ethernet jacks on two Macs, or you're connecting to a Mac and one Ethernet printer, you need a "crossover" cable, which you can get at almost any computer store. If you're going to hook up to a network with more than two devices, you'll need a little box called an Ethernet hub. A hub is a component that is the central connection point of a network.

## Begin

### 1 Attach the Cables Between Macs

Take your network cable and attach it to both Macs or to the Mac and another computer.

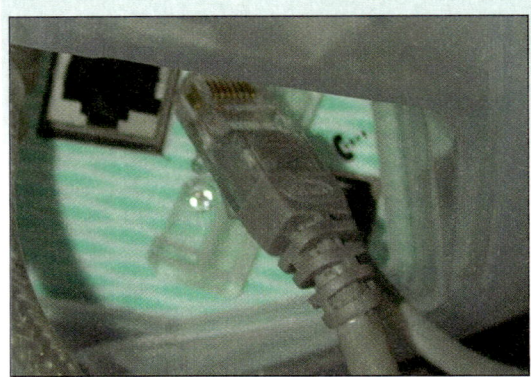

### 2 Connect to a Hub

If your network has more than two connections, use a regular Ethernet cable with a hub. Plug in one end of a cable on each Mac or printer, and the other end into a free jack on the hub.

### 3 Access the AppleTalk Control Panel

On each Mac on your network, go to the **Apple** menu, select **Control Panels**, and choose **AppleTalk** from the sub-menu.

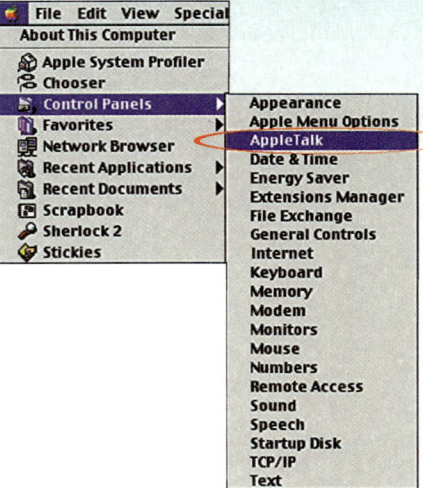

## 4 Choose Ethernet

Click on the **Connect via** pop-up menu and choose **Ethernet**.

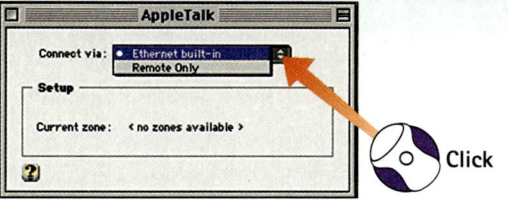

Click

## 5 Save Your Changes

If you've changed your network selection, you'll get a dialog box asking if you want to save the change. Click **Save** to store the network change.

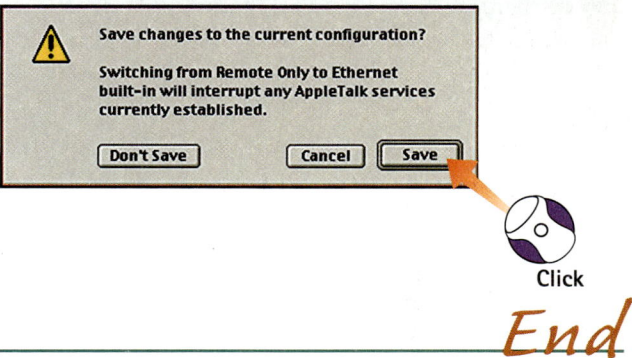

Click

*End*

---

## How-To Hints

### Use the Control Strip
If your File Sharing Control Panel is set up with the computer and owner's name, you can easily activate file sharing via the **File Sharing Control Strip**. Just click on it and then select **Turn File Sharing On**. It'll work the same as the File Sharing Control Panel.

### Don't Have Ethernet
Should you have an older Mac without an Ethernet jack, check with your dealer. Add-on cards are available for many Macs, and they're not all that expensive. Figure on paying from $25 to $100, depending on the sort of network adapter card you need.

### Can't Switch Networks
If the AppleTalk Control Panel doesn't detect a working network connection, it will flash an error. Should this happen, recheck your cables. Remember that if you are connecting directly to another Mac or printer and not an Ethernet hub, you'll need a crossover cable. Make sure that your dealer has sold you the right cable. A crossover is made by swapping the first two wires on just one side of the cable with the second two. If your cable has a clear jack, you can check this for yourself.

# Task 2

## How to Set Up File Sharing

The Mac OS gives you the ability to use **File Sharing**. This feature lets you share files on your drive with other users on your network and vice versa. And it only takes a minute to set up.

# Begin

## 1 Open the File Sharing Control Panel

Go to the **Apple** menu, choose **Control Panels**, and select **File Sharing** from the sub-menu. The File Sharing dialog will appear.

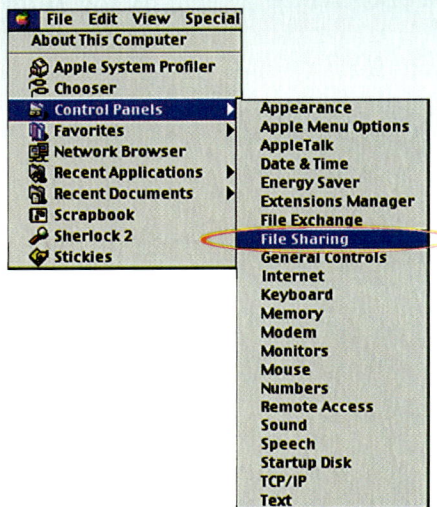

## 2 Name the Computer

If necessary, check on the **Start/Stop** tab. If you haven't already filled it in, enter the proper information in the **Computer Name**, **Password**, and **Owner Name** boxes. Remember that the **Computer Name** has to be unique and not duplicated on the network.

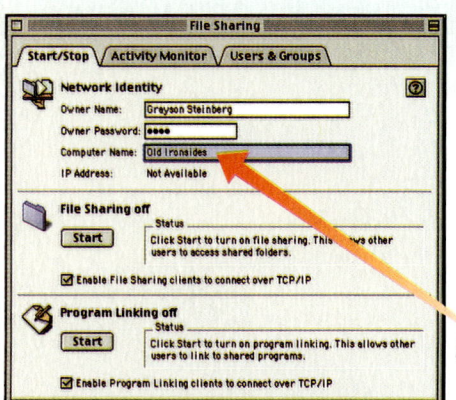

## 3 Turn on File Sharing

Click the **Start** button on the **File Sharing** Control Panel. It'll take anywhere from a few seconds to a few minutes for sharing to become active.

184  PART 13: NETWORKING YOUR MAC

## 4 Share Your Mac

After sharing is activated, have the user of the other Mac go to the **Chooser** and click on **AppleShare**. You'll see a list of networked computers on the right pane of the Chooser screen.

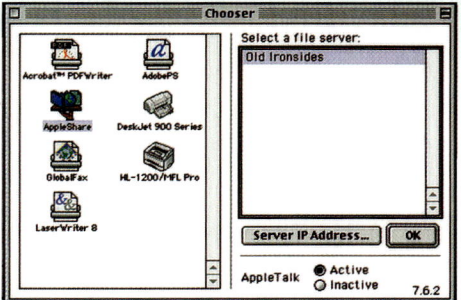

## 5 Select the Networked Computer

Click on the **Computer's Name**, which brings up a password prompt. Enter the **Owner's Name** and then the **password** to connect. Click **OK**.

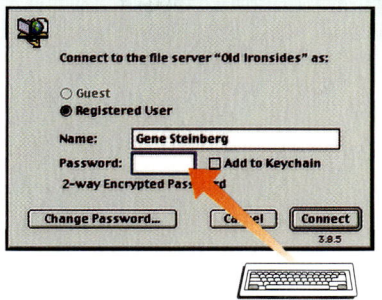

## 6 Select the Drive

After you've connected, you'll see a list of shared volumes (which can be folders or drives). Click on **one** or Shift+click on **more than one volume**; then click **OK**. The shared volume's icon will appear on the other Mac's desktop as another disk.

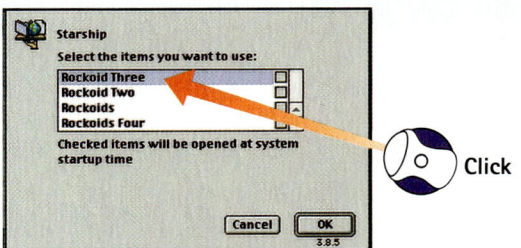

*End*

# How-To Hints

## Can't Start Sharing

In order to make file sharing active, you must give your Mac a network identity. At the very least, name the computer and owner. If you're using a network where security isn't a problem (your home or a small office), you don't have to enter a password.

## No File Sharing Control Panel

On other versions of the Mac OS, it was called Sharing Setup. But you'll find that the basic information you enter to identify your Mac is the same.

How to Set Up File Sharing  **185**

TASK 3

# How to Set Permission Levels

If your Mac network is at home, and the only ones who will be logging in are members of your family, security may not be that important. And the same may be true in a small office, where everyone knows everybody else, and there are no secrets.

But if you intend to set up a network in a larger office, and you need to limit the access of other users to the shared Macs, you'll want to make some additional file sharing settings.

## Begin

### 1 Turn on File Sharing

Following the steps listed in the previous section, switch on **File Sharing**. When the "File Sharing Starting Up" message changes to "File Sharing On," click on the close box in the upper left.

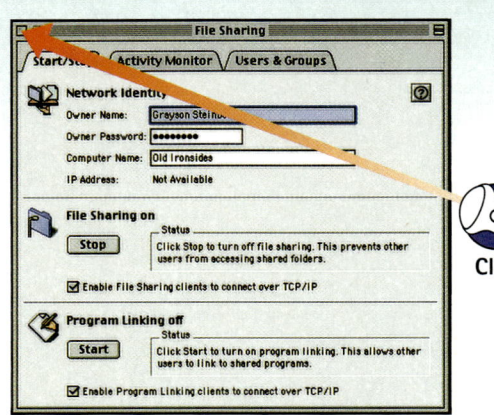

### 2 Select the Items You're Sharing

Return to the desktop and display the folders and files you want to share. Click once on the item you want to control access to. Shift+click if you're selecting more than one item for sharing.

### 3 Bring Up Get Info

Go to the **File** menu, choose **Get Info**, and select **Sharing** from the sub-menu.

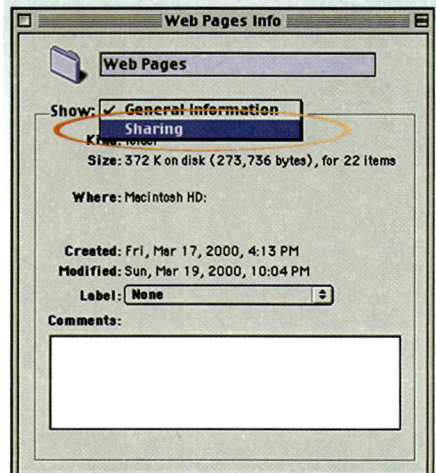

186  PART 13: NETWORKING YOUR MAC

## 4 Set Access Privileges

Check the boxes that describe the kind of privileges you want to set. You can control whether another user can change the item. You can also allow **Guest** access, which means anyone can read and write the shared item from your Mac.

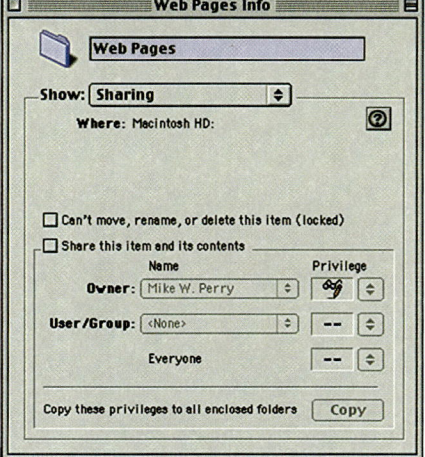

## 5 Copy Settings

If you want all folders inside the item you're sharing to have the same privileges, click the **Copy** button. Then click the **close** box to store the settings; it'll take anywhere from a minute to several minutes for the **Get Info** screen to close, depending on how many actual files are in the selected item.

Click

*End*

## 6 Confirm Settings

Always take warning windows seriously. Think about the privileges you are about to bestow and, if they make sense, click on the **Copy** button. If they do not, click on the **Cancel** button.

Click

## How-To Hints

### Don't Forget Users & Groups
You can decide whether to allow others to connect to your Mac via file sharing via the Users & Groups Control Panel. For Mac OS 9.0, it's accessed by clicking the **Users & Groups** tab in the **File Sharing Control Panel**.

### Don't Allow Guest Access if You Have a Cable Modem
When you use a cable modem to access the Internet, you are joining a huge network. Depending on how the cable service sets it up, your Mac network may appear on the network, so you'll want to make sure that Guest access isn't permitted. Contact your cable provider to find out about their security methods.

HOW TO SET PERMISSION LEVELS   **187**

## Task 4

# How to Turn Off File Sharing

When you decide that you no longer want to allow others to share files on your Mac, it takes but a moment to turn off the feature.

## Begin

### *1* Open File Sharing Control Panel

Go to the **Apple** menu, choose **Control Panels**, and select **File Sharing**.

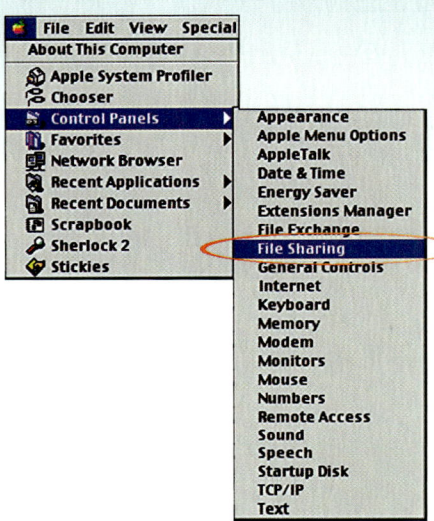

### *2* Stop File Sharing

If necessary, click on the **Start/Stop** tab. Then under **File Sharing on** click the **Stop** button.

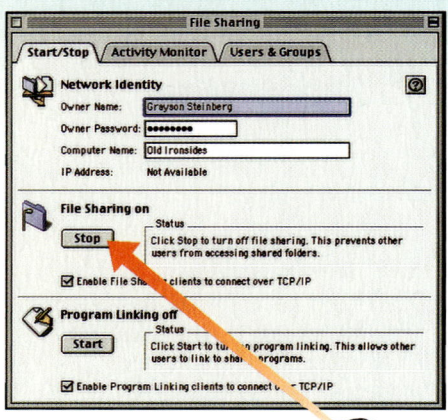

Click

### *3* Set the Time Limit

If other users are sharing your Mac's files, in the next dialog box, you'll need to **OK** how long it will take for sharing to actually switch off. This gives other users on the network time to finish file transfers or to close documents on your Mac that they're working on.

Click

PART 13: NETWORKING YOUR MAC

## 4 Or Use the Control Strip

Another way to quickly turn off file sharing is via the **File Sharing Control Strip**. Just click it and choose **Turn File Sharing Off**.

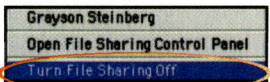

## 5 Others Get a Warning

Make sure that others on your network remove the shared volume icons from their Mac's desktops. Otherwise, they'll get a notice that sharing was shut down. If they get the message, a click of the **OK** button will close it.

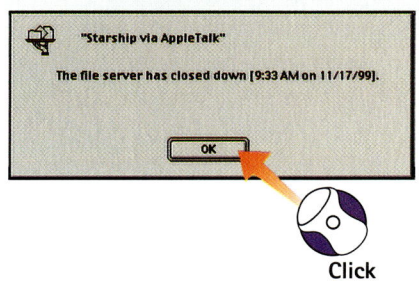

Click

*End*

## 6 Monitoring Activity

If you would like to see how busy the network is, select the **Activity Monitor** tab in the **File Sharing Control** panel window.

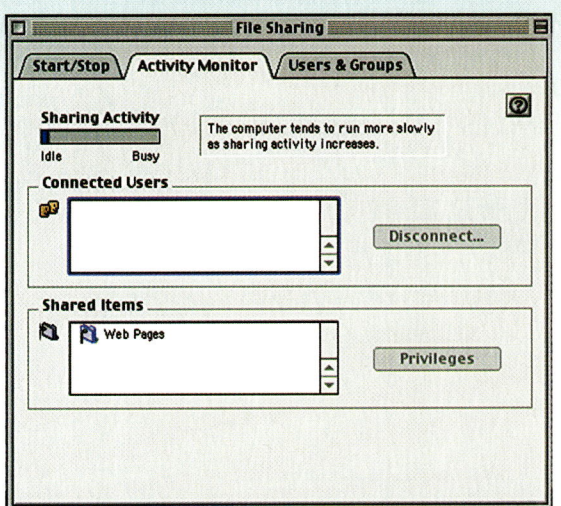

## How-To Hints

### Don't Forget to Close Shared Items

If you're working on a document or a program that's being shared on a networked Mac, don't forget to close it when you learn that sharing is being shut down. Otherwise, you'll risk doing damage to the document or having a system crash.

HOW TO TURN OFF FILE SHARING  **189**

## Task 5

# How to Diagnose Network Problems

Normally, file sharing is a transparent process. You turn it on, or turn it off, after a brief setup process, and it works fine. But what if you cannot activate it or connect to your Mac's network at all? Here are some hints on what to do.

## Begin

### 1 Check the Cables

Make sure that all the network cables are properly connected.

### 2 Check the Hub

If you are using an Ethernet hub, make sure it's plugged in and a light displays for each jack that has a cable.

### 3 Check the AppleTalk Control Panel

Even if the cables are connected properly, you may have failed to set the proper network in the **AppleTalk** Control Panel. (See Task 1.)

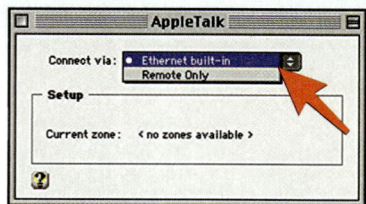

190   PART 13: NETWORKING YOUR MAC

## 4 Make Sure File Sharing is On

Go to the **File Sharing** Control Panel and verify that a **File Sharing on** label is present. (See Task 2.)

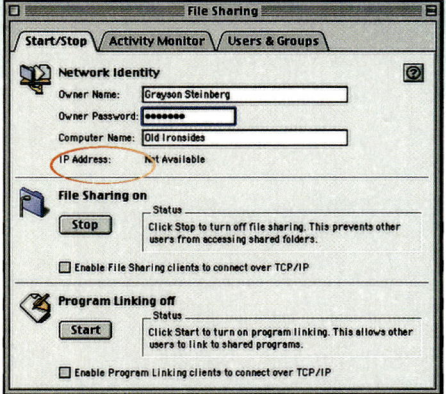

## 5 Make Sure AppleTalk Is On

If you're using a personal printer on a Mac with a regular printer port, such as an inkjet printer from Canon, Epson, or HP, normally you turn off AppleTalk to work with these printers. But it has to be on to share files. Go to the **Chooser** and activate **AppleTalk**. You can turn it off if you have to print (but you lose the network connection). Fortunately, Macs with built-in USB ports using such devices don't have this problem.

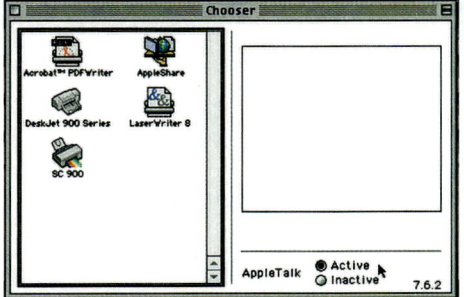

*End*

---

# How-To Hints

### Dump the Preferences
If all of the above steps can't fix your networking problem, go to the **Preferences** Folder inside the **System Folder**. Drag files labeled **AppleShare Prep**, **AppleTalk Preferences**, the **File Sharing** folder, and **File Sharing CP Prefs** to the **Trash**. **Restart**. You will have to redo your File Sharing setup information, but this will cure many potential problems.

### Eject Removable Disk Media
If you have media in a removable disk drive, it may prevent sharing from starting up. If this happens, drag the disk icon to the trash in order to eject the disk and activate file sharing. Once you've done that, you can place the disk in the drive again.

# Task

1. How to Install the Mac Operating System  194

2. How to Do a Clean System Install  196

3. How to Merge System Folders  198

4. How to Do a System Update  202

# Chapter 14

# Working with the System

The single most important piece of software you'll ever use on your Mac is the Mac OS.

The Mac OS is the heart and soul of your Mac, giving it its unique look and feel. It's what makes a Mac a Mac. Without it, your computer would just sit there, not able to display a desktop, open a file or a program or, well, compute.

The operating system is your Mac's traffic cop, directing the flow of data between all the components of your Mac and the devices attached to it.

In this section, I'll show you how to install or reinstall the Mac OS and what a clean install is all about, and the best way to make it work for you. I'll also show you how to merge old and new system folders, so none of the unique features you added get lost when you do a clean install.

TASK 1

# How to Install the Mac Operating System

As complex as a computer operating system is, installing it is not a daunting process. The simplest way involves just a few clicks of your mouse.

## Begin

### 1 Start with Your System CD

Place your **Mac OS CD** in your Mac's CD drive and wait till the CD's icon appears on your Mac's desktop.

### 2 Restart

Choose **Restart** from the **Special** menu.

### 3 Hold Down the "C" Key

As soon as you hear your Mac's startup chord, hold down the **"C"** key. This will ensure that your Mac starts from the CD and not from your hard drive. (If you have one of the newest Macs, the iBook, second-generation iMac, or Power Mac G4, hold down the **Option** key instead, and, when you see a CD icon on the screen, click the icon and then the right arrow to continue.)

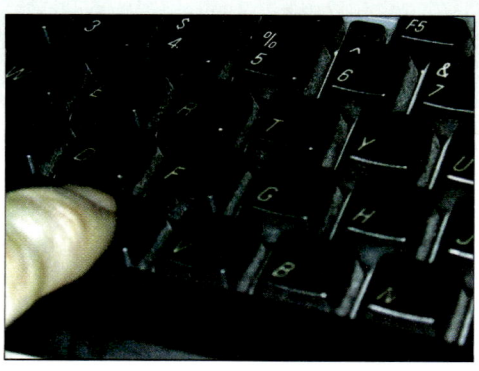

## 4 Begin the Install

Look at your CD's directory and locate the icon labeled **Mac OS Install** and double-click on it to bring up the **Welcome** screen. Click **Continue**.

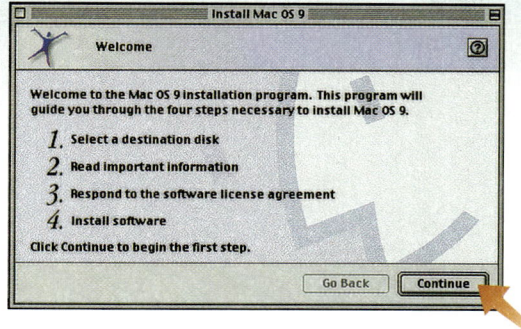

Click

## 5 Choose Your Destination

Your startup drive is automatically selected as the destination. If you want another location, click on the **pop-up** menu and pick another disk. Then click **Select**.

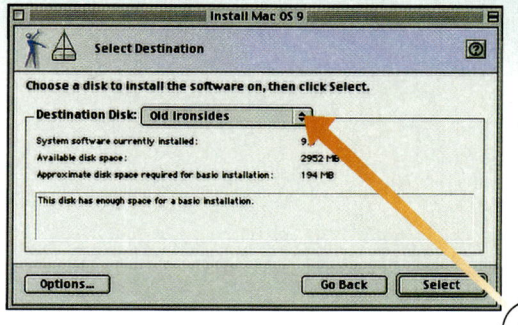

Click

## 6 Check the ReadMe and License

Check the **Important Information** screen; then **Continue** to the software license agreement.

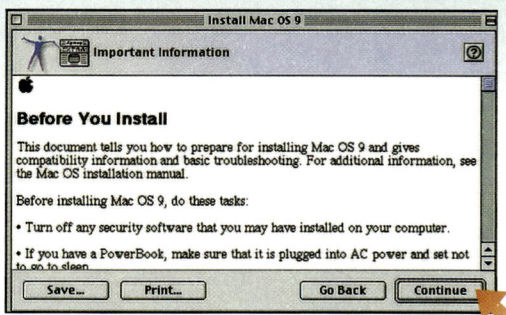

Click

## 7 Start Your System Installation

Click **Start**. When the installer's done, click the **Quit** button.

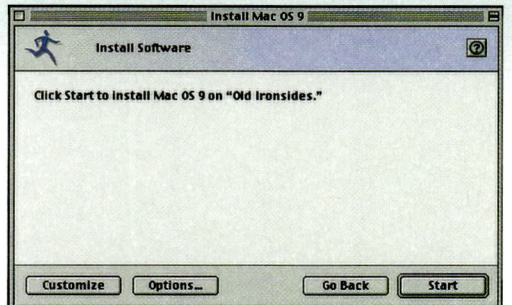

*End*

---

## How-To Hints

### Watch for the Add/Remove Prompt

If you're simply reinstalling the same system version on your Mac, you'll see an option to **Reinstall** or **Add/Remove** at the start of the process. Reinstall means what it says, that the entire system installation will be done again. Add/Remove lets you add custom components to your installation (just follow the "i" icons on the setup screens to see what the components do).

How to Install the Mac Operating System    **195**

## Task 2

# How to Do a Clean System Install

The normal system installation process simply updates the system software you have. If you're reinstalling, you'll end up with the same version you already had. If you're upgrading to a new version, it will replace the existing Apple system components in your System Folder.

A clean installation, however, will create a brand new System Folder. It's worth a try if you are experiencing system crashes with your existing version, and want to eliminate the possibility of a problem hurting your system upgrade.

## Begin

### 1 Start with Your System CD

Place your **Mac OS CD** in your Mac's **CD drive** and wait until the CD's icon appears on your Mac's desktop.

### 2 Restart

Choose **Restart** from the **Special** menu.

### 3 Hold Down the "C" Key

As soon as you hear your Mac's startup chord, hold down the **"C"** key. This will ensure that your Mac starts from the CD and not from your hard drive. (If you have one of the newest Macs, the iBook, second-generation iMac or Power Mac G4, hold down the **Option** key instead, and, when you see a CD icon on the screen, click the icon, then the right arrow to continue.)

## 4 Begin the Install

Look at your CD's directory, locate the icon labeled **Mac OS Install** and double-click on it. This will bring up the **Welcome** screen. Click the **Options** button and on the checkbox to **Perform Clean Installation;** then click **Continue**.

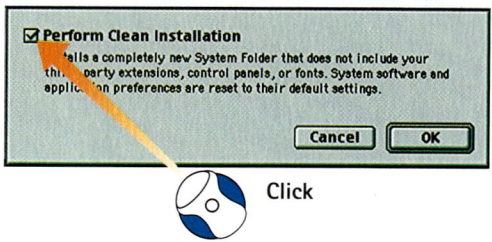

Click

## 5 Choose Your Destination

Your startup drive is automatically selected for installation. If you want another location, click on the **pop-up** menu and pick another disk. Then click **Select**.

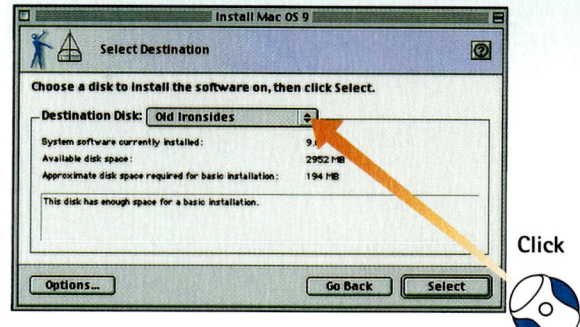

Click

## 6 Read the ReadMe and License

Read the **Important Information** screen; then **Continue** to the software license agreement.

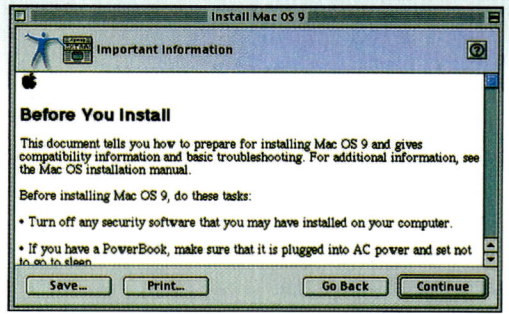

## 7 Start Your System Installation

Click **Start**. When the install is done, click the **Quit** button. Go to the next task to merge the original and new System Folders.

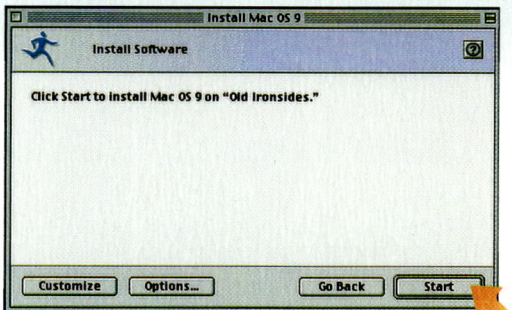

Click

*End*

## How-To Hints

### You Have Two System Folders

When you do a clean system installation, nothing is changed with the original System Folder. Instead it's renamed "Previous System Folder" and made inactive (the term is "deblessed"). Even if things are working just fine, you'll need to move parts of your Previous System Folder to your new one to continue to use some of your programs and to be able to access the Internet without having to reconfigure everything.

## Task 3

# How to Merge System Folders

All right, you have reinstalled your system software, but you've performed a clean installation to rid yourself of problems with your original System Folder.

Now, you have a second System Folder, which your Mac starts from. But you also have the original, previous System Folder. You could trash this one right away, but instead I recommend you look over the contents and merge it with your new System Folder. This will ensure that your non-Apple programs work properly, and you'll be able to access the Internet without having to redo all of your settings.

# Begin

## 1 Find the Folders

Look on your hard disk for the new System Folder and the old System Folder (renamed Previous System Folder). Double click on each to display what's inside. You will be transferring files in the Previous System Folder that are not in the new System Folder to the new folder. You will need to be very careful not to go in the wrong direction.

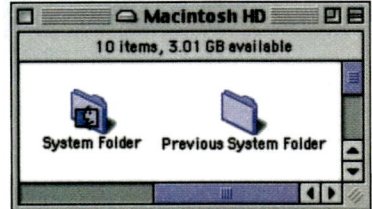

## 2 Put Them Side by Side

Place the two System folders side by side, the old on the left, the new on the right. Use whatever view (icon or list) that suits you best. Here we will be using the as icons view.

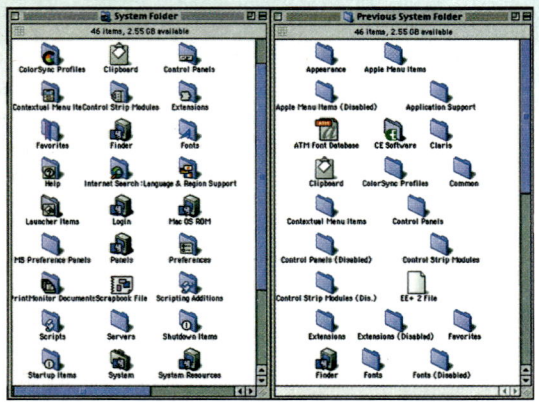

## 3 Compare the Control Panels Folder

Examine the **Control Panels** folder in the previous **System Folder**, and look for the files not duplicated in the **Control Panels** folder in the **new System Folder**. Select these files only. Then hold down the **Option** key and drag them to the **new Control Panels** folder.

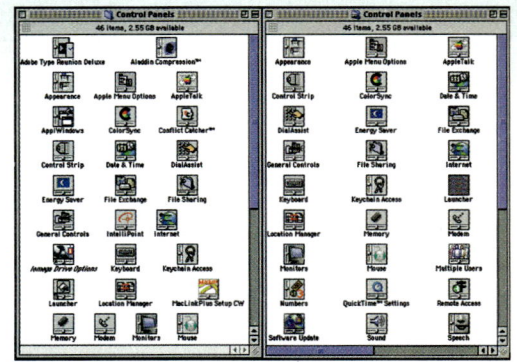

198   PART 14: WORKING WITH THE SYSTEM

## 4 Compare the Extensions Folder

Look at the **Extensions** folder in the **previous System Folder**, and compare it to the contents of the **Extensions** folder in the **new System Folder**. Select these files only. Then hold down the **Option** key and drag them to the new **Extensions** folder.

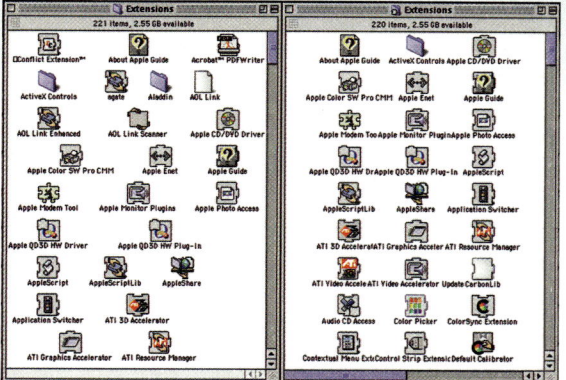

## 5 Compare the Preferences Folder

Use the same process explained in the previous steps. Compare the Preferences folder in the Previous System folder with the one in the new System Folder. Select those files; then hold down the **Option** key and drag those files to the **new Preferences** folder. (If you have had problems with a particular program, such as frequent crashes, you may want to avoid bringing over its Preference files.)

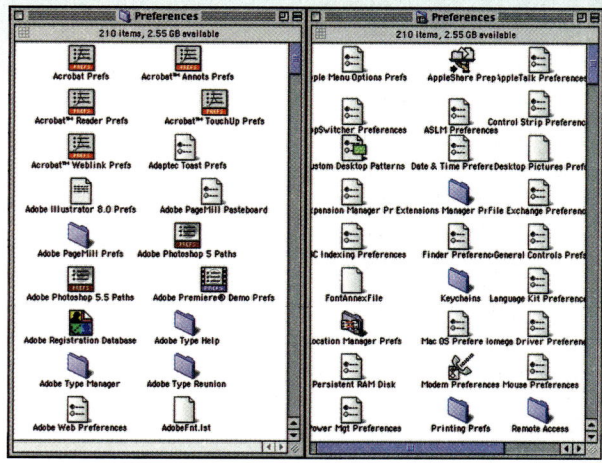

## 6 Transfer Internet Settings

Now look at files in your **old Preferences** folder and select ones that are marked with such labels as America Online, Eudora, Fetch, Explorer, and Netscape. Hold down the **Option** key and drag those files to your **new Preferences** folder. Also remove and replace the **Remote Access** folder, to make sure that your Internet connection setup is also included.

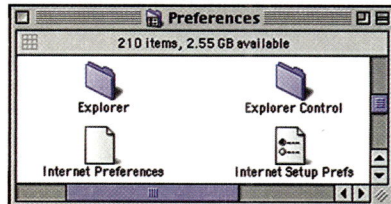

*Continues*

## How to Merge System Folders Continued

### 7 Check and Compare Other Folders

Following the above steps, go ahead and compare the contents of such folders as Apple Menu Options, Contextual Menu Items, Control Strip Modules, Fonts, and Startup Items. **Option+drag** the necessary files.

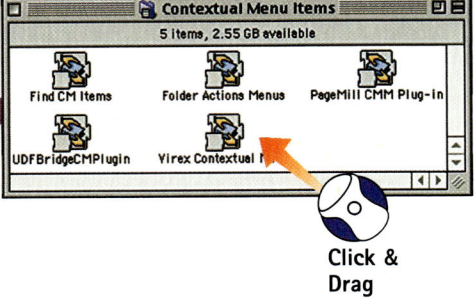

Click & Drag

### 8 Restart Your Mac

Recheck the files you've transferred, in case you forgot something. Then **restart**, after which you'll want to make sure that everything is running properly. Should you run into performance problems, you may want to recheck the non-Apple files in your System Folder and see if they need to be updated. If performance is what you expect, you may go ahead and trash the previous System Folder.

 Click

*End*

## How-To Hints

### Don't Replace Files
If you see a message notifying you that there are files in the new location with the same name as the old ones, don't copy them. You may be replacing something you need to keep. The only exception would be your Internet software, which you need to replace to restore your proper settings.

### Holding Down Option Key Preserves Previous System Folder
When you hold down the Option key when you drag a file to another location on your drive, the file is copied, not moved. By doing that, you won't be changing anything in your previous System Folder. This way you'll have an intact System Folder in the event of trouble.

### Yes, You Can Go Back!
The reason I asked you to preserve the previous System Folder is to have a fallback in the event the new system installation isn't successful, and your Mac continues to misbehave. If you have to go back, simply rename the new System Folder **"Replaced System Folder,"** and remove the System or Finder files. Then rename the previous System Folder to **"System Folder,"** open and close it (to reactivate it), and restart. You'll be back where you started.

### Give Your Hard Disk An Attic
If you're nervous about throwing away that old system folder, suspecting that it might just contain something you'll need later, you need not do so. Instead, create a folder that functions much like your attic at home. Toss all sorts of things into it, things that you don't think you'll ever need but can't quite bear to trash. Later, if you find your hard disk is getting crowded, this junk folder can be the first place to clear out some extra space.

## Task 4

# How to Do a System Update

From time to time, Apple releases a system update. This is not a full system upgrade, but a set of files designed to fix problems and improve performance with your existing system software.

When you get an update like this, it'll only work on the version of the Mac OS that it updates. So, for example, the Mac OS 8.6 update is designed to work with Mac OS 8.5 or 8.5.1. The Mac OS 8.1 update works with 8.0.

Such updates are not meant to give you a no-cost upgrade path from an older version.

## Begin

### 1 Get Your Update

Apple makes system updates available at their Web sites, and you may also get them on a CD, in case you don't have Internet access (or the time it takes to download is too long). If you are using Mac OS 9, there's also a Control Panel called Software Update that you can use to connect to the Internet and check for new program updates direct from Apple. Just click **Update Now** to start the checking process (sorry, it doesn't work for older Mac OS versions).

### 2 Double-Click the Update File

System updates from Apple come in the form of a **Disk Image** file. This is a file that is an exact match of an original on a floppy disk. To use it, double-click the file, which will create a disk icon on your drive that contains the installation software.

### 3 Locate the Installer icon

Locate and double-click on the **disk icon** created by the previous step. Locate the **installer icon** and double-click on it.

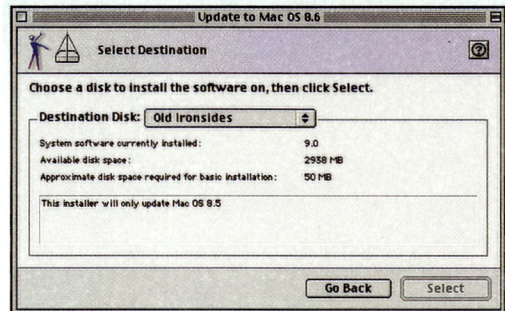

202   PART 14: WORKING WITH THE SYSTEM

## 4 Select Destination

By default, the update installer will select your startup drive for the update. If you want to choose another location, click on the **pop-up** menu next to the **Destination Disk** icon and select another disk (it must contain the system version you want to update).

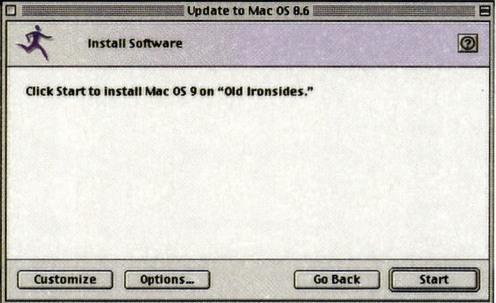

## 5 Check the ReadMe

Look at the **ReadMe** or **Important Information** screen and check Apple's instructions about the installation process. They may list potential problems with software you have or suggest special steps to follow when you do your system update.

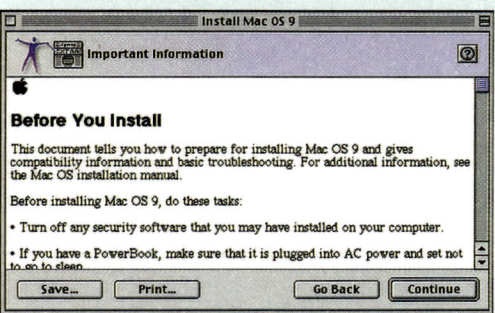

## 6 Continue to Start screen

Agree to the software license, and you'll be taken to the main installation screen. Click the **Start** button to begin the process. When it's done, you'll just have to click a **Restart** button to make your Mac restart with the updated system version.

*End*

## How-To Hints

### Turn Off Virus Software

Virus detection software examines system changes carefully and may interfere with a software update. You'll want to disable such software before you perform one of these installations. One virus program, Norton Anti-Virus, will put up a prompt giving you the chance to temporarily disable it at the start of a software installation.

### Check the System Version

After you do a system update, choose **About This Computer** from the **Apple** menu and verify that the new system version is active. If you still see the old version displayed there, check your Mac's startup drive (or another drive) to see if there's another System Folder that may have been updated instead. If the System Folder on another drive was updated by mistake, you can do the system update again, this time making sure the right drive is selected.

How to Do a System Update 203

# Task

1. How to Deal with System Crashes  206
2. How to Use the Extensions Manager  208
3. How to Find Extension Conflicts  210
4. How to Deal with Memory Problems  212
5. How to Rebuild the Desktop  214
6. How to Free Space on a Hard Drive  216
7. How to Cope with a Hard Drive Crash  218
8. How to Use Virus Software  220

# PART 15

# Solving Problems

It may be in a day, a week, or a month. But it is inevitable with any personal computing system that things will eventually go wrong.

With your Mac, it may be a freeze while you're working in a program, or a program may up and quit with a strange message, such as a Type 1 or Type 2 error.

One day, all those fancy, colorful icons on your desktop may become all white, looking like plain old documents. And when you try to launch an application by double-clicking on a document, you may get a message that you don't have the application. Yet you know you do.

You will also run into problems using your hard drive, because it's filled or because you get error messages when you try to copy files.

I'll cover the often-complicated process of troubleshooting your Mac with simple step-by-step information that'll get you past most problems.

TASK 1

# How to Deal with System Crashes

You are typing away on a brand new document, or just surfing the World Wide Web. Suddenly your Mac stops working. You click the mouse, touch a key, nothing happens. What to do?

## Begin

### 1 Force Quit!

Press the **Command+Option+Esc** keys, all at the same time.

### 2 Accept the Force Quit

Under most circumstances, you'll see a screen message asking if you want to **Force Quit**. You will have regained at least a little control over your computer. Click this **button**.

Force "Norton FileSaver Extension" to quit? Clicking Force Quit causes you to lose any unsaved changes. To avoid further problems, restart your computer after you click Force Quit.

### 3 Restart Your Mac

With luck you'll be returned to your Finder's desktop. Click on the **Special Menu** and choose **Restart**.

## 4 Force Quit Fails?

Life can be difficult. A Force Quit doesn't always work and sometimes you'll find yourself still staring at your document and a frozen cursor. Give Steps 1 to 3 yet another try before moving on.

## 5 Force a Restart (Older Macs)

If you have an older Mac with an ADB keyboard, hold down the **Command+Control+Power On** keys at the same time to force your Mac to restart.

## 6 Force a Restart (New Macs)

New Macs with USB input devices don't recognize those keystrokes. For these models, locate a little **push button** with a triangle above it (it's on the connection panel at the right side of an iMac, for example). You may have to use a straightened paper clip to get at the switch. Press the **button** to restart.

*End*

## How-To Hints

### Doesn't Work

If your Mac continues to freeze up on a regular basis, you'll want to check the rest of this section of the book for additional troubleshooting hints.

### Be Careful about Installing Older Software

Older programs may not necessarily be compatible with the newest Apple computers or Mac OS 9. It's a good idea for you to check with the publisher to make sure that there are no problems in using the program before you install it.

## TASK 2

# How to Use the Extensions Manager

Apple has a control panel that you can use to control which system software components run when you start your Mac. It can also be used to help you diagnose a problem.

## Begin

### 1 Launch Extension Manager

Click on the **Apple** menu, choose **Control Panels**, and then select **Extensions Manager** from the sub-menu.

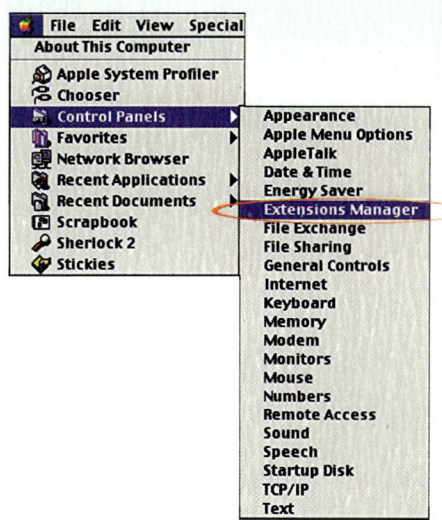

### 2 Look at the Setup

You can store your startup lineup in a **Selected Set**, which is a collection of System Folder items that work at startup.

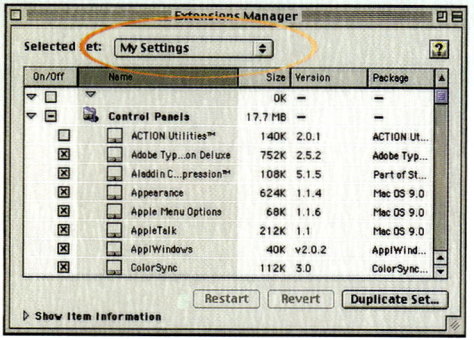

### 3 Disable an Extension

If you want to turn off a system extension, click on the **checkbox** at the left of its name to remove the check and turn it off.

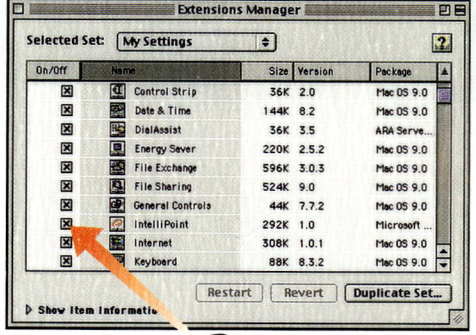

Click

208 PART 15: SOLVING PROBLEMS

## 4 Activate an Extension

To activate an extension, click the **checkbox** at the left of its name to turn it on. Click the close box to exit the **Extension Manager**.

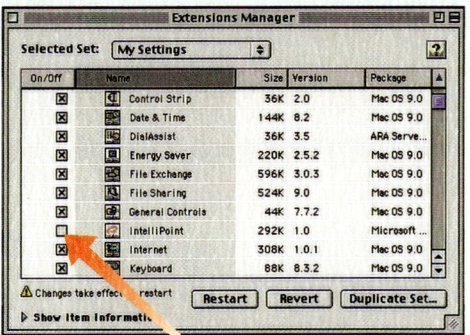

Click

## 5 Restart

For the changes to take effect, you must choose **Restart** from the **Special** menu. After you restart, your Mac will only use the extensions you've activated.

Click

## 6 Change it Back

If you want to reactivate an extension you've disabled, feel free to open **Extensions Manager** again and check the item; then **Restart** to make it run.

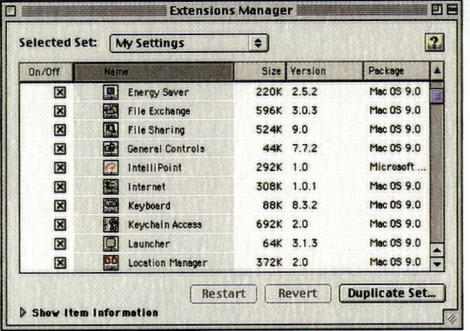

*End*

## How-To Hints

### Be Careful What You Disable!
Some system extensions are necessary for certain programs to run. The best thing to do is only turn off items to test to see if they stop your Mac from crashing (see the next task).

### Create Custom Sets
You can easily create a new set with **Extensions Manager** simply by clicking on the **File** menu and selecting **New Set**. Once you give the set a name, you can turn the items on or off as needed.

TASK 3

# How to Find Extension Conflicts

Extensions Manager is a valuable tool to help isolate the cause of constant system crashes on your Mac. Here's how it's done.

## Begin

### 1 Launch Extension Manager

Click on the **Apple** menu, choose **Control Panels**, and then select **Extensions Manager** from the sub-menu.

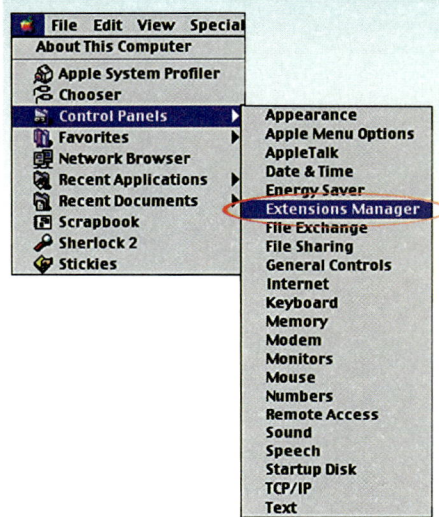

### 2 Change Setups for Diagnosis

If you have repeated freezes, you can use **Extensions Manager** to help you diagnose the problem. First, look at your sets.

### 3 Change to a Base Setting

Select **Mac OS 9 Base** (or whatever system version you're using). This set is the minimum for running OS 9, and should give you no conflict problems.

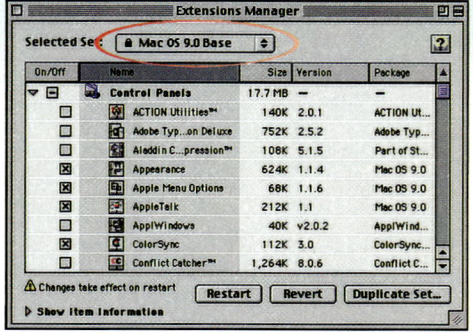

210   PART 15: SOLVING PROBLEMS

## 4 Click Restart

After the setting is changed, click the close box to exit the Extension Manager. Then choose **Restart** in the **Special** menu to start with the selected set.

Click

## 5 Test Performance

Try repeating whatever it was you were doing when your Mac froze or an application quit.

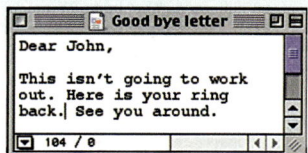

## 6 Continue the Test

If everything works, go back to the **Extensions Manager FIle** and choose **New Set**. Make a set called **Diagnostic Set** and turn on half the extensions you disabled. Then **restart**.

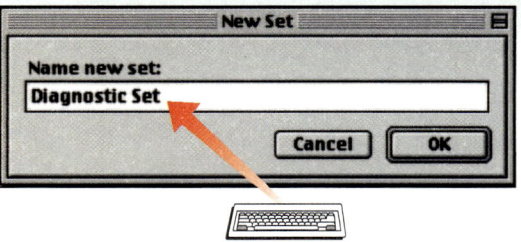

## 7 Try Again

Test again. If everything works, return to the Extension Manager and turn on the other half of the exstensions and test yet again. If your Mac froze, return to the Extension Manager and turn on only half of the first set. Keep narrowing those you turn on until you find the culprit.

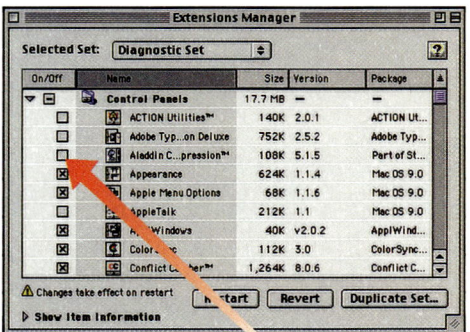

Click

*End*

---

## How-To Hints

### Be Careful with Microsoft and AOL Extensions

The system extensions used with Microsoft's software are required for their programs and also for AOL to run. If you try to run them without activating those extensions, they may refuse to launch. For Microsoft's newest software, simply reinstall all the Microsoft extensions you turned off.

### Remember to Switch Back

After you've finished diagnosing your problem, restore all your system extensions except the one that caused your crash; then restart. Contact the company who made the software for help.

## Task 4

# How to Deal with Memory Problems

When you run a Mac application, it takes a portion of the memory you have on your Mac for itself. While most applications are designed to work just fine with the normal amount of memory assigned to them, some work faster if you give them more memory.

## *Begin*

### *1* Select the Application's Icon

To change the memory setting, first make sure that you've **quit** the application. Then click **once** on it's icon to select it (not double-click, which launches it).

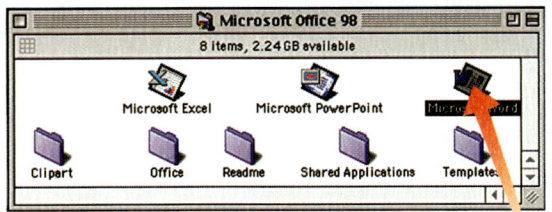

Click

### *2* Choose Get Info

Go to the Finder's **File** menu, and choose **Get Info** and **Memory**.

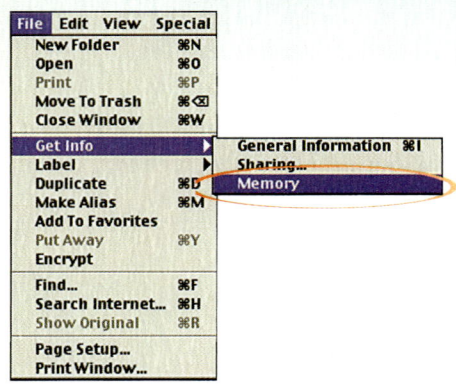

### *3* Enter the Preferred Setting

Click on the **Preferred** text box and enter a new figure, which is at least **500K** to **1000K** above the setting already there.

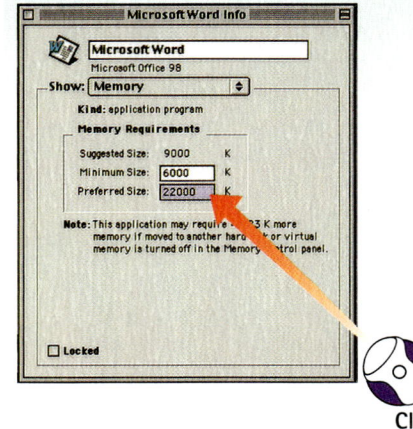
Click

## 4 Store the Setting

Press **Return**, **Enter**, or **tab**; then click the **close** box on the **Get Info** window.

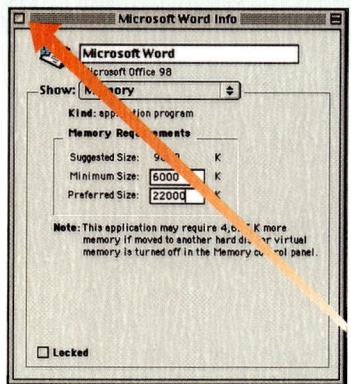

Click

## 5 Launch the Application

Double-click on the applications icon to launch it and test performance. If it still doesn't seem to perform the way you like, **quit** the application and try giving it a greater allocation of memory.

Double-click

*End*

## How-To Hints

### You Can't Give It Too Much Memory

Your Mac cannot run a program if the amount of memory it needs exceeds what you have available. You must also make sure that the amount of system memory plus what you give to the program isn't too much. To check how much memory is available, quit all your open programs, go to the **Apple Menu**, and choose **About This Computer**. The **Largest Unused Block** will show you how much memory is available for another program to use.

### Consider More RAM for Your Mac

Some Macs come with just enough memory to run a few simple programs. If you find that you don't have enough to run the programs you like, contact your dealer and ask about buying extra memory. Some Macs are easy to upgrade. Others are hard. You'll want to ask your dealer what steps to take for memory upgrades.

## TASK 5

# How to Rebuild the Desktop

The ability to launch a program when you double-click on a document and the capability to display colorful icons is due to what are called desktop files. They are used by the Mac OS Finder to keep track of this information. If either one of the files gets damaged, you may not be able to launch a program when you click on a document, or the colorful icons may become white and indistinct. Should this happen, you'll want to rebuild the desktop.

## *Begin*

### *1* Restart Your Mac

First, choose **Restart** from the Finder's **Special** menu.

### *2* Wait for the Startup to Finish

As the startup icons are displayed at the bottom of your Mac's screen, get ready. As soon as the boot process is about to end, hold down the **Command+Option** keys. (You could, of course, just hold them down right after restarting your Mac, but might as well give your fingers a rest.)

### *3* Do You Want to Rebuild?

You'll see a message asking if you want to rebuild the desktop? **OK** this message.

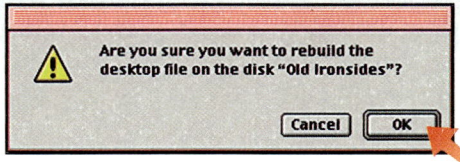

Click

214   PART 15: SOLVING PROBLEMS

## 4 Watch the Progress Bar

You'll see a progress bar indicating the status of your desktop rebuild. If you have more than one drive connected to your Mac, you'll have another desktop rebuild request to **OK** for each drive.

## 5 Check Performance

Have a look at your desktop icons or try launching your applications. If the problem is gone, fine. If not, try **rebuilding** again. Sometimes, it takes two rebuilds to fix a problem.

*End*

## How-To Hints

### Another Desktop Rebuild Technique

A free program, TechTool, from MicroMat, can be used to make a more thorough desktop rebuild. You'll find a copy on the World Wide Web at http://www.micromat.com. There's also a retail version, TechTool Pro, which comes with lots of handy system and hard drive diagnostic tools.

TASK 6

# How to Free Space on a Hard Drive

You try to copy a file on your Mac's hard drive, but you get a message that says there's no room. Or you want to install a program that uses more available space than what you have. Is there a way to solve the problem? Indeed there is.

*Begin*

## *1* Check the Space

The first thing you'll want to do is check how much space is available on your drive. To do that, open your hard drive's directory by double-clicking on its **icon**.

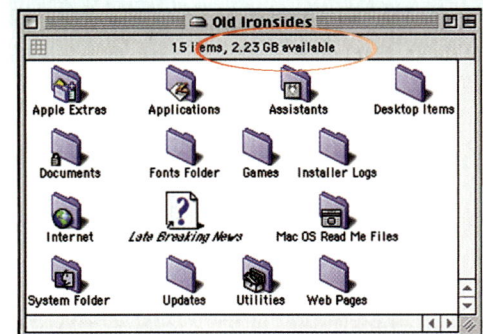

## *2* Check What You Need

When you install a new program, consult its **ReadMe** file to see if it mentions how much space is required to install the program.

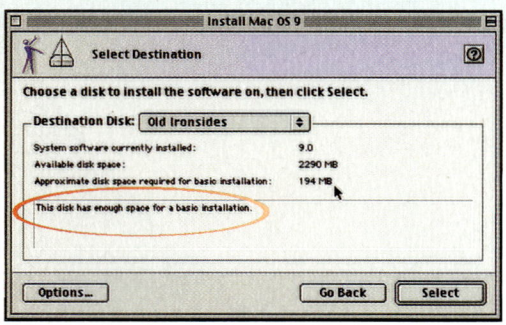

## *3* Backup and Remove Documents

The first way to get more disk space is to store documents you don't need elsewhere. You can do that by copying them to another **hard drive** or to a **Zip** or **SuperDisk** drive.

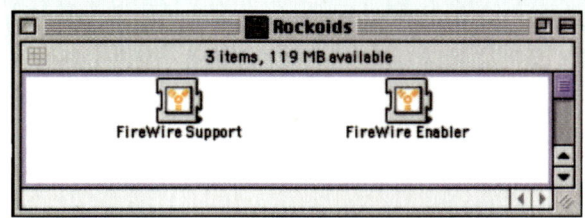

216  PART 15: SOLVING PROBLEMS

## 4 Delete Unneeded Files

If there are files you don't need, or they've been copied to another drive, drag them to the trash and empty the trash. But be careful about things in the System Folder or application folders. You may end up removing files you need.

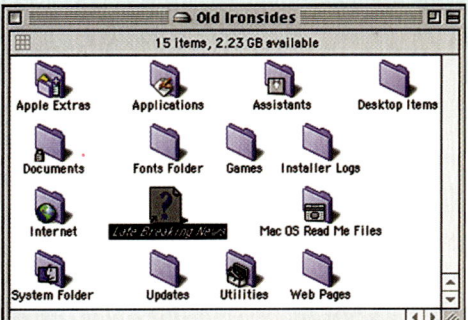

## 5 Check Available Space

Now look at your hard drive's directory again to see how much space is available. If you still need more, go ahead and **delete** more files (but watch out for stuff you may need later).

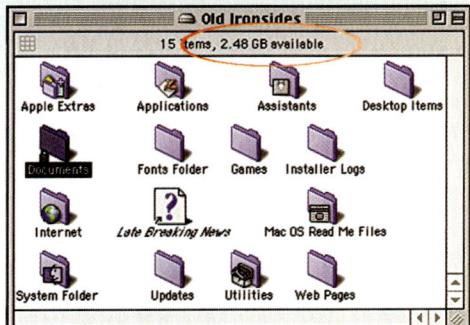

*End*

## How-To Hints

### Delete a File by Mistake?

In the rush to remove files, you may accidentally trash something you truly need. The best solution here is to reinstall a program. If it's a valuable document file, you may be stuck. First thing, don't copy any more files to your drive. Then try installing MicroMat's TechTool Pro or Symantec's Norton Utilities. Both programs have the capability to recover some deleted documents. But they work best when you install them before you need to recover the files.

### Still Need More Space?

If all that work you've done to remove files doesn't give you enough space, consider getting another hard drive. Some Macs let you install more than one drive inside. Others require you to hook up an external drive. Depending on the kind of Mac you have, you may be able to get a SCSI hard drive, a USB hard drive, or a FireWire hard drive. There are also removable drives, such as SuperDisk drives, Zip drives, and CD writers. These are convenient ways to store extra files.

HOW TO FREE SPACE ON A HARD DRIVE

## Task 7

# How to Cope with a Hard Drive Crash

Hard drives are mechanical devices. They work constantly, every second your Mac is on. Sometimes, they fail, and when you start your Mac, the Happy Mac icon is just a question mark. Or perhaps you copy files and get disk error messages. Here are solutions to these problems.

## Begin

### 1 Use Your System CD

If you cannot access your Mac's hard drive, get your **Mac OS System CD** and insert it in your Mac's CD drive.

### 2 Restart Your Mac

If your Mac is hunting for a startup drive, use the forced restart sequence mentioned in Task One.

### 3 Start from the CD

For older Macs, hold down the **"C"** key at startup to boot your Mac from the CD. For the iBook, Power Macintosh G4, and latest versions of the iMac, hold down the **Option** key instead, select the **CD drive icon** on the next screen and click the **right arrow**.

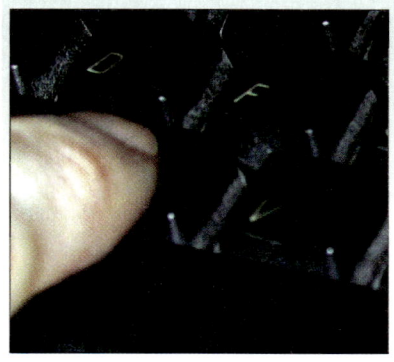

218  PART 15: SOLVING PROBLEMS

## 4 Locate Disk First Aid

After your Mac has started from the System CD, go to the **Utilities** folder on the CD, locate **Disk First Aid**, and double-click to launch it.

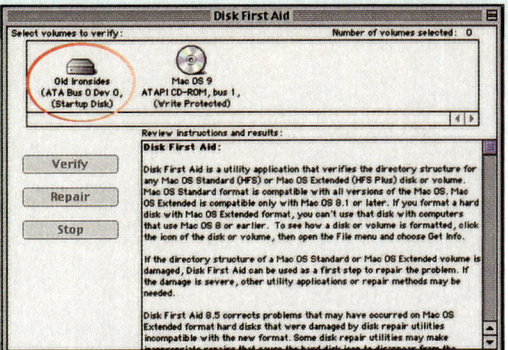

## 5 Select Your Drive

Click on the icons representing your Mac's hard drive and any other hard drives connected to your Mac.

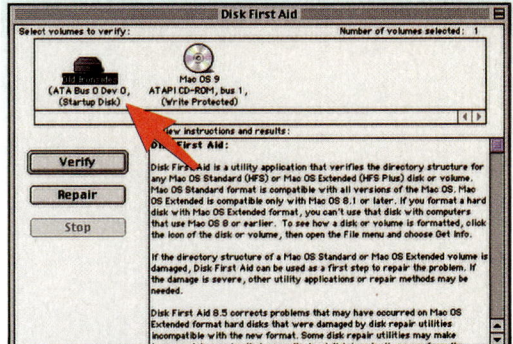

## 6 Repair the Drive

Click the **Repair** button to start the diagnostic/repair process.

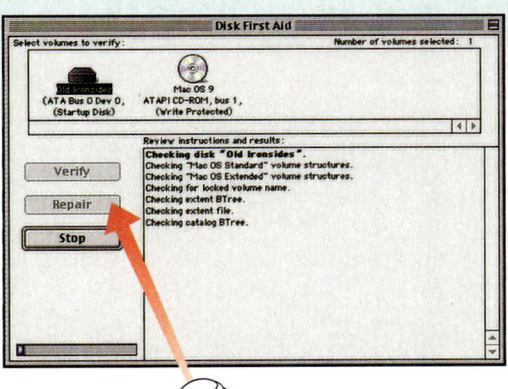

 Click

## 7 Repeat the Process

Whether or not Disk First Aid can fix the hard drive problem, run it again. That's because some hard drive directory problems will mask others. If you run it twice, you have a better chance of solving the problem. Once **Disk First Aid** is done, **restart** your Mac.

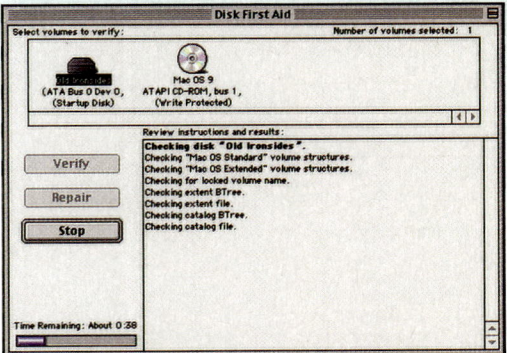

*End*

HOW TO COPE WITH A HARD DRIVE CRASH   219

TASK 8

# How to Use Virus Software

Computer viruses are present on all computing platforms. Even Mac users aren't immune. A computer virus can cause your Mac to put up a silly message. But it can also cause your Mac to crash over and over again and refuse to run. If you use files from others or download files from the Internet, the safest approach is to buy virus software.

The two major virus programs are Norton Anti-Virus from Symantec and Virex from Network Associates. Either will do the job and provide a good level of protection.

*Begin*

## 1 Install the Software

Virus software works best if you install it as soon as you get it. While it can fix problems that occur later on, those problems could cause damage to some of your files.

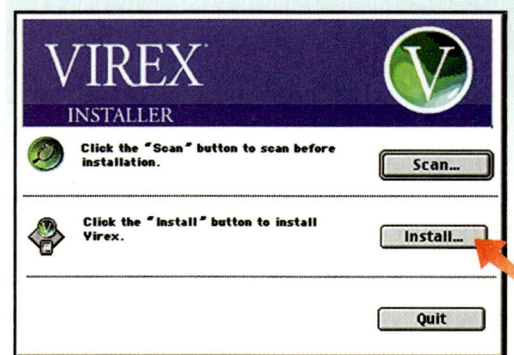

Click

## 2 Set It to Scan Removable Disks

Either **Norton Anti-Virus** or **Virex** can be set to scan removable disks you insert in a drive. Such disks may contain virus infections.

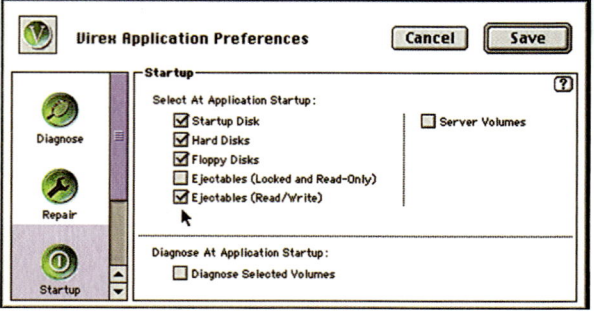

## 3 Schedule Automatic Scans

These virus programs have the option to run a full-scale scan of your Mac's drive (or any drives attached to it) at regular intervals.

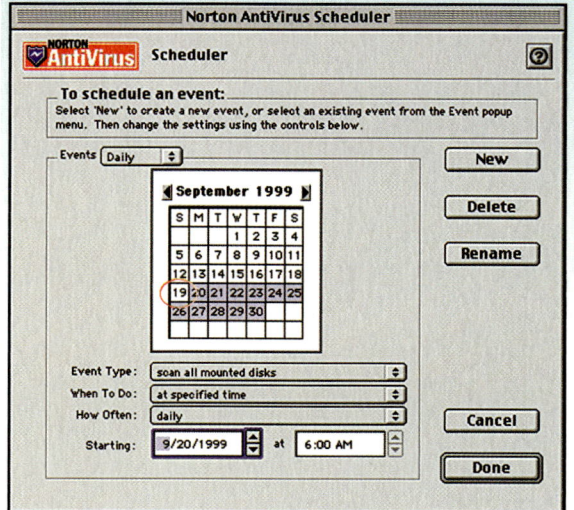

220  PART 15: SOLVING PROBLEMS

## 4 Update Regularly

Each month new virus infections are discovered. Both Norton Anti-Virus and Virex have an automatic updating feature, which checks the publisher's Internet site for new versions and downloads them to you when you want or on a schedule.

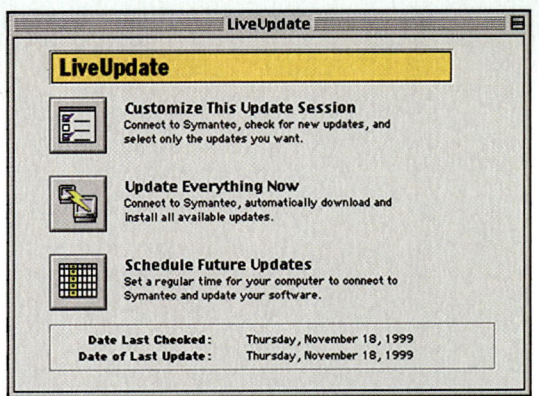

## 5 Check All Your Disks

You shouldn't assume that because your hard drive is free of virus infections that another disk is also. When you buy virus software, you should check all your disks, floppies, and removable media included, to make sure they are clean as well. Even CD-ROMs can contract a virus.

*End*

## How-To Hints

### Can't Fix It?

Disk First Aid isn't perfect by any means and sometimes it won't be able to fix the problem. Should this happen, consider trying one of the commercial hard drive repair programs. These include Alsoft's DiskWarrior, MicroMat's TechTool Pro, or Symantec's Norton Utilities. Even if the drive works all right, you should seriously consider running one of these programs. If they don't fix the damage, you should consider backing up all your files and using the Drive Setup software on your Mac's System CD to initialize the drive. This wipes the drive clean, and usually fixes all problems (but it also deletes all your files).

### Drive Still Can't Be Used

If you have initialized your drive and it still won't run, call Apple or the maker of the drive. It's possible the drive mechanism has failed. Even though hard drives are said to last for hundreds of thousands of hours, this doesn't mean that any single unit won't fail before then. Apple guarantees its products for one year (unless you buy an AppleCare extended warranty). If you bought a separate drive, check with the dealer or manufacturer about warranty policies.

### Got a Virus Infection?

If your virus software reports a possible infection, let it fix the problem. If a file is infected, you'll want to replace it. Most virus infections can be easily eradicated from your Mac's drive simply by letting the programs do their stuff. By keeping the programs active, you can avoid re-infection.

HOW TO USE VIRUS SOFTWARE

# Glossary

## A

**active window**  The frontmost window and the one you are working in. It is indicated by the presence of a gray title bar with black letters. An inactive window will have a light gray title bar with gray letters.

**alias**  A small file that points or links to the original file and can open the original in just the same way as the original itself. An alias file is a convenient way to access a frequently used item that is buried several folders deep.

**America Online (AOL)**  The world's largest online service, which provides Internet access, email, forums, chats, instant messaging, and other online features.

**AppleScript**  Apple's scripting language, which lets you automate routine tasks, such as making an alias of a file and placing it in the Apple menu.

**application**  Also referred to as a program, this is the software that actually lets you perform a given set of functions on your Mac, such as word processing, drawing, or accessing the Internet.

**application menu**  The application menu is accessed by clicking on a program's icon or name at the right side of the menu bar.

**application window**  When you open and work on a document, it opens in this window to display the contents of the document.

**attachment**  An item that is connected to an email message. An attachment may consist of any sort of file, such as a document, a picture, or a program. Typically, attachments are compressed (made smaller) in order to reduce file size and the time it takes to send and receive the file.

## B

**backup**  Making a duplicate of your files for safekeeping or replacement, in case the original is lost or damaged.

**blind carbon copy**  When you send a copy of an email message to a recipient without the recipient or others being aware of whom it went to.

**Bookmarks**  In Netscape, it's a feature that lets you store a list of the Web sites you want to revisit, so they can be easily accessed. *See also* Favorites.

**boot**  The process of starting your Mac. During this process, your Mac does a quick hardware check and then loads all the startup programs (extensions) that you have installed on your computer. Finally, the Mac's distinctive desktop pattern appears.

**bps**  Short for bits per second. A measurement of the speed with which computer data is transferred.

**browser**  *See* Web browser.

**Byte**  The term for a single character of computer data, made up of eight bits.

# C

**cache**  A cache is a storage space where frequently used information is stored for quicker access. A cache may be located on your Mac's CPU or logic board or on your hard drive. Web browsers use a cache, consisting of data previously downloaded from the Web, to speed up performance.

**carbon copy**  The process of sending a copy of an email message to one or more additional recipients. Recipients know who gets a carbon copy.

**CD-ROM drive**  Based on Compact Disc technology, a CD-ROM drive is used to read both audio and data CDs. Two variations of CD-ROM technology, CD-R and CD-RW, are used to record data.

**channel**  The name for a content area on the World Wide Web or on an online service, as typified by AOL. Such a content area contains information devoted to a specific topic, such as computers, entertainment, and news.

**check box**  A small square box in a dialog box where you can turn a function on or off.

**click**  The process of pressing and releasing the mouse switch quickly to activate a function on your Mac.

**clipboard**  A temporary holding area in your Mac's built-in memory into which items copied or cut are placed. The Mac provides a single clipboard, although some programs may provide additional clipboards.

**collapse box**  When you click on a window's collapse box, it reduces the size to just the title bar (it's an option in the Appearance Control Panel). A similar function is also available for earlier versions of the Mac operating system via a Control Panel called WindowShade.

**commands**  When you click on a menu on your Mac, you see a list of choices you can make to make your Mac perform specific functions, such as saving or printing a document. Those choices are commands.

**compression**  The act of making a file smaller, using a computer algorithm, so they take less space on a drive or transfer more quickly on the Internet. Some compression programs  make a file smaller without removing data; others remove so-called non-essential data, so the file is impacted as little as possible. The common Mac compression program, StuffIt, reduces the file's size without losing any data.

**contextual menu**  A pop-up menu displayed when you control-click an item. It displays commands related to the item on which you clicked.

# D

**dialog box**  This is a window in which you must enter information or make a selection to perform a particular function.

**desktop**  This is the decorative backdrop pattern you see on your Mac. The desktop may contain icons for disks, programs, folders, and alias files pointing to other items.

**digital camera**  Functionally similar to a regular camera, but instead of recording images on film, the images are recorded as files onto a storage medium, such as a disk or FlashCard. You can then transfer (or download) the files to your Mac so you can edit or print the pictures.

**directory**  See folder.

**double-click**  The act of quickly pressing the mouse button twice to activate a function on your Mac, such as opening a disk, folder, file, or program.

**double-click speed**  A setting in the Mouse or Trackpad Control Panel that controls how quickly you must double-click the mouse button to activate the function.

**download**  The act of receiving a file on your Mac's drive from another computer or over a network.

**drag**  After you click down on a selected item, the process of moving it to another location while holding down the mouse button.

**drag and drop**  After you drag an item to another location, you release the mouse button, which, in effect, drops the item in the new location or on to an application that will open it.

**driver**  A program that communicates with an accessory or peripheral device on your Mac so it can be used. Drivers are used for such items as printers, scanners, digital cameras, and removable drives, such as a Zip or SuperDisk.

**DVD drive**  DVD is short for Digital Versatile Disc. It's a medium, based on CD technology, used to store videos and large amounts of data. DVDs can store up to 15GB of files. A variation of the DVD, the DVD-RAM, uses a special type of disc that can store up to 5.2GB of files.

## E

**email**  The popular abbreviation for electronic mail, it's the preeminent way of communicating on the Internet. It's the act of sending and receiving messages (and sometimes files, called "attachments") via the Internet or a local computer network.

**email address**  The place you send your email to. An email address consists of a user name and a location where the computer network is located. For example, an AOL member's email address would consist of the user name (or screen name in AOL parlance) and aol.com (for example, gene@aol.com). On AOL, the location need not be specified, but on most other services, it does.

**Erase Disk**  A function in the Finder's Special menu that deletes the contents of a selected disk and prepares it to receive new files.

**Ethernet**  A popular, high-speed networking standard used to transfer data.

## F

**Favorites**  In Internet Explorer, the capability to create a list of the Web sites you want to revisit, so you can easily return to them. *See also* Bookmarks.

**file**  A single item containing computer data. It may consist of a word processing document, a program, or another piece of computer data.

**file sharing**  The ability to share files with other users on a network with your Mac. For Mac OS 9 and later versions, you can also share files over the Internet using the same technique.

**file system**  The technique by which files are stored. On the Mac, there are two methods currently in use. One is HFS, or Hierarchical File System, or Mac OS Standard. The other is HFS+, also known as Mac OS Extended. HFS+ is more efficient, by making the minimum file size much smaller on larger hard drives, so you can store more files.

**floppy disk**  The original storage medium used for the Mac and other personal computers. It consists of a small, flexible disk that can store up to 1.4MB of data. A floppy-disk variant, SuperDisk, stores up to 120MB.

**Finder**  The Mac application that controls your desktop processes. These include a desktop pattern or picture, opening and closing files, and moving and copying files. The Finder runs from the moment the startup process completes until you shut your Mac down.

**folder**  Sometimes called a directory, it is a container on your Mac's drive that can hold files or other folders.

**formatting**  1) The act of adjusting the properties of text, such as picking the font, size, style, color, and other characteristics. 2) The act of removing all data from a disk and preparing it for use to receive new data.

**fragmented**  Computer files are written in separate pieces on your Mac's drive. When the parts of many files are spread throughout the disk, it is considered to be fragmented, which may, potentially, reduce performance someone. You can use an optimizing program, such as Alsoft's PlusOptimizer, MicroMat's TechTool Pro, or Symantec's Norton Utilities, to rewrite the files to deliver slightly better performance.

## G

**gigabyte**  A total of 1024 megabytes, also referred to as a GB, or gig. The hard drives that come with Macs nowadays have capacities that are in the multi-gigabyte range.

**grow box**  A little area at the lower right of a document or Finder window used to make the window larger or smaller, by clicking and dragging.

## H

**hard disk**  The regular fixed storage medium on your Mac. It consists of a small, sealed device that contains several rapidly spinning platters that are used to carry your data.

**history**  In your Web browser, it is a list of the sites you have visited most recently (up to the capacity of the browser). It's similar to BookMarks, or Favorites, which are lists of sites you make to easily return to a site, without regard to how recent the last visit was.

**home page**  The introductory page of a Web site. A home page typically contains information about the site, a set of direct links to other pages at the site, or links to other sites with related information. You can set a default home page with your Web browser, so that you always access the site whenever you launch the browser or click the Home button.

**HTML**  Short for Hypertext Markup Language. This is the programming language of the World Wide Web, a set of text-based commands that tell your browser how to display a Web page.

**hub**  A device that provides a central connection point for an Ethernet network, or for extending a peripheral bus, such as USB and FireWire.

**hyperlink**  This is a link (underlined and in a different color) that you can click to take you to another Web page, whether it's part of that site or another. Whenever your mouse passes over a hyperlink on a Web page, the cursor changes to a hand.

## I

**icons**  The graphic or picture used to identify an item on your Mac. An icon identifies a disk, document, folder, or program.

**insertion point**  This is the area in a text box identified by a vertical bar (usually flashing) where you enter your text.

**Internet**  A huge computer network that spans the entire world. The Internet began as a U.S. government and university project, but has since become the focal point for a huge industry consisting of Web sites, online shopping centers, service providers, and more.

**Internet service provider (ISP)**  This is a service that provides Internet access. Some services provide special online content, such as custom home pages, custom start pages, or support and information areas.

## J–K

**Java**  The programming language invented by Sun Microsystems that's used to generate programs that work on different computing platforms, such as the Mac OS, Windows, or UNIX. Web site designers use Java to generate special content, such as animation, multimedia, or moving titles.

**Kbps**  A measurement of the rate of data transfer, consisting of thousands of bits per second.

**kilobyte**  Also referred to as KB, it's a measurement of the size of computer data in 1024 byte increments.

## L

**link**  *See* hyperlink.

**list box**  A window that provides a text listing of files or folders.

**log off**  The act of signing off from a computer network, ISP, or online service.

**log on**  The act of signing on a computer network, ISP, or online service.

# M

**Macintosh HD**  When a new Mac ships from the factory, this is the name given to your hard drive. You can easily rename the disk to your taste, except when the disk is networked via file sharing.

**mailbox**  Sometimes known as the inbox. It is the place where the email you've received is located.

**maximize**  The act of making a document or file window as large as possible (filling your Mac's display).

**Mbps**  Compare to Kbps, it measures the speed of data transfer in millions of bits.

**megabyte**  A measurement of the size of computer data, consisting of 1024 kilobytes. Also identified as MB.

**menu**  This is the pop-up or pull-down listing of commands available in a program, available from a menu bar, dialog box, or a list displayed via the Mac's contextual menus feature.

**menu bar**  The Mac OS menu bar is a horizontal, shaded bar at the top of your screen that contains labels that represent a specific category of commands. Click on a label to access those commands.

**modem**  This is the device typically used to transfer computer data over telephone lines. The latest data transfer device technology, DSL (for Digital Subscribers Line), uses digital technology to speed data transfer up to 100 times that of a regular modem (which uses analog technology).

**multitask**  The act of performing more than one function on your Mac at the very same time. The Mac OS uses "cooperative multitasking," where each program decides how to cooperate with others. Compare to the technique to be used in Mac OS X (not released when this book was written), preemptive multitasking, where the operating system does the multitasking chores (in theory, giving much faster performance).

# N

**network**  Whenever you connect two or more computers together, or a computer to a printer that can be shared by more than one user, you have a network.

# O

**online service**  Compared to an Internet service provider, an online service provides not only Internet access but its own content in areas that are available only to members. AOL, CompuServe, and Prodigy are examples of online services.

# P

**password**  This is a set of letters or numbers that you must enter to access an Internet or online service, or a secured Web site or network. You can password protect your Mac, to limit access if it's networked. A good password uses a mixture of numbers and letters, so it cannot be guessed too easily.

**point**  The act of taking the mouse cursor or pointer on your Mac and putting it at a specific location on your Mac's display.

**pop-up window**  When you click on a dialog box or use the contextual menus feature, it's the act of bringing up a menu containing different commands.

**port**  The place where you connect a cable on your Mac to hook up a specific device. Macs have a number of different ports, depending on the model, for such functions as Ethernet, FireWire, your modem and printer, or USB.

**PostScript** A technology for describing documents and fonts that was created by Adobe Systems. PostScript allows a document or font to be used at the maximum resolution available on your Mac's display or in a printed document.

**preferences** This is a group of settings that you can use to customize how your Mac or a Mac program works. You can, for example, use the Mouse Control Panel to make your mouse run faster, so the cursor speeds across the screen more quickly.

**pull-down menus** The list of commands you access when you click on a menu bar.

## Q

**QuickTime** This is Apple's technology for creating and viewing multimedia content containing animation, audio, and video. All Macs (except the oldest models) come equipped with QuickTime.

## R

**radio button** A small round button in a dialog box that is used to turn a function on or off. When one button is selected, the others are deselected.

**RAM** The abbreviation for Random Access Memory, computer chips that are used to temporarily store computer data. All Macs come with RAM that is used for the Mac OS and all the programs you run.

**RAM disk** This is a setting in the Memory Control Panel that dedicates a portion of RAM for use as storage space that is like a hard drive. While it can get you much faster performance for some programs, the memory you devote to the RAM disk takes that memory away from use by your programs.

**reset switch** A little switch on your Mac (usually with or below a triangular icon) that's used to force a restart. It's intended as an emergency measure when your Mac locks up and you cannot make it run. On some Macs (such as the first generation iMac), you need a paper clip to access the reset switch.

## S

**scalable font** A font that can be displayed in any available size on your Mac. It is also known as an outline font and comes in PostScript or TrueType formats. Such Mac OS fonts as Helvetica and Times are scalable fonts.

**screen name** This is the handle or user name AOL members use to identify themselves.

**scrollbar** This is the vertical or horizontal bar in a Finder or document window used to move to a different location on the window.

**serial port** On older Macs, this is a port used to connect a modem or printer. It has since been replaced by the USB (Universal Serial Bus) port.

**SuperDisk** A special type of removable drive that can use both floppy disks with an HD label on them (high-density) and a special 120MB disk.

**surf** Internet slang for visiting the World Wide Web and checking out sites.

## T

**text box** This is the rectangular or square area on your Mac's screen in which you insert text.

**title bar** The top of a document or Finder window that identifies the item you're working on.

**toolbar** This is a set of buttons, usually with an icon of some sort, that are used to activate a program's functions. While a toolbar usually appears just below the menu bar, some programs let you break the toolbar off and move it to another location.

**TrueType** A scalable font technology that, like PostScript fonts, lets you display and print fonts in all the sizes available in your application.

**type size** The size that the characters display and print. Sizes are specified in points, based on 72 points to an inch (a measurement technique used in the printing industry).

**type style** The various ways in which a character may appear, such as regular, bold, italic, bold italic, and, in some programs, underline, shadow, or strikethrough (with a line in the middle of the character).

**typeface**   A single set of characters, numbers, and symbols that comprise a single unique style. There are thousands of typefaces available for your Mac.

## U

**upload**   The act of sending a file from your Mac to another computer or service.

**URL**   Short for Uniform Resource Locator. This is the address of a Web or FTP site on the Internet. Examples of URLs include `http://www.samspublishing.com`, and `http://www.apple.com`, Apple's popular Web site.

**USB**   The abbreviation for Universal Serial Bus. This is the peripheral standard used on all new Macs for such items as a keyboard, a mouse, a camera, a hard drive, and a scanner.

## V

**virtual memory**   A way to extend the amount of memory available for your Mac's programs by setting aside a portion of hard drive space in which to exchange or swap the data. A small amount of virtual memory (one MB above the amount of RAM your Mac has) is normal and won't hurt performance. Too much virtual memory may mean the Mac has to constantly pull data from your hard drive, which reduces performance.

**virus**   The bane of the computing experience. A virus is a program that attaches itself to a program or document and then spreads, or infects, other computers that run the program or document. A virus may put up a silly message or trash files and cause system crashes.

## W

**Web browser**   This is a program that interprets the contents of a Web page and reproduces them in your Mac's display. Your Mac comes with two highly popular Web browsers—Microsoft Internet Explorer and Netscape Navigator and Communicator.

**Web page**   A single document, containing text and perhaps pictures and animation, that is available on the World Wide Web.

**Web site**   An Internet location containing one or more Web pages that belong to an individual or business.

**window**   A container on your Mac with the contents of a directory or a document.

**World Wide Web**   The feature of the Web that combines animation, pictures, sound, and text into a graphical page that displays on your Mac's screen. You view a Web page via a program called a browser, such as Microsoft Internet Explorer.

## Z

**Zip drive**   A removable drive that uses a disk which resembles a fat floppy disk. It stores, depending on the model drive and type of disk you have, 100MB or 250MB of data.

**Zoom box**   This box is located at the left of the collapse box on a Finder or document window. It toggles the current size of the window between two sizes.

# Index

## Symbols

**56K modems,** 174-175

## A

**About This Computer command (Apple menu),** 203
**accessories, installing**
  digital cameras, 172-173
  hubs, 178-179
  keyboards, 170-171
  modems, 174-175
  pointing devices, 170-171
  scanners, 168-169
  speakers, 176-177
**Acrobat Reader,** 109
**activating extensions,** 209
**Activity Monitor,** 189
**add-ons (system add-ons), installing,** 103
**Address Book button (email software),** 89
**addresses**
  email addresses, 91
  Web page addresses, entering into browsers, 79, 84
**adjustable controls,** 31
**alert boxes,** 59
**alias icons,** 25
**aliases**
  creating, 32-33
  moving, 33
  naming, 33
  placing, 35
**Alsoft DiskWarrior,** 161
**America Online folder,** 81
**AOL (America Online), logging on with Sherlock 2,** 57

**AOL extensions,** 211
**Appearance Control Panel,** 98, 118-119
**Apple Extras folder,** 15, 40-41
**Apple menu,** 29
  About This Computer command, 203
**Apple Menu Items folder,** 35
**Apple software, updating,** 99
**Apple Web site,** 79
**AppleTalk Control Panel,** 139, 178-179, 182, 190
**AppleWorks,** 106
  documents
    *creating, 62-63*
    *editing text, 64-65*
    *exporting, 70-71*
    *importing, 70-71*
    *moving text between, 68-69*
    *resizing document windows, 69*
    *restoring, 66-67*
    *selecting text, 63*
    *typing text, 63*
    *Undo/Redo commands, 66-67*
  launching, 62
**application icons,** 25
**applications**
  assigning memory to, 112-113, 212-213
  deleting, 115
  launching, 34
  menu bar, 29
  opening, Open dialog box, 40
  preferences, setting, 110-111
  quitting, 13, 35
  running, 13
  uninstalling, 114-115

**Arrange command (View menu),** 22
**arranging icons/windows,** 22
**Assistants folder,** 11-13
**ATI Graphics Accelerator extension,** 94
**audio**
  speakers
    *display distortion (monitor), 177*
    *installing, 176-177*
  system alert sounds
    *recording, 128-129*
    *setting, 126-127*
**automatic shut downs,** 130-131
**available hard drive space, checking,** 217

## B

**Back button (Web browsers),** 80
**backing up drives,** 164-165
**batteries (laptops), charging,** 7
**Bcc (blind carbon copy),** 90
**brightness and contrast settings,** 133
**browsers (Web browsers),** 78-80
  Back button, 80
  connecting to the Internet, 78
  Download button, 84
  Favorites, 79-80
  Forward button, 80
  links, 79
  logging off, 81
  Print button, 80-81
  Refresh button, 80
  Stop button, 80
  Web page addresses, entering, 79, 84

as Button command (View menu), 26
buttons, default buttons (dialog boxes), 41

## C

cables, printer cables, 139
calibrating colors (monitors), 133
cameras (digital cameras), installing, 172-173
Cc: window (email), 90
CD-ROMs, starting the Mac from, 162-163
Channels (Sherlock 2), creating, 57
check boxes, 31
checking email, 87
chime setting (clock options), 124
Chooser, 29
clean system installations, 196-197
   merging System Folders, 198-200
Clean Up command (View menu), 22
clearing paper jams (printers), 151
closing windows, 13, 21
collapsing windows, 21
color calibration (monitors), 133
color depth, changing, 132
Color Picker, 30
Command+Control+Power On key combination, 207
Command+Option key combination, 214
Command+Option+Esc key combination, 206
commands
   Apple menu, About This Computer, 203

Edit menu
   Preferences, 100
   Redo, 66
   Revert, 66
   Undo, 66
File menu
   Make Alias, 32
   New Folder, 23
   Open, 40, 42
   Print Desktop, 23
   Print Window, 23
   Save, 45
   Save As, 44, 46
Help menu, Tutorial, 14
Printer menu, Set Default Printer, 147
Special menu
   Empty Trash, 25, 37
   Restart, 16
   Shut Down, 16
View menu
   Arrange, 22
   as Button, 26
   Clean Up, 22
   as List, 26
   List, 59
Conflict Catcher, 95
conflicts (extension conflicts), finding, 210-211
connect scripts, 76
connections
   cameras, 172
   drives, 154
   hubs, installing, 178-179
   Internet connections (Web browsers), 78
   keyboard, 6, 170
   modems, 7, 174
      troubleshooting, 81
   mouse, 7
   networks, 182-183
   printers, 139
      setting, 10
   scanners, 169
   speakers, 176
contacts (email), saving in Address Book, 89
Contextual Menu, 96-97
contextual menus, 30-31

contrast and brightness settings, 133
Control Panels, 29, 98
   Appearance, 98, 118-119
   AppleTalk, 139, 178-179, 182, 190
   Control Strip, 99
   Date & Time, 122-125
   Energy Saver, 130-131
   Extensions Manager, 208-211
   File Sharing, 184-185, 188-189, 191
   Internet, 99
   Modem, 174
   Monitors, 99, 132-133
   Monitors & Sound, 127
   Mouse, 120-121, 171
   Multiple Users, 134-135
   Software Update, 99, 202
   Sound, 126-129, 177
   Startup Disk, 158-159
   Trackpad (laptops), 121
   Users & Groups, 187
Control Panels folder, 98-99
Control Strip, 96-97
Control Strip Control Panel, 99
Control Strip Modules folder, 96-97
copying
   files/folders, 59
   icons, 59
   text, 64
crashes
   hard drive crashes, 218-219
   system crashes, 206-207
cutting text, 64

##

damaged drives, repairing, 160-161
Date & Time Control Panel, 122-125
date and time
   chime setting, 124
   clock options, setting, 124
   Day Light Savings Time setting, 123

display formats, 124
displaying, 125
setting, 9, 123
**default buttons (dialog boxes), 41**
**deleting**
applications, 115
files, 36-37
*freeing hard drive space, 216-217*
Folder Extension items, 95
sounds from system, 127
**desktop, 12-13**
patterns, selecting, 119
pictures, selecting, 98
rebuilding the desktop, 214-215
themes, selecting, 118
viewing desktop items, 27
**desktop cameras, installing, 172-173**
**desktop icons, 24-25**
**desktop printer icon, 144-145**
**desktop printing feature, 146-147**
**Desktop Skills tutorial, 15**
**diagnosing network problems, 190-191**
**dialog boxes, 30-31**
default buttons, 41
File Sharing, 184-185
Get Info, 112-113
New Document, 62
Open, 40-43
Page Setup, 140-141
Preferences, 30-31, 110-111
Print, 142-143
Save As, 44-46
**digital cameras, installing, 172-173**
**Direct Connections (printers), 10**
**Disabled folders, 97**
**disabling extensions, 208**
**Disk First Aid, 160-161, 219**
**disk icons, 24**
**Disk Image file, 202**

**DiskWarrior, 161**
**display distortion from speakers, 177**
**display fonts, selecting, 119**
**display settings, 99, 132-133**
**document icons, 13, 25**
**document windows, closing, 21**
**documents**
creating, 62-63
exporting, 70-71
importing, 70-71
previewing (Open dialog box), 43
printing, 140
*desktop printing feature, 146-147*
*drag-and-drop printing, 147*
*image size, changing, 141*
*more than one copy, 142*
*page layout, 140*
*Page Setup dialog box, 140-141*
*paper dimensions, checking, 141*
*paper orientation, 140*
*paper size, changing, 141*
*Print dialog box, 142-143*
*print order, changing, 143, 149*
*print quality, selecting, 143*
*PrintMonitor, 148-149*
*scheduling later printing, 147*
*selected pages, 142*
*stopping/resuming print jobs, 144-145*
resizing document windows, 69
restoring, 66-67
text
*editing, 64-65*
*entering, 63*
*moving between documents, 68-69*
*selecting, 63*
*undo/redo an action, 66-67*
*See also* files
**Domain Name Servers, 76**
**Download button (Web browsers), 84**
**downloading software, 83-84**

**drag-and-drop editing, 65**
**drag-and-drop printing, 147**
**driver extension, 94**
**drivers, printer drivers, 139**
**drives**
available space, checking, 217
backing up, 164-165
Fire Wire Hard Drive, 154, 159
formatting, 156-157
freeing up hard drive space, 216-217
hooking up, 154-155
Jaz drives, 155
optimizing, 162-163
repairing damage, 160-161
scanning with virus software, 220-221
SCSI drives, 155
selecting
*Open dialog box, 42*
*Save As dialog box, 46*
startup disks, selecting, 158-159
USB drives, 159
Zip drives, 155
*See also* hard drives

# E

**Edit menu, 28**
Preferences command, 100
Redo command, 66
Revert command, 66
Undo command, 66
**editing text, 64-69**
**email**
accounts, setting up, 76-77
addresses, 91
checking, 87
contacts, saving in Address Book, 89
flagging messages, 89
forwarding messages, 88
junk email, 89
reading, 87
replying to messages, 88
sending messages, 88, 90-91
writing messages, 88
**email software, 86-91**
Address Book button, 89
Flag button, 89

Forward button, 88
launching, 87
New button, 90
Reply button, 88
Send & Receive button, 87
Send Now button, 88, 91

**Empty Trash command (Special menu), 25, 37**

**Energy Saver Control Panel, 130-131**

**energy-star compliance, 131**

**Ethernet hubs**
connecting to, 182-183
installing, 178-179

**Eudora, 89**

**expanding windows, 20**

**exporting files, 70-71**

**extensions, 8**
activating, 209
AOL extensions, 211
ATI Graphics Accelerator extension, 94
conflicts, finding, 210-211
disabling, 208
driver extension, 94
High Sierra File Access extension, 95
Microsoft extensions, 211
network extensions, 95
QuickTime extension, 95
shared library extension, 95

**Extensions folder, 94-95**

**Extensions Manager Control Panel, 208-211**

## F

**Favorites (Web browsers), 79-80**

**Favorites icon, 43**

**File menu, 28**
Make Alias command, 32
New Folder command, 23
Open command, 40, 42
Print Desktop command, 23
Print Window command, 23
Save As command, 44, 46
Save command, 45

**File Sharing Control Panel, 184-185, 188-189, 191**

**File Sharing Control Strip, 183, 189**

**File Sharing dialog boxes, 184-185**

**files**
backing up, 164-165
copying, 59
deleting, 36-37
*freeing hard drive space, 216-217*
Disk Image file, 202
exporting, 70-71
finding with Sherlock 2, 52-53
importing, 70-71
JPEG files, 173
list of recent files, 43
locked files, 37
Mac OS ROM file, 103
moving, 58-59
*to the Trash icon, 36-37*
naming, 32-33
*Save As dialog box, 45, 47*
opening (Open dialog box), 40, 43
ReadMe files, 108-109
removing from Trash, 37
restoring, 66-67
selecting, 58
sharing, 184-185
*diagnosing network problems, 190-191*
*permission levels, setting, 186-187*
*turning off file sharing, 188-189*
sound files, adding to system, 127
System Enabler file, 103
System File, 103
System Resources file, 103
text, finding with Sherlock 2, 54-55
text-clipping files, 69
*See also* documents

**finder preferences, 9**

**finding**
extension conflicts, 210-211
files with Sherlock 2, 52-55

people, 84
software, 83-84

**Fire Wire Hard Drive, 154, 159**

**First Run installers, 107**

**Flag button (email software), 89**

**flagging email messages, 89**

**folder icons, 24**

**folders, 12**
America Online, 81
Apple Extras folder, 15, 40-41
Apple Menu Items folder, 35
Assistants folder, 11-13
backing up, 164-165
Control Panels folder, 98-99
Control Strip Modules folder, 96-97
copying, 59
creating, 23, 48-49
*Save As dialog box, 45, 47*
Disabled folders, 97
Extensions folder, 94-95
Fonts folder, 102
layout of folders within folders, 23
Map Control Panel folder, 40-41
moving, 27, 58-59
naming, 49
*Save As dialog box, 45, 47*
Preferences folder, 100-101, 111
selecting, 58
System Folder, 96-97, 102-103
*clean installations, 196-197*
System Folders, merging, 198-200
viewing, 26-27

**fonts**
display fonts, selecting, 119
displaying in WYSIWYG style, 110

**Fonts folder, 102**

**Force Quit, 206-207**

**forcing restarts, 207**

**formatting drives, 156-157**

**Forward button**
email software, 88
Web browsers, 80

**forwarding email messages, 88**

**freeing up hard drive space, 216-217**

## G

**Get Info dialog box,** 112–113
**graphics, JPEG files,** 173
**graphics tablets, installing,** 170
**grays, setting monitor to,** 133
**grid spacing,** 23
**Guest access, setting,** 187

## H

**hard drives**
available space, checking, 217
backing up, 164–165
crashes, troubleshooting, 218–219
FireWire Hard Drive, 154, 159
freeing up space, 216–217
hooking up, 154–155
opening, 12
optimizing, 162–163
repairing damage, 160–161
scanning with virus software, 220–221
SCSI hard drives, 155
startup disks, selecting, 158–159
*See also* drives

**Help icon (Save As dialog box),** 47
**Help menu,** 29
Tutorial command, 14
**High Sierra File Access extension,** 95
**hooking up drives,** 154–155
**hooking up the Mac,** 6–7
**hubs**
connecting to, 182–183
Ethernet hubs, 182–183
installing, 178–179
**hypertext links,** 79

## I

**iBook**
batteries, charging, 7
power button, 7
starting from CD-ROMs, 163
Trackpad Control Panel, 121

**icons,** 12
alias icons, 25
application icons, 25
arranging, 22
copying, 59
desktop printer icons, 144
disk icons, 24
document icons, 13, 25
Favorites icons, 43
folder icons, 24
grid spacing, 23
Help icons (Save As dialog box), 47
lining up, 22
Macintosh HD icons, 12
moving, 27, 58–59
moving between (Tab key), 25
naming, 21
organizing, 22–23
printer icons, 24
question mark icon, 159
selecting, 58
sorting, 22
Trash icon, 25
*moving files to,* 36–37
*removing files from,* 37
*stopping print jobs,* 145

**image size (printing),** 141
**importing files,** 70–71
**initializing drives,** 156–157
**ink (printers),** 151
**Installation Log,** 115
**Installer,** 106–107
uninstalling applications, 114–115
**installing**
digital cameras, 172–173
hubs, 178–179
keyboards, 170–171
Mac Operating System, 194–195
*clean installations,* 196–197
*merging System Folders,* 198–200
modems, 174–175
pointing devices, 170–171
printer software, 138
scanners, 168–169

software, 106–107
speakers, 176–177
system add-ons, 103

**Internet**
search engines, 82
searching with Sherlock 2, 56–57

**Internet accounts, setting up,** 74–77
**Internet Assistant,** 74–77
**Internet Control Panel,** 99
**Internet Explorer,** 78–81
Back button, 80
Download button, 84
Favorites, 79–80
Forward button, 80
links, 79
logging off, 81
Print button, 80–81
Refresh button, 80
Stop button, 80
Web page addresses, entering, 79

**Internet settings, changing,** 99
**IP addresses,** 76
**ISPs (Internet Service Providers), joining,** 74–77

## J–K

**Jaz drives,** 155
**joysticks, installing,** 170
**JPEG files,** 173
**junk email,** 89

**keyboards**
Command+Control+Power On key combination, 207
Command+Option key combination, 214
Command+Option+Esc key combination, 206
connecting to the Mac, 6
installing, 170–171
Option key, 21, 37
Tab key, 25

## L

**laptops**
   batteries, charging, 7
   Energy Saver options, 131
   starting from CD-ROMs, 163
   Trackpad Control Panel, 121

**launching**
   AppleWorks, 62
   applications, 34
   email software, 87
   Internet Assistant, 74
   Outlook Express, 87

**libraries, searching, 83**

**Library of Congress Web site, 83**

**lining up icons/windows, 22**

**links, 79**

**as List command (View menu), 26**

**List command (View menu), 59**

**list of recent files, 43**

**locked files, 37**

**logging in/out of Macs, 135**

**logging off Web browsers, 81**

**logging on to AOL (Sherlock 2), 57**

**low ink (printers), 151**

**low toner (printers), 151**

**low-power mode, 17**

## M

**Mac Operating System**
   installing, 194-195
      *clean installations, 196-197*
      *merging System Folders, 198-200*
   system updates, 202-203

**Mac OS ROM file, 103**

**Mac OS Setup Assistant, 8-11**
   finder preferences, 9
   passwords, 9
   printer connections, 10
   regional preferences, 8
   time and date settings, 9

**Mac OS tutor, 14-15**

**Macdownload.com Web site, 83**

**Macintosh HD icon, 12**

**MacTopia Web site, 89**

**Make Alias command (File menu), 32**

**Map Control Panel folder, 40-41**

**memory**
   assigning to applications, 212-213
   giving applications more memory, 112-113
   troubleshooting memory problems, 212-213

**memory requirements**
   changing, 113
   viewing, 112-113

**menu bar, 28-29**

**menus**
   Apple menu, 29
      *About This Computer command, 203*
   Contextual Menu, 96-97
   contextual menus, 30-31
   Edit menu, 28
      *Preferences command, 100*
      *Redo command, 66*
      *Revert command, 66*
      *Undo command, 66*
   File menu, 28
      *Make Alias command, 32*
      *New Folder, 23*
      *Open command, 40, 42*
      *Print Desktop command, 23*
      *Print Window command, 23*
      *Save As command, 44, 46*
      *Save command, 45*
   Help menu, 29
      *Tutorial command, 14*
   Printer menu, 147
   Scaling menu, 141
   Special menu, 16, 29
      *Empty Trash command, 25, 37*
   View menu, 28
      *Arrange command, 22*
      *as Button command, 26*
      *Clean Up command, 22*
      *as List command, 26*
      *List command, 59*

**merging System Folders, 198-200**

**Metcrawler Web site, 82**

**MicroMat TechTool Pro, 37, 161**

**MicroMat Web site, 215**

**microphones, 129**

**Microsoft extensions, 211**

**Microsoft Outlook Express, 86-91**
   Address Book button, 89
   Flag button, 89
   Forward button, 88
   launching, 87
   New button, 90
   Reply button, 88
   Send & Receive button, 87
   Send Now button, 88, 91

**Modem Control Panel, 174**

**modems**
   56K modems, 174-175
   connecting to the Mac, 7
   installing, 174-175
   setting up (Internet Assistant), 75
   troubleshooting, 81

**monitoring activity, 189**

**monitors**
   color calibration, 133
   color depth, changing, 132
   contrast and brightness settings, 133
   display distortion from speakers, 177
   grays, setting to, 133
   resolution setting, 132

**Monitors & Sound Control Panel, 127**

**Monitors Control Panel, 99, 132-133**

**mouse**
  connecting to the Mac, 7
  installing, 170-171
  tracking speed, adjusting, 120-121

**Mouse Control Panel, 120-121, 171**

**Mouse Skills tutorial, 14**

**moving**
  aliases, 33
  between icons (Tab key), 25
  files, 58-59
  folders, 27, 58-59
  icons, 27, 58-59
  text, 64-65
    *between documents, 68-69*

**multiple undos/redos, performing, 67**

**Multiple Users Control Panel, 134-135**

**naming**
  aliases, 33
  files, 32-33
    *Save As dialog box, 45, 47*
  folders, 49
    *Save As dialog box, 45, 47*
  icons, 21

**Netscape Navigator, 81**

**Network Connections (printers), 10**

**network extensions, 95**

**networks**
  Activity Monitor, 189
  connecting to, 182-183
  diagnosing network problems, 190-191
  file sharing, 184-185
    *permission levels, setting, 186-187*
  hubs, installing, 178-179
  selecting
    *Open dialog box, 42*
    *Save As dialog box, 46*

**New button (email software), 90**

**New Document dialog box, 62**

**New Folder command (File menu), 23**

**newsgroups, setting up, 77**

**Norton Anti-Virus, 107, 220-221**

**Norton Utilities, 37, 161**

**Open command (File menu), 40, 42**

**Open dialog box, 41-43**
  Standard Open dialog box, 40

**Open Transport technology, 95**

**opening**
  applications, 34, 40
  files, 40, 43
  hard drive, 12
  pop-up windows, 27
  Web Browsers, 78
  windows, 20

**operating system**
  installing, 194-195
    *clean installations, 196-197*
    *merging system folders, 198-200*
  system updates, 202-203

**optimizing hard drives, 162-163**

**Option key, 21, 37**

**organizing icons/windows, 22-23**

**Outlook Express, 86-91**
  Address Book button, 89
  Flag button, 89
  Forward button, 88
  launching, 87
  New button, 90
  Reply button, 88
  Send & Receive button, 87
  Send Now button, 88, 91

**page layout (printing), 140**

**Page Setup dialog box, 140-141**

**paper dimensions (printing), 141**

**paper orientation (printing), 140**

**paper size (printing), 141**

**passwords, 9**
  voices as passwords, 135

**pasting text, 65**

**patterns (desktop patterns), selecting, 119**

**people, finding, 84**

**permission levels, setting (file sharing), 186-187**

**Personal Backup, 165**

**phone directories, searching, 84**

**pictures (desktop pictures), selecting, 98**

**placing aliases, 35**

**pointing devices, installing, 170-171**

**pop-up lists, 30**

**pop-up windows, 27**

**ports, USB ports, 171**

**power button (iBook/PowerBook), 7**

**Power Mac, starting from CD-ROMs, 163**

**power on switch, 7**

**PowerBook**
  batteries, charging, 7
  power button, 7
  Trackpad Control Panel, 121

**preferences**
  application preferences, setting, 110-111
  changing, 100-101

**Preferences command (Edit menu), 100, 110**

**Preferences dialog box, 30-31, 110-111**

**Preferences folder, 100-101, 111**

**previewing documents (Open dialog box), 43**

**Print button (Web browsers), 80-81**

**Print Desktop command (File menu), 23**

**Print dialog box, 142-143**

**Print Window command (File menu), 23**

**printer cables,** 139

**printer connections, setting,** 10

**printer drivers, selecting,** 139

**printer icons,** 24

**Printer menu, Set Default Printer command,** 147

**printers,** 138
   connections, 139
   low toner/ink, 151
   paper jams, clearing, 151
   restarting, 150
   setting up, 138-139
   software, installing, 138
   troubleshooting, 150-151

**printing**
   desktop printing feature, 146-147
   drag-and-drop printing, 147
   image size, changing, 141
   more than one copy, 142
   page layout, 140
   Page Setup dialog box, 140-141
   paper dimensions, checking, 141
   paper orientation, 140
   paper size, changing, 141
   Print dialog box, 142-143
   print order, changing, 143, 149
   print quality, selecting, 143
   PrintMonitor, 148-149
   ReadMe files, 109
   scheduling later printing
      *desktop printing, 147*
      *PrintMonitor, 149*
   selected pages, 142
   stopping/resuming print jobs, 144-145

**PrintMonitor,** 148-149

**privileges, setting (file sharing),** 186-187

**programs**
   launching, 34
   menu bar, 29
   opening, Open dialog box, 40
   quitting, 13, 35
   running, 13

**proxy servers,** 77

## Q

**? (question mark icon),** 159

**QuickMail Pro,** 89

**QuickTime extension,** 95

**quitting applications,** 13, 35

## R

**radio buttons,** 31

**RAM (random access memory)**
   assigning to applications, 112-113, 212-213
   memory problems, troubleshooting, 212-213

**reading email,** 87

**ReadMe files,** 108-109

**rebuilding the desktop,** 214-215

**recording system alert sounds,** 128-129

**Redo command,** 66-67

**reducing windows,** 21

**Refresh button (Web browsers),** 80

**regional preferences,** 8

**reinstalling operating systems,** 195

**Remote Access,** 78

**removable media (backup storage),** 164-165

**removing**
   applications, 114-115
   files from Trash, 37

**renaming**
   aliases, 33
   files, 32-33

**repairing hard drive damage,** 160-161

**Reply button (email software),** 88

**replying to email messages,** 88

**resizing windows,** 20-21
   document windows, 69

**resolution setting,** 132

**restarting**
   Macs, 16-17
   *forcing restarts, 207*
   *from CD-ROMs, 162-163*
   *rebuilding the desktop, 214-215*
   printers, 150

**restoring files,** 66-67

**resuming print jobs,** 144-145

**Retrospect,** 165

**Revert command,** 66-67

**running applications,** 13

## S

**Save As command (File menu),** 44, 46

**Save As dialog box,** 44-46

**Save command (File menu),** 45

**Scaling menu,** 141

**scanners, installing,** 168-169

**scheduling**
   Macs, 131
   printing
      *desktop printing, 147*
      *PrintMonitor, 149*

**scrolling windows,** 20

**SCSI hard drives,** 155

**search engines,** 82

**searching**
   files with Sherlock 2, 52-55
   Internet with Sherlock 2, 56-57
   libraries, 83
   phone directories, 84
   software, 83-84

**selecting**
   drives
      *Open dialog box, 42*
      *Save As dialog box, 46*
   files, 58
   folders, 58
   icons, 58
   networks
      *Open dialog box, 42*
      *Save As dialog box, 46*
   text, 63

**Send & Receive button (email software),** 87

Send Now button (email software), 88
sending email messages, 88, 90-91
servers, 123
Set Default Printer command (Printer menu), 147
setting up the Mac, 6-7
    Mac OS Setup Assistant, 8-11
shared library extension, 95
sharing files, 184-185
    diagnosing network problems, 190-191
    permission levels, setting, 186-187
    turning off file sharing, 188-189
Sherlock 2, 29
    Channels, creating, 57
    finding files, 52-53
        *by contents, 54-55*
    logging on to AOL, 57
    searching the Internet, 56-57
shutting down the Mac, 16-17
    automatically, 130-131
sizing windows, 20-21
    document windows, 69
Sleep feature, 17
sleep mode, 130-131
software
    downloading, 83-84
    email software, 86-91
        *Address Book button, 89*
        *Flag button, 89*
        *Forward button, 88*
        *launching, 87*
        *New button, 90*
        *Reply button, 88*
        *Send & Receive button, 87*
        *Send Now button, 88, 91*
    finding, 83-84
    installing, 106-107
    printer software, installing, 138
    updating Apple software, 99
    virus software, 220-221
        *disabling for software installation, 107*
        *disabling for system updates, 203*

Software Update Control Panel, 99, 202
sorting icons/windows, 22
Sound Control Panel, 126-129, 177
sound files, adding to system, 127
sounds
    deleting from system, 127
    system alert sounds
        *recording, 128-129*
        *setting, 126-127*
speakers
    display distortion, 177
    installing, 176-177
Special menu, 29
    Empty Trash command, 25, 37
    Restart command, 16
    Shut Down command, 16
Speed Disk, 162-163
Standard Open dialog box, 40
starting the Mac, 7
    from CD-ROMs, 162-163
Startup Disk Control Panel, 158-159
startup disks, 158-159
Stop button (Web browsers), 80
stopping
    file sharing, 188-189
    print jobs, 144-145
Subject box (email), 90
surge protectors, 6
Symantec Norton Anti-Virus, 107
Symantec Norton Utilities, 37, 161
system add-ons, installing, 103
system alert sounds
    recording, 128-129
    setting, 126-127
system crashes, 206-207
System Enabler file, 103
System File, 103
System Folder, 96-97, 102-103
    clean installations, 196-197
    merging System Folders, 198-200

System Resources file, 103
system updates, 202-203
system versions, checking, 203

## T

Tab key, 25
TechTool, 37, 161, 215
text
    copying, 64
    cutting, 64
    entering into documents, 63
    finding files by contents (Sherlock 2), 54-55
    moving, 64-65
        *between documents, 68-69*
    pasting, 65
    selecting, 63
text-clipping files, 69
themes (desktop themes), selecting, 118
time and date
    chime setting, 124
    clock options, setting, 124
    Day Light Savings Time setting, 123
    display formats, 124
    displaying, 125
    setting, 9, 123
    time zones, setting, 122
toner (printers), 151
trackballs, installing, 170
tracking speed (mouse), adjusting, 120-121
Trackpad Control Panel (laptops), 121
Trash icon, 25
    moving files to, 36-37
    removing files from, 37
    stopping print jobs, 145
troubleshooting
    extension conflicts, 210-211
    hard drive crashes, 218-219
    memory problems, 212-213
    modems, 81
    network problems, 190-191
    printers, 150-151
    system crashes, 206-207

**TROUBLESHOOTING**    **239**

**turning off file sharing,** 188–189
**turning on the Mac,** 7
  automatically, 131
**tutorials,** 14–15
**typing text,** 63

## U

**Undo command,** 66–67
**uninstalling applications,** 114–115
**updating Apple software,** 99
**updating systems,** 202–203
**US WEST Dex Web site,** 84
**USB devices, hub connections,** 179
**USB drives,** 159
**USB hubs, installing,** 178–179
**USB ports,** 171
**users, Multiple Users feature,** 134–135
**Users & Groups Control Panel,** 187

## V

**versions (system versions), checking,** 203
**View menu,** 28
  Arrange command, 22
  as Button command, 26
  Clean Up command, 22
  as List command, 26
  List command, 59
**viewing**
  desktop items, 27
  folders, 26–27
**Virex,** 220–221
**virus software,** 220–221
  disabling for software installation, 107
  disabling for system updates, 203

**voices as passwords,** 135
**volume level, setting,** 127
**VST Technologies Fire Wire Hard Drive,** 154, 159

## W

**Web browsers,** 78–80
  Back button, 80
  connecting to the Internet, 78
  Download button, 84
  Favorites, 79–80
  Forward button, 80
  links, 79
  logging off, 81
  opening, 78
  Print button, 80–81
  Refresh button, 80
  Stop button, 80
  Web page addresses, entering, 79, 84
**Web sites**
  Apple, 79
  Library of Congress, 83
  Macdownload.com, 83
  MacTopia, 89
  Metacrawler, 82
  MicroMat, 215
  US WEST Dex, 84
**windows,** 12, 20
  arranging, 22
  closing, 13, 21
  collapsing, 21
  grid spacing, 23
  lining up, 22
  opening, 20
  organizing, 22–23
  pop-up windows, 27
  resizing, 20–21
  scrolling through, 20
  sorting, 22
**word processing**
  documents
    *creating,* 62
    *exporting,* 70–71
    *importing,* 70–71

  *moving text between,* 68–69
  *resizing document windows,* 69
  *restoring,* 66–67
  *Undo/Redo commands,* 66–67
  text
    *editing,* 64–65
    *entering,* 63
    *selecting,* 63
**writing email messages,** 88

## X-Z

**ZIP drives,** 155
**Zoom command,** 69

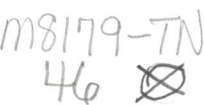